# UNDERSTANDING
## INFLUENCE FOR LEADERS
## AT ALL LEVELS

# UNDERSTANDING
## INFLUENCE FOR LEADERS AT ALL LEVELS

## MANAGEMENT
### TODAY SERIES

*Series Editors*
Carolyn Barker
and
Robyn Coy

Sydney  New York  San Francisco  Auckland  Bogotá  Caracas
Lisbon  London  Madrid  Mexico City  Milan  Montreal  New Delhi
San Juan  Singapore  Tokyo  Toronto

Reprinted 2006
Text © 2005 Australian Institute of Management
Illustrations and design © 2005 McGraw-Hill Australia Pty Ltd
Additional owners of copyright are named in on-page credits.

Apart from any fair dealing for the purposes of study, research, criticism or review, as permitted under the *Copyright Act*, no part may be reproduced by any process without written permission. Enquiries should be made to the publisher, marked for the attention of the Permissions Editor, at the address below.

Every effort has been made to trace and acknowledge copyright material. Should any infringement have occurred accidentally the authors and publishers tender their apologies.

**Copying for educational purposes**
Under the copying provisions of the *Copyright Act*, copies of parts of this book may be made by an educational institution. An agreement exists between the Copyright Agency Limited (CAL) and the relevant educational authority (Department of Education, university, TAFE, etc.) to pay a licence fee for such copying. It is not necessary to keep records of copying except where the relevant educational authority has undertaken to do so by arrangement with the Copyright Agency Limited.

For further information on the CAL licence agreements with educational institutions, contact the Copyright Agency Limited, Level 19, 157 Liverpool Street, Sydney NSW 2000. Where no such agreement exists, the copyright owner is entitled to claim payment in respect of any copies made.

Enquiries concerning copyright in McGraw-Hill publications should be directed to the Permissions Editor at the address below.

---

**National Library of Australia Cataloguing-in-Publication data:**

Understanding influence for leaders at all levels.

Includes index.
ISBN 0 074 71380 9.

1. Leadership. 2. Self-actualization (Psychology). 3. Personnel management.
I. Australian Institute of Management.

303.34

---

Published in Australia by
**McGraw-Hill Australia Pty Ltd**
**Level 2, 82 Waterloo Road, North Ryde NSW 2113**
Acquisitions Editor: Eiko Bron
Production Editor: Sybil Kesteven
Editor: Sharon Nevile
Proofreader: Tim Learner
Indexer: Glenda Browne
Designer (cover and interior): Lucy Bal
Illustrator: Alan Laver, Shelly Communications
Typeset in Bembo by Post Pre-Press Group
Printed on 80 gsm woodfree by 1010 Printing International Limited, China

*McGraw·Hill Australia*
A Division of The *McGraw·Hill Companies*

# CONTENTS

| | |
|---|---|
| Preface | vii |
| 1 Power and influence—*Nick Forster* | 1 |
| 2 Persuasion and influence—*Caroline Hatcher* | 39 |
| 3 Charisma and influence—*Desmond Guilfoyle* | 67 |
| 4 The power of positive spin—*Thomas Murrell* | 99 |
| 5 The power of networking—*Robyn Henderson* | 135 |
| 6 The power of knowledge—*Alastair Rylatt* | 163 |
| 7 Influencing behaviour in organisations—*John Eales* and *Liza Spence* | 193 |
| 8 Influencing fundamental change—Phil Harker | 225 |
| Index | 255 |

# PREFACE

*Leader as influencer* is one of the key roles that managers today must play. So say the world's leading management and business commentators . . . as does the Australian Institute of Management.

Never before has there been a greater need to get things done by influencing. In a world full of 'noise' and overloaded with signals, the ability to influence others is now a skill that is central to job function and role responsibility for leaders at all levels.

Influence is the subject of this book, which is the sixth in the *Management Today Series*. Like the earlier titles in this best selling business book series, it pulls apart what it means to be an effective leader in today's business world.

Some time ago, Carolyn Barker, Co-Series Editor, was invited to lunch with a group of interesting and articulate leaders. The inevitable topic of 'people' dominated the conversation, especially how to manage the context in which people work, live and play. From there, the conversation turned to the concepts of persuasion, power and influence, and how these were now the skills that make for better leadership.

Afterwards, it dawned upon us that this would be a fascinating direction for our next book . . . an examination of what it means to have influence and to be influential, and the role that personal influence and power play in workplace leadership.

Simply defined, power is the ability to change the behaviour, attitudes and beliefs of others. Influence is the exercise of that power. In other words, power is something that you may have or strive for; influence is what you do with it.

In our initial research for this book, we discovered two things. First, when people think about power and influence, they are unused to consciously considering the subject. 'The political entity, the organisation, the company or someone else (who is bigger, faster, stronger or wealthier) has power and influence . . . not me.' It seems that there is a general belief that power and influence cannot be possessed or exercised by ordinary individuals in their everyday environments.

Second, for many people, power and influence are negative words. Even those who have formal leadership positions or hierarchical authority often cringe if their power and influence over others is articulated (especially if that articulation links leadership aspirations with the drive for power). Influence, whether it is over others or over the organisational agenda, has been associated with deceitful, covert behaviour—the realm of Machiavelli and political backroom boys and girls.

And yet, in today's organisation, leaders must know how to influence others.

'Command and control' is being replaced by 'collaboration and consensus', dramatically affecting the way leaders go about getting things done. In the modern management environment, influence and leadership are inextricably combined.

The Australian Institute of Management has a strong philosophical view that leadership is not the exclusive mantle of the formally anointed—the one at the top, the executive class. Rather, leadership is the engagement of followers in the pursuit of shared goals. Implicit in this simple but elegant definition is that leadership occurs at every tier of the organisation.

Like leadership, influence starts from an intrinsically neutral position. Whether it is good or bad depends on how you use it. However, one of the underpinning contentions of this book is that influence is more effective when exercised within an ethical framework and deployed with a working knowledge of emotional intelligence. It is for this reason that each of the chapters provides advice for leaders who wish to be influential without destroying the trust of their peers or followers.

This book is an unashamedly eclectic collection of chapters on the role of influence. It is not a neat and tidy 'textbook'; rather, it is a collection of the thoughts and writings of nine Australian management commentators. Although there are several themes common to all of the chapters, each reflects the contributors' deeply held views on how leaders and managers can use and increase their influence, yet act with integrity and a clear conscience.

The opening chapter sets the scene by examining the nature of power, influence and leadership within organisations. The following four chapters examine some tools or strategies that leaders can use for increasing personal influence; namely persuasion, charisma, spin and networks. The authors provide guidelines so that leaders can master each of these strategies and achieve their organisational goals. Influencing, like every other skill, can be learned.

We have chosen to group the most challenging chapters in the second half of the book. They concentrate on strategies for leaders who wish to influence fundamental changes in the direction, culture and behaviour of their organisations. Why are these chapters challenging? Because they each address the question most frequently asked of our leaders today: 'Why won't you change your behaviour to match what you are telling us to do?' Regardless of how much money, time and effort an organisation spends on major reform and change programs, unless the leader or the leadership team can demonstrate a change in their own belief structures, they will not have any real or sustainable influence on the organisation's desired reforms.

*Understanding Influence* is true to the philosophy of the *Management Today Series*, in that each chapter combines background theory with real world application, challenging and thought provoking concepts with practical guidance, and intellectual rigour with passionate opinion.

In total, AIM's *Management Today Series* has presented the work of almost 50 authors and has explored over 70 management and leadership topics. The feedback that we get from people throughout Australasia and beyond usually takes the shape of comments on their favourite chapter in their favourite book, and the reasons why it struck a chord with them. Many have also remarked that as time has gone on and their roles have changed, so too has their 'favourite' chapter. We think this reflects the depth of the collection and the strength of the multi-authored approach.

We hope you enjoy this book and, as always, we look forward to your feedback. If you wish to provide comment on this book or any of the others in the *Management Today Series*, please email us at editor@aim.com.au or visit <www.aim.com.au>.

Carolyn Barker, FAIM and Robyn Coy, AIMM
Series Editors
Australian Institute of Management

# POWER AND INFLUENCE

# 1

Nick Forster

Introduction

The two-sided nature of power and influence

    Power and empowerment

Sources of power and influence

    Personal power

    Personal attributes of leaders that people *willingly* follow

    Expert power

    Legitimate, reward and coercive power

The most effective sources of power

The dark side of power

    Power and the toxic personality

    Machiavellian power games

    Beyond Machiavelli

Conclusion

For further exploration

Notes

# About the author

Nick Forster, BA (Hons), MSc, PhD

Professor Nick Forster works at the Graduate School of Management at the University of Western Australia.

He has published four books, written more than seventy articles for a variety of international journals, produced numerous research and consulting reports for organisations in Australia and the UK, and contributed to several professional and practitioner publications. His latest book (endorsed by Michael Chaney) is *Maximum performance: a practical guide to leading and managing people at work* (Edward Elgar, 2004).

Nick has worked with the AIM/GSM Integral Leadership Centre in the delivery of leadership and management development workshops to several of Western Australia's largest companies and public sector organisations, and has been a facilitator in AIM's Action Learning Programs, run in conjunction with the Harvard Business School. He has also collaborated in research, training and consultancy work with more than fifty UK and Australian companies, and was on the judging panel for the Australian Human Resource Management Awards during 2003–04.

Nick also teaches on the MBA and Executive MBA programs at the Graduate School of Management, and has received ten MBA-nominated commendations and awards for excellence in teaching. He was nominated by his peers for a National Australian Universities Teaching Award in 2000.

To find out more about Nick Forster's expertise, research and publications, visit <www.wamcg.com.au>.

Nick Forster can be contacted at <nforster@ecel.uwa.edu.au>.

# Executive summary

Power and influence are two of the most important attributes of successful business and organisational leaders, and yet they are often among the most difficult to acquire and use effectively and ethically. Three key questions are addressed in this chapter:
- What are the principal sources of power and influence in organisations?
- How can leaders and managers acquire and use these to maximum effect?
- What power and influence strategies can be employed when dealing with toxic or political organisational cultures?

In order to answer these questions, the personal qualities, attributes, skills and competencies of the leaders that most employees would *willingly* follow are identified. The chapter then discusses how these form the bedrock of personal power and authority for leaders at any level in contemporary organisations. Other important sources of power and influence, and their limitations, are also identified.

Last, the chapter examines the issue of toxic leadership and describes eight Machiavellian power and influencing strategies that can be employed if the situation demands it, as well as the potential pitfalls and dangers of operating within the 'dark side' of leadership and power.

# Introduction

Looking back at the most successful business leaders of the twentieth century, such as Robert Goizueta (Coca-Cola), Jack Welch (General Electric), Alfred Sloan (General Motors), Sam Walton (Wal-Mart), Bill Marriot (Marriot Hotels) Bill Hewlett and Dave Packard (HP), Akio Morita (Sony), Konosuke Matsushita (Matsushita), Andy Grove (Intel) and others, it becomes clear that they all shared several important qualities and characteristics:

- They had superb practical business acumen and were tough and pragmatic, but always had one imaginative and visionary eye looking towards the future.
- They paid attention to their employees, realising that they truly were the most important assets their companies possessed.
- They regularly experimented with new business processes and people management techniques without becoming reactive 'fad surfers'.
- They led from the front, always by example, and were people both of action and of contemplation.
- They were curious about the world and were lifelong learners.

All, by the standards of their day, operated within acceptable ethical and moral codes. But, above all else, they were able to inspire their followers to achieve great things because they *possessed power and used it to full effect*. Their collective influence has since spread far beyond the companies that they built into some of the greatest commercial enterprises in human history.

## The two-sided nature of power and influence

So, what are power and influence? Both terms are derived from Latin words: *potere*, meaning 'to be able' and *influere*, meaning 'to flow in'. Hence, power can be described as the ability to change the behaviour, attitudes and beliefs of others, while influence is the *exercise* of this power.

When used in the 'right' way, power and influence can be positive forces for good. They can give individuals increased freedom, choice and strength, and an enhanced ability to mobilise people and resources in order to accomplish personal goals, work tasks and organisational objectives.

Within organisations, leaders and managers who have power can achieve more for their followers because they possess 'clout'. People will work harder for bosses that they believe have status, credibility and influence within organisations. In contrast, employees are much less willing to work for weak leaders who lack genuine personal authority and credibility, or are bossy and dictatorial.

In one well-known study of ninety people who had been nominated by their peers as being the most influential leaders in the USA in business, politics and society in the 1980s, it was discovered that they shared three characteristics:

1 They made other people feel powerful.
2 They used their power to enable their followers to aspire to and realise exceptional achievements.
3 They learned early in their careers how to build strong personal power bases within their organisations, businesses or spheres of influence.[1]

Some people may view power and influence as 'black arts'. They are, however, essential parts of the repertoire of successful business leaders. They are natural and inevitable facts of organisational life, as individuals and groups seek to gain influence and control over finite resources in order to achieve their objectives. Having said this, there certainly is a Janus-like[2] quality to power and influence, as shown in Table 1.1.

Table 1.1 The two faces of power and influence[3]

| Positive | Negative |
| --- | --- |
| Assertive | Aggressive |
| Social | Unsocial |
| Influential | Domineering |
| Persuasive | Exploitative |
| Inspiring | Brutish |
| Win–win | Win–lose |

The truth is that power and influence are neutral concepts. Whether you choose to operate within the 'light' or 'dark' sides of power and influence will depend on your personal intentions and goals. How you use power will be determined by your personality, perceptions about what constitutes effective leadership and management, the culture of the organisation in which you work, and the leadership and management practices of the people you work with.

## Power and empowerment

In many business contexts, to become a more powerful leader means being prepared to *give power away* by empowering your followers and, as far as possible, not using power in a coercive way.

The use of the negative face of power, including hoarding it, is ultimately ineffective. In the words of David McClelland:

> *The negative face of power is characterised by the dominance–submission mode: if I win, you lose. It leads to a simple and direct means of feeling powerful (such as being aggressive). It does not often lead to effective social leadership for the reason that such a person tends to treat other people as pawns. People who feel they are pawns tend to be passive and useless to the leader who gets his satisfaction from dominating them. Slaves are the most inefficient form of labour ever devised by man. If a leader wants to have far-reaching influence, he must make his followers feel powerful and able to accomplish things on their own. Even the most dictatorial leader does not succeed if he has not instilled in at least some of his followers a sense of power and the strength to pursue the goals he has set.*[4]

McClelland made these comments 30 years ago, but they are even more relevant today. By empowering their followers, leaders actually increase their own power and influence. Power and empowerment are closely related and have an iterative effect on each other: first, we have to acquire power, then give it away to others and, as a result, become more powerful—then give it away again to our followers and so forth. This does not mean that we give up *control*—we still remain in charge—but the locus of control passes to our employees.

However, giving up formal, positional power and command-and-control authority can be a very threatening prospect to old-school leaders and managers. Very few people will voluntarily give up power, particularly if they have fought hard to obtain it during their careers ('Well, I did it the hard way and there's no reason why they can't.'). They might also be fearful about losing their status, special perks or privileges. Other old-school leader/managers may 'look down' on their followers, believing that they are incapable of being empowered, without the ability to do anything more than obey orders. However, this viewpoint runs counter to all the evidence that has been accumulated on high performing leader/managers and consistently successful organisations over the last 20 years.[5] And, in the words of Kouzes and Posner, two of the most influential leadership commentators of the last decade:

> *In examining powerless and powerful times, there is one clear and consistent message: feeling powerful—literally feeling 'able'—comes from a deep sense of being in control of our lives.*
> - *When we feel able to control our own destiny, and when we believe we are able to mobilise the resources necessary to complete a task, then we will persist in our efforts to achieve.*
> - *Conversely, when we feel that others control us, when we believe that we lack support or resources, we show no commitment to excel (although we may comply).*
>
> *Thus, any leadership practice that increases another's sense of self-confidence, self-determination, and personal effectiveness makes that person feel more powerful and greatly enhances the possibility of success. The leader who is most open to influence, who listens, and who helps others is the leader who is most respected and most effective—not, as traditional management myth has it, the highly-controlling tough-guy boss . . . The more people believe that they can influence and control the organisation, the greater organisational effectiveness and member performance will be. Shared power results in higher job fulfillment and performance throughout the organisation.*[6]

## Sources of power and influence

Where do power and influence come from? A close examination shows that there are just five sources of power and influence in organisations: personal, expert, legitimate (positional), reward and coercive power. Each of these is reviewed in detail in the following sections.

## Personal power

For many leaders, real power derives from *personal power*; that is, their personal attributes and qualities. This is especially true for those who lack formal, legitimate power or positional authority—for them, personal power may be their *only* source of power and influence. For this reason, personal power and the attributes of those who have it will be examined in some depth here.

To a considerable extent, our ability to influence others stems from the images, impressions or perceptions that the people we work with have of us and, crucially, how we routinely *present* ourselves to others through our words, actions and deeds. In other words, if people *believe* that a leader has power and influence, they are more likely to be inspired and motivated by them (although there can be a dark side to this relationship, an issue we will return to later in this chapter).

Conversely, leaders who are perceived to be ineffectual or weak find it much harder to motivate, energise and inspire their followers—regardless of any positional authority they may have. In the words of Steve Carey, a former advisor to Bill Clinton, 'I obey a manager because I have to. I follow a leader because I want to.'

So, what exactly are the mysterious qualities that differentiate leaders who are perceived to have power and influence from those who are perceived to lack them? In order to begin answering this question, please complete the following exercise.

### What kind of leader do you want to follow?[7]

*The following is a list of qualities, attributes and competencies that have been associated with business leaders and organisational leadership. Take a few minutes to reflect on these, and then identify the six that you would consider to be essential characteristics of a leader you would willingly follow now or in the future.*

| | | |
|---|---|---|
| Ambitious | Good communicator | Mature |
| Brave | Honest | Modest |
| Caring | Humorous | Motivational |
| Charismatic | Imaginative/creative | Powerful |
| Credible/competent | Inspirational | Rational |
| Decisive | Intelligent | Self-motivated |
| Dependable | Logical | Supportive |
| Equitable/fair minded | Loyal | Visionary/forward looking |
| Experienced | | |

List your six choices.

1 _____
2 _____
3 _____
4 _____
5 _____
6 _____

Now, compare your choices with the results of the two surveys outlined in Tables 1.2 and 1.3.

Table 1.2 Survey results: qualities of leaders we would willingly follow

| What do you admire in a leader you would willingly follow? | What are the qualities of leaders you admire? |
|---|---|
| 1 Honesty and integrity | 1 Honesty and integrity |
| 2 Competence and credibility | 2 Competence and credibility |
| 3 Vision and ability to be forward looking | 3 Inspiration and motivation |
| 4 Inspiration and motivation | 4 Ability to create direction and vision |
| 5 Fair mindedness and equity | 5 Good two-way communication skills |
| 6 Communication that appeals to people's hearts, hopes and dreams | 6 Parity and equity |

Sources: Data in left column based on international surveys of 220 000 managers and leaders by Barry Posner, 1980–2004;[8] data in right column summarises results from surveys of 478 MBA students, 1997–2004. Another desired quality that often appeared in the top six was a good sense of humour.[9]

On a cultural and symbolic level it appears that most people respond in a very positive way to leaders who exhibit these leadership qualities and characteristics. So it is not surprising how often these leadership qualities appear in the repertoire of admired fictional leaders. To illustrate this point, Table 1.3 describes the desired leadership qualities of two well-known fictional characters.

Table 1.3 Desired leadership qualities

| Albus Dumbledore, headmaster of Hogwart's School for Wizards and Witches | Jean-Luc Picard, captain of the starship *Enterprise* |
|---|---|
| Honesty and integrity | Honesty and integrity |
| Competence and credibility | Competence and credibility |
| Inspiration and motivation | Inspiration and motivation |
| Bravery and decisiveness | Bravery and decisiveness |
| Good communication skills | Good communication skills |
| Fairness and equity | Fairness and equity |
| (Sense of humour) | (Sense of humour) |

Sources: The first five Harry Potter books; *Star trek: the new generation*

Table 1.4 provides a comparison of the leadership qualities described in the earlier two tables. How do your choices from the exercise compare? It doesn't matter if they are different—desired leadership qualities vary depending on the person and their current profession, organisation and situation.

## Personal attributes of leaders that people *willingly* follow

Of course, there are other important elements that play their part in successful leadership and in the acquisition and use of power. However, the qualities outlined in Table 1.4 appear to be essential, and if you possess them you will be able to effectively exercise personal power and influence as a leader/manager, both now and in the future.

Let's now look at these leadership qualities and attributes in a little more depth.

### *Honesty and integrity*

Honesty comes from the Latin word *honestas*, meaning 'quality' or 'honour', and integrity is derived from *integra*, meaning 'wholeness'.

Table 1.4 Comparison of desired leadership qualities

| Barry Posner survey | MBA student surveys | Albus Dumbledore | Jean-Luc Picard |
|---|---|---|---|
| Honesty and integrity | Honesty and integrity | Honesty and integrity | Honesty and integrity |
| Competence and credibility | Competence and credibility | Competence and credibility | Competence and credibility |
| Vision and ability to be forward looking | Ability to create direction and vision | Bravery and decisiveness | Bravery and decisiveness |
| Inspiration and motivation | Inspiration and motivation | Inspiration and motivation | Inspiration and motivation |
| Communication that appeals to people's hearts, hopes and dreams | Good two-way communication skills | Good communication skills | Good communication skills |
| Fair mindedness and equity | Parity and equity | Fairness and equity | Fairness and equity |
| (Sense of humour?) | (Sense of humour) | (Sense of humour) | (Sense of humour) |

Power and influence

Honesty and integrity are almost always identified as being the most important qualities of leaders that people would willingly follow. Research shows that employees have great respect for leaders who do not engage in Machiavellian power games, and who exude professional trust, integrity, empathy and reliability (characteristics that are closely associated with emotional intelligence).[10] Such leaders do not make promises they cannot keep, and do not break their promises once they have been made.

Effective and benevolent leaders adhere reasonably strictly to codes of ethics, values and principles, and have a clear sense of right and wrong when making business decisions. Those that don't will, sooner or later, find themselves on the slippery downward slope to the dark side of leadership.

*Competence and credibility*

Not surprisingly, competence and credibility are highly valued leadership attributes, and are often associated with industry-relevant experience, practical business knowledge, intelligence and dynamism. There is little doubt that followers respond more positively to leaders who they believe have 'clout', possess 'smarts', can best represent the interests of their followers, are able to make difficult and important decisions, and can see their ideas through to execution.

For example, all of the leaders mentioned at the beginning of this chapter were able to combine their passion for the work they did and the companies they created and led, with high level practical business acumen and knowledge, toughness and pragmatism. They also led from the front, led by example and asked to be judged on results—not fine words or promises. Their natural energy and enthusiasm also rubbed off on their staff, encouraging them to reach for ever-higher personal goals and objectives.

*Inspiration and motivation*

A willingness to treat their followers as intelligent, creative human beings who will contribute more to an organisation with encouragement, opportunities and rewards is ranked by many managers and professionals as the most important attribute of leaders. To be more accurate, this ability is actually a consequence of understanding how not to *demotivate* or *disempower* one's followers.

Inspirational and motivational leaders demand something more than robotic compliance from their followers. They have the capacity to change their followers' basic beliefs, values and attitudes in order to get from them superior levels of performance and achievement. Sometimes described as 'super bosses', they are perceived to lead by virtue of their ability to inspire devotion, loyalty and extraordinary effort from their followers. Above all else, they understand power and, whether they are benevolent or malevolent leaders, they understand something about human behaviour and how to motivate and influence or, if required, manipulate people to do their bidding. They can be exhausting bosses to work for, because they expect very high levels of motivation and performance from their followers. An often cited example of this kind of boss is the legendary Jack Welch, the former CEO of General Electric, voted 'Business Man of the 20th Century' by *Fortune* magazine in December 2001.

*Vision for the future and sense of direction*

The origin of the word leadership in all English-speaking cultures is *loedan*, an Anglo-Saxon word meaning 'a way, road, path or journey'. For almost all of the time that modern humans have inhabited this planet (about 130 000 years according to the most recent estimates), the primary function of leaders has been to act as the heads of nomadic clans or tribes; leading them from one region to another as the seasons changed, as animals migrated or as the environment changed. In fact, the origin of the word leadership in all cultures throughout the world is—you guessed it—a way, road, path or journey.

Today, human beings still respond to this pathfinding capability in the same way that they have done for millennia. Leaders are often required to take people on journeys to the future and, consequently, they have to be able to get their followers to question existing realities and embrace new ones. Without a vision, or some sense of direction about the future, a leader cannot move an organisation forward or mobilise its employees. The ability to do this has been described as something that often sets true leaders apart from the crowd; a unique ability to spot new business opportunities and new markets, like hounds sniffing out truffles in the woods. Hence, leaders who are capable of envisioning the future and articulating this vision to their followers have another potent form of power to draw on.[11]

Peter Drucker once observed, with his customary clarity, that the only true definition of a leader is 'someone who has followers'.[12] This is something that can be easily forgotten when we create long shopping lists of the skills and qualities of 'great leaders' and 'charismatic CEOs'. In this two-way relationship, the leader helps subordinates achieve valued rewards by directing them towards goals desired by the organisation. In return, subordinates help the leader by performing well, and the better subordinates perform, the better their leaders will perform. In this symbiotic relationship, the leader becomes *a servant* to all of his or her followers, not a directive 'boss' with an in-group of favourites.

### Good communication skills

It has often been said that 'leadership is communication', and so it is no surprise that this invariably appears in employee surveys of desirable leadership qualities. The word communication is derived from the Latin *communicare*—'to make common'—and can be described simply as a process of respectfully sharing information with others in order to improve mutual understanding. Although this sounds deceptively simple, effective communication results from a complex cluster of competencies including:
- the capacity to listen actively to others
- the ability to appeal to hearts and minds
- the capacity to build strong relationships through dialogue
- an understanding of the language of leadership
- good formal presentation skills
- the capacity to communicate with everyone in an organisation in a direct and personal way.

Research in organisations has consistently demonstrated that employees want their leaders to communicate with them more often and involve them in decision-making processes.[13] One study, involving thousands of employees from eighty Australian companies, asked respondents: 'What would improve your workplace more than anything else?' The answer was not 'more perks' or 'higher wages', or even 'more time off'. The top two responses were, 'more effective leadership' and 'good communication with management'.[14]

*Equity/parity*

Leaders who treat all their followers fairly, equitably and with respect, and who do not create in-groups of favourites, retain power over longer periods of time than those who fail to do this. They don't make irrational, prejudicial judgments about people on the basis of their ethnicity, culture, race, gender, sexual orientation or physical abilities. When they do make judgments about other people, these are made on the basis of their character, values, abilities, work performance and the tangible contributions they make to their organisations.

Surprisingly, many political and business leaders still have an unconscious tendency to separate their followers into distinct groups, recruiting an 'in-group' of people they instinctively like, and creating an 'out-group' of people they like less. The consequence of this separation of subordinates into favourites and non-favourites is that each group is treated differently, with the inner group being allowed more latitude in behaviour and much closer relationships with the leader. Being in the in-group also leads to higher motivation and performance and greater loyalty to the organisation.[15]

However, there are many obvious dangers in this behaviour. There may be a tendency to hire only those people who are 'like us', leading to the emergence of a management team of sycophantic 'yes' men and women and, over time, to widespread organisational sclerosis, nepotism and groupthink. This phenomenon can often be found in business organisations, when leaders become arrogant, inward-looking and complacent, surrounded by obsequious acolytes.

Before reading the next paragraph, can you guess which US president this quote describes?

---

*He knew that true leadership is often realised by exerting quiet and subtle influence on a day to day basis, by frequently seeing followers and other people face to face. He treated everyone with the same courtesy and respect, whether they were kings or commoners. He lifted people out of their everyday selves and into a higher level of performance, achievement* and awareness. He obtained extraordinary results from ordinary people by instilling purpose in their endeavours. He was civil, open, tolerant and fair and he maintained a respect for the dignity of all people at all times.[16]

The answer is *Abraham Lincoln*, but notice how contemporary this description of his leadership style sounds. There are clear parallels between this and the leadership style of business leaders like Andy Grove, Akio Morita, Bill Hewlett and Dave Packard, Bill Marriot and Alfred Sloan.

Many successful business leaders have regarded themselves as *primus inter pares* (first among equals) and they understand that true leadership (and power) is influenced by this two-way process with their followers. Hence, genuine power and influence has little to do with 'telling people what to do'. It is rather, at the most fundamental level, the ability to *empower* others.[17]

*Sense of humour*

When you have some free time, browse through the hundreds of job advertisements for senior managers and business leaders that appear in local newspapers or on job sites. In these, frequent references are made to the need for 'exceptional communication skills', 'enhanced ability to lead teams', 'the ability to motivate and mentor staff', 'highly developed people management skills', 'exceptional leadership abilities' and so forth. Almost all job advertisements are very predictable, repetitive, stale shopping lists of competencies and qualities that often have little connection with the characteristics that some recruits actually exhibit, once appointed. Remarkably, one essential factor missing from every single job advertisement I've ever seen is 'having a good sense of humour', the seventh attribute of effective leaders identified earlier in this chapter.

Why might this be an important source of power and influence? Humour comes from the Latin word *umor*, meaning 'fluidity' or 'flexibility', and has been the subject of research since at least the mid-nineteenth century.[18] Contemporary research indicates that this is an overlooked management attribute, even though it would appear to be common sense that it should be an important part of leadership. For example, evidence presented at the British Psychological Society's Annual Conference in January

1999 indicated that staff give far greater credence to humorous senior managers than they do to intelligence and are more productive than staff who work for humorless managers.[19] A survey of fifty-three medium and large businesses, conducted by the Business Council of Australia and the Australian Chamber of Commerce and Industry, revealed that employers are looking for certain personal qualities in addition to technical job skills. These included positive self-esteem, a balanced attitude to work and family life, excellent communication skills, motivation, enthusiasm, commitment and, above all, a sense of humour.[20] This indicates that an important quality for aspiring leaders to acquire is a good sense of humour.

Intuition tells us that a sense of humour is an important but often overlooked personal attribute of influential leader/managers. Humorous people often have the desirable leadership attributes described earlier in this chapter in abundance, because they are usually psychologically healthy, possess emotional intelligence, manage stress well, don't take themselves too seriously and have a genuine interest in other people and their welfare. In contrast, humorless people often have overbearing egos, are unable to listen to others and are toxic to some extent. Some companies have even built the concept of fun into their organisational cultures.[21] Although humour alone will never create a great company or high performing employees, it can be a powerful tool to employ at work; and while it may not be essential for effective leadership, it definitely helps.[22]

### Expert power

Although personal attributes and qualities can be potent sources of influence and authority, there are other important sources of power in business organisations. The first of these is expert power, and its importance is exemplified in the ancient saying 'knowledge is power'. This refers to the authority individuals derive from the specific technical expertise and/or professional knowledge they possess, and this can often be a significant component of individuals' perceived competence and credibility.

Expert power has become increasingly important in businesses characterised by rapid technological change, and knowledge and intellectual capital have emerged as important drivers of organisational growth, adaptability and success in all industrial and technology enterprises. All current indications suggest that expert power and intellectual knowledge/capital will become even more important in the future, as products quickly become obsolete; as markets grow, die, shift and change with increasing rapidity; and as new technologies continue to proliferate at a mind-boggling speed. The most successful organisations in the future will be those that can access their employees' ideas and knowledge, disseminate them rapidly, and quickly embody them in new products or services.

Knowledge is fast becoming one of the most important renewable resources that a company can capture and leverage in order to improve its effectiveness and competitiveness. One of the key roles of business leaders now is to ensure the generation and application of new expert knowledge at a faster and faster rate in their organisations.[23]

Although expert knowledge can be a significant source of personal power and influence, it is important that you do not allow it to become the only source. You might come to be regarded as a niche player, or as someone whose opinions might not be sought in areas outside a narrow range of expertise. You might also be overlooked for promotion to middle management positions because you lack cross-functional expertise and knowledge, or generalist managerial and leadership experience.

## Legitimate, reward and coercive power

These are the most easily recognised and widespread forms of power, derived from the formal structural power and authority of an office, position or role in an organisation. They can have quite remarkable effects on people's perceptions of, and obedience to, authority figures and how they exercise power.

Perhaps the two most famous examples of the effects of positional power and authority were the Milgram studies at Yale in 1961–62, and the Stanford Prison Experiment, conducted during the summer of 1971.

In the first experiment, a laboratory was set up where participants, acting in the role of 'teachers' were told to administer electric shocks to 'learners' who failed to accurately repeat two words that were read to them. The electrical generator had thirty switches, ranging from 'Slight shock' (15 volts) through 'Severe shock' and up to 'Danger: fatal shock'. The last two switches, at 430–450 volts, were labelled 'XXX'. The 'teachers' were told that their learners were strapped into a chair in an adjacent sealed room; and that they were to increase the shock level each time the learner got an answer wrong. What was remarkable about this experiment was that 65% of the participants in the study obeyed orders to administer the shocks and, when instructed by the experimenter, compliantly delivered the maximum possible—and in real life potentially lethal—dose of 450 volts. No participant in the experiment stopped before they had reached 300 volts, and most continued administering shocks even when they could see their victims writhing in agony.

Of course this was a set-up; no actual electric shocks were administered, but the participants did not know this. Before Milgram conducted this experiment he had asked mental health professionals to estimate what proportion of people would administer apparently dangerous levels of shock. The consensus was 1–2%.[24] This study was replicated over a 25-year period, from 1961 to 1985, with similar results reported in Australia, South Africa and several European countries.

In the second experiment (in many respects the forerunner of reality TV shows like *Big brother* and *Survivor*), the participants were divided into two groups—'guards' and 'prisoners'—in a realistic mock-up of a prison, and instructed to role-play as if it was the real thing. Nine students were 'arrested' at their homes, taken to 'jail', strip-searched and processed as if they really were prisoners.

The guards were given full authority to set the prison rules and allocate punishments for infractions by the prisoners. Soon, they were routinely humiliating the prisoner group in an effort to break their will. After the guards had put down a prisoner protest on day two, they steadily increased their coercive tactics and dehumanisation of the prisoners. The worst instances of abuse took place at night, when the guards thought the staff running the experiment were not watching them. For example, they made prisoners clean out the toilets with their bare hands.

What is most interesting about this experiment, which formed the basis of the 2002 German film, *Das Experiment*, was that all the participants were put through a barrage of psychological tests during the initial screening process and had been judged to be the most normal, average and healthy members of an original group of seventy students. And yet, when given positional authority, these apparently normal people started behaving like sadistic monsters within a very short time period.

Even after three decades, the creator of this experiment still expresses surprise at how willingly and enthusiastically the students took on the guard roles, observing that: 'within a few days, the role dominated the person. They became real guards and real prisoners'. So disturbing was the experiment that he cancelled it after just 6 days, rather than allowing it to run for the planned 14 days.[25] It has never been repeated.

These two examples highlight the influence that legitimate/positional power can have on people's behaviour, although it is important to emphasise that formal authority of this kind is quite different to leadership. The examples also demonstrate that legitimate power is often associated with *reward* and *coercive power*. Reward power arises from the opportunities leaders have to use rewards as a way to influence people. This has some parallels with coercive power, because the threat of removing rewards can be regarded as a form of punishment.

Coercive power refers to the use of rewards, exclusion, threats, sanctions, pain and punishment to influence people's behaviour. As history has shown, these have all too often been used for truly monstrous reasons.

The examples cited above also remind us that almost anyone who acquires power and authority has within themselves the potential to abuse them.[26]

## The most effective sources of power

Which of the five forms of power are the most effective in influencing other people? One of the best-known large-scale studies of how 750 managers use power revealed that they typically used seven influencing strategies when dealing with their bosses, subordinates and co-workers. Ranked in order, these were:

1 using reason, data or logic (expert power)
2 friendliness and assertiveness (personal power)
3 forming coalitions with others (personal power)
4 bargaining and/or negotiation (expert and personal power)
5 ordering compliance (legitimate/positional, reward and coercive power)
6 relying on the support of a higher authority (legitimate/positional power)
7 sanctions or punishments (legitimate/positional, reward and coercive power).[27]

There is considerable research evidence to support the view that the use of reason and logic is a powerful influencing strategy. Leaders and managers who use information, facts and data to support their decisions are rated far more highly by their subordinates, when compared to those who use either coercive or legitimate power to force through their ideas. Those who consistently use these latter two strategies have less motivated, more stressed and poorer performing employees. Those who habitually use force, coercion or Machiavellian strategies to drive through their decisions also end up making more bad decisions than good ones.[28]

Coercive and legitimate power strategies also act as *extrinsic* motivators; that is, they simply reward compliance and punish inappropriate behaviours. Forty years of research into motivation shows that these strategies are the least effective ways of motivating people because, over time, they diminish the capacity of individuals to change, improve and develop *themselves*.

By comparison, high *intrinsic* employee motivation—the internal passion and commitment employees have about their work—is one of the primary drivers of both individual and organisational excellence.[29] Further support for this position can be found in numerous research experiments on small work groups. For example, in one study work groups were divided into two sub-groups. The first groups were given the freedom to make influential decisions about their work tasks, and the other groups were prohibited from doing this. The managers of the powerless groups reported that their employees were not motivated to work hard, were unsuitable for promotion, and evaluated their overall work performance less favourably than the leaders of the empowered work groups.[30]

The most effective and productive power and influence strategies are:
- using reason, data or logic (expert power)
- friendliness and assertiveness (personal power)
- forming coalitions with others (personal power)
- bargaining and/or negotiation (expert and personal power).

The least effective and most divisive power and influence strategies are:
- ordering compliance (legitimate, reward and coercive power)
- relying on the support of a higher authority (legitimate power)
- sanctions or punishments (legitimate and coercive power).

Effective leader/managers use personal and expert power as much as possible, but will occasionally draw on the other three if the situation demands it. Although coercive or Machiavellian power strategies may have to be used in emergency or life-threatening situations (more about this later), in most organisational contexts these strategies should only be used as a last resort because they are the most ineffective way of influencing others.

## The dark side of power

Earlier I suggested that most managers and professionals have great respect for leaders who exude professional honesty, integrity, empathy and reliability. I also focused on the qualities of what can be broadly described as 'good' leaders—men and women who bring added value to the organisations they lead, and have positive effects on the people they work with.

There is, of course, a dark side to leadership and power. During their careers most people will encounter not only incompetent leaders, but also individuals in positions of power who enjoy undermining, bullying or intimidating their staff. Bullying can range from sexual harassment to more subtle behaviours, such as imposing unrealistic deadlines and unpaid overtime on employees, or constant criticism and sarcasm.

People who behave in this manner have been described as having 'toxic' personalities, and their toxicity can have a damaging effect on the health, wellbeing and performance of those people who are unfortunate enough to encounter them.

## Power and the toxic personality

How can we spot potential bullies and toxic personalities? People who are tyrants and bullies in adulthood became little tyrants and bullies during their formative years. Although a detailed discussion of exactly how this happens is beyond the scope of this chapter, many childhood bullies do evolve into cunning and manipulative adults. According to psychologists, toxic personalities will exhibit most of the following traits:

- They are impatient, arrogant, perfectionist, defensive, rigid and blunt, with a large capacity for holding grudges.
- They are likely to be highly intelligent, but use this entirely for their own ends and their own self-aggrandisement.
- They have little empathy with other people and any decisions they make are driven by one consideration: 'What's in this for me?'
- They will use an autocratic management style with their subordinates, but behave compliantly towards their superiors.
- They will often lack a sense of humour, and take themselves and their own opinions *very* seriously.

People with deeply toxic personalities can affect others in a similar fashion to the evil Dementors in the popular Harry Potter series, who 'glory in decay and despair, and drain peace, hope and happiness out of the air around them' and—literally—eat people's souls.[31]

Some toxic personalities may become fully-fledged psychopaths. In some widely publicised research on 105 psychopaths in Scottish jails in 1996, the British psychologist Lisa Marshall revealed that politicians and stockbrokers share many of the same characteristics as criminal psychopaths. The only difference is that career high-flyers (a category that includes people in business) usually manage to stay within the law, or at least not get caught.[32]

To be labelled psychopathic, an individual needs to display ten of these psychopathological tendencies:[33]

- selfishness
- callousness
- remorseless use of others
- tendency to lie

- cunning
- failure to accept responsibility for actions
- extreme egotism
- extreme sense of self-worth
- emotional instability
- antisocial tendencies
- need for constant stimulation
- irresponsibility
- unrealistic long-term goals
- a sexually deviant or promiscuous lifestyle
- behavioural and emotional problems in childhood
- juvenile delinquency.

Like an unwelcome virus, they seem to have spread themselves around almost all organisations. As Alistair Mant has observed, there is a disturbing number of toxic leaders and managers 'who seem to survive and flourish, spewing their neuroses all about them right to the bitter end'.[34] They also appear to be particularly attracted to careers in politics, the law, finance and stockbroking or to get-rich-quick scams. In a few cases, they even manage to juggle two or three of these at the same time. In the words of one Wall Street commentator:

*Something is wrong with—what shall we call it?—Wall Street, Big Business. We'll call it Big Money. Something has been wrong with it for a long time, at least a decade, maybe more. I don't fully understand it. I can't imagine it's this simple: a new generation of moral and ethical zeroes rose to run Big Money over the past decade, and nobody quite noticed that they were genuinely bad people who were running the system into the ground. Those who invested in and placed faith in Global Crossing, Enron, Tyco or Worldcom have been cheated and fooled by individuals whose selfishness seems so outsized, so huge, that it seems less human and flawed than weird and puzzling. Did they think they would get away with accounting scams forever? Did they think they'd never get caught? We should study who these men are—they are still all men—and try to learn how they rationalised their actions, how they excused their decisions, and how they thought about the people they were cheating. I mention this because I've been wondering if we are witnessing the emergence of a new pathology.*[35]

Toxic behaviour can cause other significant problems in any workplace. It may result in lower morale and work performance as well as increased absenteeism, and possible legal costs associated with handling workplace bullying claims. In one survey, it was estimated that workplace bullying claims cost one Australian State, Victoria, A$26 million a year.[36] Ray Catanzarita, a senior partner in the law firm Clayton Utz, made these comments at the time:

> Examining the figures independently has highlighted the significant costs of bullying in the workplace. Aside from the immense financial cost, bullying can result in severe emotional and even psychological damage. With this point in mind, it may be timely to consider national standards to provide employers and employees with guidance on how to prevent, or at least minimise, workplace bullying. Violence and bullying are undesirable in any workplace, and any measure which may facilitate their reduction is a step in the right direction.[37]

The question is: 'What strategies can be employed if you have to have to deal with bullies and toxic personalities who are in power?'

## Machiavellian power games

Several books appeared in the 1990s and early 2000s with the stated intention of putting Machiavelli back into business. These included Grifin's *Machiavelli on management: playing and winning the corporate power game*,[38] McAlpine's *The new Machiavelli: the art of politics in business*,[39] *The 48 laws of power* by Robert Greene[40] and some tongue-in-cheek advice from a real-life coup leader, Andre de Guillaume, in *How to rule the world: a handbook for the aspiring dictator*.[41] These books suggest a number of extremely devious and underhand strategies that can be used to gain power, although it has to be said that some of their suggestions are rather nebulous or vague, and a few may even be illegal in some countries.

Nevertheless, as discussed earlier, even with the best possible intentions there will be times and situations when you may have to operate within the dark side of power. So the question is, what strategies can you use if that is the case, or if your organisation has a very political organisational culture that is underpinned by

power games? The authors mentioned suggest a range of strategies that can be employed in these situations. I have condensed them into the following:
1. Treat power as a social game.
2. Protect your reputation.
3. Praise your leaders.
4. Make people dependent on you.
5. Avoid people who are toxic, negative, self-obsessed, unhappy or unlucky.
6. Don't say more than you have to.
7. Conceal your intentions and don't take sides in haste.
8. Don't fight battles you can't win and ensure that you crush your opponents when the time is right.

*Treat power as a social game*

The word 'game' is often used synonymously with power and politics, and for a very good reason. Like chess, this is a game that must be played with a clear idea of our personal strategies (and alternative strategies), and a good understanding of what our opponents' strategies are likely to be (and where their strong and weak points are).

Our energy must be focused at all times on the best strategies to use, as well as the personalities of our opponents. To use power well, we have to be both master players and master psychologists, recognising the needs and motivations of others while at the same time not becoming emotionally involved with them. An understanding of these hidden needs and motives is the greatest power tool that we can ever possess, because we will then be able to appeal to, and make use of, the self-interests of others while pursuing our own goals and objectives.

*Protect your reputation*

As discussed earlier, your personal reputation (how others perceive you) is the bedrock of personal power. If this slips, you are vulnerable.
- Make your reputation unassailable.
- Maintain a professional (but friendly) space between yourself and work colleagues.

As a former mentor of mine once observed: 'I look at it this way. You don't have to make love with these people, you don't have to socialise with them after work or be their lifelong buddies. I deliberately maintain a space between myself and everyone else who works here. What you have to try to do is develop good working relationships and maintain a professional, impartial approach with everyone, even if they do sometimes behave like w★★★★★rs.'

*Praise your leaders*

Or at least do not criticise them by name in public. Sooner or later, someone will report back to them what you have said.
- Act as the perfect courtier; yield to superiors and flatter them when the opportunity arises.
- Don't upstage your superiors in public.
- Learn about their private interests and personal goals.
- Support their ideas in public, but offer critical advice, tactfully, in private.

Your power and influence will also increase if you are willing 'to go the extra mile' for them, and help them out with problems and difficulties they may encounter at work.

*Make people dependent on you*

To maintain your independence, you must be *needed* by other people. The more you are relied on, the more freedom, influence and power you will have.
- Cultivate relationships at every opportunity—with your peers, your bosses and your clients.
- Act as a mentor for junior staff.
- Be a team player and share in your colleagues' accomplishments.
- Support your colleagues' ideas and suggestions and be responsive to their problems without endangering your own interests.
- Be seen as someone people can chat with confidentially about work issues.
- Be honest with the people who do rely on you, but keep your cards close to your chest.
- Don't reveal more than you need to.
- Find allies and mingle—isolation is dangerous.

Work on people's hearts *and* minds. If you have to ask other people for help, appeal to their self-interest. Try to find or uncover something that will benefit them if they help you. Professional politicians know this as the 'reciprocity strategy'.

*Avoid people who are toxic, negative, self-obsessed, unhappy or unlucky*

Associate with people who make you feel good and valued, or whose positive reputation will reflect well on you. Avoid people who are always negative, self-obsessed or just interested in their own agendas, but try to deal professionally and calmly with second-rate, difficult or toxic employees at all times. When you are dealing with such people, focus on their actions and strategies, and what these mean.

Anger and emotion are counter-productive because they cloud reason and clarity of thought.
- Try to remain calm and objective at all times.
- Remember that other people cannot *make* you angry, only you can allow yourself to *become* angry (and toxic personalities thrive on the emotional discomfort of others).
- Learn from previous occasions when you have allowed emotions to damage your case and don't repeat them.

Train yourself to take nothing personally and never show defensiveness or vulnerability. If you do, you might expose an Achilles heel that your opponent can strike at. But, if you can make an opponent lose control of his or her temper in a public space, you will gain an advantage.

*Don't say more than you have to*

The more you talk, or seek to hog the limelight, the less effective you will be.
- Only talk when you have to and when you really have something valuable, insightful or pertinent to contribute to discussions or decision-making processes at work.
- Use logic, data and facts to support your position—not bluster, polemic or personal opinions.
- Whenever you can, let your actions persuade others, because they will often speak louder than any words you use or any arguments you win.

- Nobody likes to feel less intelligent than another person. The trick is to make other people feel smarter than you. Once convinced of this, they will not suspect that you may have ulterior motives or be a threat to them.
- Never say or do anything that could be held against you.
- Control how you use valuable information.
- If you can act on information before an opponent knows about it, you can often gain an advantage.

*Conceal your intentions and don't take sides in haste*

If you are going to create a stir, keep people in the dark.
- Do not reveal your intentions in advance.
- Don't be predictable—occasionally surprise and confound your colleagues.
- The only cause you should concentrate on is your own.
- If you have to choose sides, take your time to carefully evaluate which will be the winning one. In this context, recall the adage: 'Fools rush in to take sides'.

*Don't fight battles you can't win and ensure that you crush your opponents*

- Surrender the occasional battle if you have to, but stay focused on winning the war.
- Concentrate your energies and resources on important victories, not the Pyrrhic ones.
- Life is short, opportunities are few and you only have so much energy to expend in locking horns with people at work.
- If you want to neutralise an opponent, you must know as much as possible about them.
- Everyone has weaknesses or skeletons in the cupboard—find out what these are, but only use them when the time is right.
- Timing is everything and support is vital. Make sure that you have enough supporters to enable the removal or deposition of your opponent before this is proposed.
- Make sure that you crush your opponents completely, or they may come back to get you at some point in the future. As the master of political skulduggery, Machiavelli, once observed: 'When he seizes power, the new ruler must determine all the injuries he will need to inflict. He must inflict them once and for all.'

### Beyond Machiavelli

Although there may be times when our survival, or the survival of a project we're involved in, forces us to make use of the 'dark side' of power, this is ultimately self-destructive. Sooner or later, it will involve cheating and lying, as well as deceitful and malicious behaviour towards others. In time, these will lead to significant personal or organisational problems.

Furthermore, engagement with the dark side of power and Machiavellian political strategies uses up a tremendous amount of time, energy and resources—at the individual, group or organisational level. These are precious commodities in all businesses these days, and highly politicised working cultures are characterised by time-wasting, turf battles, in-fighting, backbiting and cheap point-scoring, rather than active engagement with the productive and creative aspects of organisational leadership and management.

In companies like Enron, Worldcom and many others, the abovementioned toxic attributes were also closely associated with a psychopathic level of personal greed, avarice, egoism and selfishness, resulting in some of the biggest corporate scandals in history.

## Conclusion

There is one question that remains to be addressed in this opening chapter. Is there anything to learn about the use of power and influence that our ancestors were not familiar with?

More than 2300 years ago the Greek philosopher, Aristotle, suggested that prospective leaders, having acquired self-awareness and wisdom, needed to develop three additional clusters of competencies:
- *Ethos* the ability to convince their followers that they were trustworthy, reliable and fair (honesty and integrity; equity and parity)
- *Pathos* the ability to appeal to their followers' values, emotions and motivations (vision; communication; motivation and inspiration)
- *Logos* knowledge and expertise (credibility and competence; expert knowledge).

This indicates that the core attributes of leaders who wield power and influence have been understood for a very, very long time. Although there have been significant technological, political, economic and social changes over the last 2000 years that have modified the way that power and influence are now understood and exercised, the ancient leadership qualities described by Aristotle (and many other historical figures of note) are as relevant today as they have always been. If we can enhance or develop these qualities, then we can truly start to make things happen in new and exciting ways.

In summary, leaders who possess genuine power and influence are capable of:
- taking calculated gambles that lead to successful results
- quickly learning how to use, or change, organisational rules to their best advantage
- sharing power with their followers (which reinforces and enhances their personal power bases)
- acquiring, using and sharing information to further their interests and those of their followers
- exploiting new opportunities that come their way, but also of having the capacity to create these.

As a result, such leaders are better able to compete and win, and to achieve their objectives without resorting to the dark side of power. And, although they may be highly driven individuals, they do not step over the line into unethical leadership and business practices.

The use of power and influence is a complex art, not an exact science, and there is no single best power and influencing strategy to adopt. The strategy you choose to use will be strongly influenced by your personality traits and leadership/management styles; the kind of organisation you work for and its political culture; and the nature of the problems or conflicts that you routinely deal with.

Having said this, it is important that leaders and managers work on developing all their power bases (primarily personal and expert, but also legitimate, reward and coercive), because all will be needed at some point in their careers. The more 'tools' they have at their disposal, the more effective they will be in dealing with any problems that arise in their organisations.

The more strategies you prepare in advance, the greater your chances of success; the fewer strategies, the more limited your options and the chances of success within your organisation and in your career, both now and in the future.

## Wise sayings about power and influence

1 *Honesty and integrity are non-negotiable organisational values at Wesfarmers.*

> Michael Chaney, CEO of Wesfarmers, during a talk to MBA students at the University of Western Australia Graduate School of Management, April 2004[42]

2 *Leaders should have clean hands, warm hearts and cool minds.*

> James Sarros and Oleh Buchatsky, 1999[43]

3 *Power is the ultimate aphrodisiac.*

> Henry Kissinger, foreign secretary to former US president 'Tricky-Dicky' Nixon, 1975[44]

4 *You do not lead by hitting people over the head—that's assault, not leadership.*

> General Dwight D Eisenhower, Supreme Allied Commander during World War II.

5 *Power corrupts and absolute power corrupts absolutely.*

> Lord Acton, 1895

6 *A leader is best when people hardly know he exists, not so good when people obey and acclaim him, worse when they despise him. But of a good leader, who talks little, when his work is done, his aim fulfilled, they will say, 'We did it ourselves'.*

> Lau-Tzu, 6th century Chinese philosopher

7 *Most powerful is he who has himself in his own power. He who has great power should use it lightly.*

> Seneca, 1st century Roman senator and historian

# For further exploration

- D Carnegie, *How to win friends and influence people*, Simon & Schuster, New York, 1994.
  More than 15 million copies of this influential book have been sold and it is packed with useful ideas and insights.
- J Collins, *Good to great: why some companies make the leap and others don't*, Harper Business, New York, 2001.
- J Collins & J Porras, *Built to last: successful habits of visionary companies*, Century, London, 1996.
  These two books are, to date, the most definitive books on the 'secrets' of sustained corporate success and longevity, and the use of power and influence, by their mainly modest, honest, self-effacing and uncharismatic leaders.
- N Forster, *Maximum performance: a practical guide to leading and managing people at work*, Edward Elgar, Cheltenham, 2004.
  This book contains hundreds of practical tips and suggestions on many facets of contemporary organisational leadership and people management (including power, politics and influencing strategies) from business and political leaders, managers and professionals, MBA and Executive MBA students, management consultants and business academics.
- J Kouzes & B Posner, *The leadership challenge*, Jossey-Bass, San Francisco, 1997.
  One of the best books on leadership, power and influence written in the last 20 years—practical, grounded, full of useful insights and intellectually rigorous.
- A McAlpine, *The new Machiavelli: the art of politics in business*, Wiley, London, 1999.
  One of several more recent books that explore ways of utilising the dark side of power—to be read with a pinch of salt.
- R Semler, *Maverick: the success story behind the world's most unusual company*, Century, London, 2001.
  The classic text about the numerous benefits that arise when leaders surrender their power, abandon command-and-control style management and empower their employees.

# Notes

1. W Bennis & B Nanus, *Leaders: the strategies of taking charge*, Harper and Row, New York, 1985.
2. Janus was the two-headed (and two-faced) Roman deity, who had two sets of eyes—one pair focusing on challenges that lay ahead and the other focusing on what lay behind.
3. Adapted from D McClelland, *Power: the inner experience*, Irvington, New York, 1975.
4. D McClelland, 1975, p. 263.
5. For example, see N Forster, *Maximum performance: a practical guide to leading and managing people at work*, Edward Elgar, Cheltenham, 2004; J Collins, *Good to great: why some companies make the leap and others don't*, Harper Business, New York, 2001; J Collins & J Porras, *Built to last: successful habits of visionary companies*, Century, London, 1996.
6. Abridged from J Kouzes & B Posner, *The leadership challenge*, Jossey-Bass, San Francisco, 1997, pp. 184, 186–7.
7. Exercise adapted from J Kouzes & B Posner, 1997.
8. Professor Barry Posner, Australian Institute of Management Leadership Conference, Hyatt Regency Hotel, Perth, Western Australia, 10 March 2004.
9. Graduate School of Management, Perth, Western Australia, Master of Business Administration Leadership Seminars, 1997–2004.
10. A discussion of emotional intelligence (EI) is beyond the scope of this chapter, but this cluster of leadership traits really stands out from the recent literature on leadership effectiveness. Advocates of EI contend that EQ is the single most reliable indicator of leadership effectiveness, far outweighing traditional IQ measures or even technical competence. In many ways, EI leadership is the polar opposite of dysfunctional, toxic, domineering and corrupt leadership. There is also evidence that EI principles can be learnt by organisations, leading to enhanced employee performance, productivity and bottom line results.

    For more information, see D Goleman, 'What makes a leader?', *Harvard Business Review*, January 2004, pp. 91–2; D Goleman, R Boyatzis & A McKee, *The new leaders: transforming*

*the art of leadership into the science of results,* Little Brown, London, 2002; D Goleman, 'Leadership that gets results', *Harvard Business Review,* March–April 2000, pp. 78–90.
11 For further information on this ability, see N Forster, 2004 (see note 5).
12 P Drucker, *The effective executive,* Prentice-Hall, Englewood Cliffs, 1966.
13 J Brownell, 'Perceptions of effective listeners: a management study', *Journal of Business Communication,* vol. 27, 1990, pp. 401–15.
14 N Pope & P Berry, 'Top down approach doesn't work', *Australian Financial Review,* 1 December 1995.
15 D Kipnis & S Schmidt, 'Why do I like thee: is it your performance or my orders', *Journal of Applied Psychology,* vol. 66, no. 3, 1983, pp. 324–8.
16 DT Phillips, *Lincoln on leadership: executive strategies for tough times,* Warner Books, USA, 1993.
17 See also D Uren, 'Smart thinkers bring passion to power roles', *Weekend Australian,* business section, 9–10 October 1999; N Forster, 2004, chs 1, 4 and 7 (see note 5).
18 J Spencer, *The physiology of laughter,* 1863.
19 N Forster, 2004, ch. 1 (see note 5).
20 S Stock, 'Laughing yourself into a job', *Australian,* business section, 29 May 2002.
21 These include The SAS Institute (the largest privately owned software company in the world), Scandia, Cisco Systems, Southwest Airlines, Google, Deloittes and Diageo (formerly Guinness UDV). All of these companies have been extremely successful in their respective markets over the last decade. For example, although almost every airline in the world struggled during the meltdown of the world's airline industry during 2002–03, Southwest Airline's performance was nothing short of remarkable. During 2001–02, it was was the only top ten US airline company to post a profit and became the sixth largest airline company in the USA during 2003. It was also declared the best performing US stock of the last decade by *Money* magazine in December 2002 ('Southwest skirts the storm: with the industry in crisis, Southwest is the airline others are

watching with increasing interest', *Australian,* business section, 2 May 2003). For more information on the role of humour and fun in organisations, see N Forster, 2004 (note 5).

22 N Forster, 2004 (see note 5).
23 N Forster, 2004, ch. 10.
24 S Milgram, 'Behavioural study of obedience', *Journal of Abnormal and Social Psychology,* vol. 67, 1963, pp. 371–8.
25 P Zimbardo, 'Stanford prison experiment: a simulation study of the psychology of imprisonment conducted at Stanford University', 1999 at <www.prisonexp.org>.
26 Adapted from J French & B Raven, 'The bases of social power', in D Cartwright (ed.), *Studies in social power,* University of Michigan Institute for Social Research, Michigan, 1959, pp. 150–67; J Carlopio, G Andrewartha & H Armstrong, *Developing management skills: a comprehensive guide for leaders,* 2nd edn, Pearson Education, Frenchs Forest, NSW, 2001, pp. 260–80; J Pfeffer, *Managing with power,* Harvard Business School Press, Boston, 1992.
27 Adapted from D Kipnis, 'Patterns of managerial influence: shotgun managers, tacticians and bystanders,' *Organizational Dynamics,* Winter 1984, pp. 58–67; R Lippitt, 'The changing leader–follower relationships of the 1980s', *Journal of Applied Behavioural Science,* vol. 18, 1982, pp. 78–81.
28 For example, see S Schmidt & D Kipnis, 'The perils of persistence', *Psychology Today,* vol. 21, 1987, pp. 32–3; D Kipnis & S Schmidt, 1983 (see note 15).
29 Among many examples of this, see Corporate Research Foundation, *The best companies in Australia to work for,* Harper-Collins, Crows Nest, NSW, 2003; R Semler, *Maverick: the success story behind the world's most unusual company,* Century, London, 2001; C O'Reilly & J Pfeffer, *Hidden value: how great companies achieve extraordinary results with ordinary people,* Harvard Business School Press, Boston, 2000; J Collins & J Porras, 1996 (see note 5); D McClelland & D Burnham, 'Power is the great motivator', *Harvard Business Review,* January–February 1995, pp. 126–32; V Vroom, *Work and motivation,* Wiley, New York, 1964.
30 D Kipnis, 1984 (see note 27).

**31** J Rowling, *Harry Potter and the prisoner of Azkaban*, Bloomsbury, London, 1999, p. 140.
**32** Lisa Marshall, cited by J Bennetto in 'Q: What's the difference between a politician and a psychopath? A: None', *The Independent*, 7 July 1996.
**33** I Murray, 'Bullies score top marks for cunning', *Australian*, 21 January 2002.
**34** A Mant, *Leaders we deserve,* Blackwell, Oxford, 1993.
**35** Abridged from P Noonan, 'White collar big money psychopath', *Wall Street Journal On-Line*, 1 July 2002. For many other examples of the behaviour of toxic personalities, see N Forster, 2004, chs 1, 7 and 12 (note 5). Many of the traits of real-life toxic leaders can be found in the fictional character of David Brent, Manager of Wernham-Hogg, in the comedy series *The office* (BBC Productions 2002–03). For more on this wonderful take on work and dysfunctional management, visit <www.bbc.co.uk/comedy/theoffice>.
**36** J Catanzariti, 'Code tackles problem of workplace bullies', *Weekend Australian*, 2–3 March 2002.
**37** J Catanzariti, 2002.
**38** G Grifin, *Machiavelli on management: playing and winning the corporate power game*, Praeger Publications, New York, 1991.
**39** A McAlpine, *The new Machiavelli: the art of politics in business*, Wiley, London, 1999.
**40** R Greene, *The 48 laws of power*, Hodder, Sydney, 1999.
**41** A de Guillaume, *How to rule the world: a handbook for the aspiring dictator*, Allen & Unwin, Crows Nest, NSW, 2002.
**42** Michael Chaney, CEO of Wesfarmers, during a talk to MBA students at the UWA Graduate School of Management, April 2004.
**43** J Sarros & O Buchatsky, *Leadership and values*, Harper-Collins, Sydney, 1996.
**44** H Kissinger, D Eisenhower, Lord Acton, Lau-Tzu and Seneca quotes viewed at <http://www.quotationspage.com>.

# PERSUASION AND INFLUENCE 2

Caroline Hatcher

Introduction

What is persuasion?

Persuasion and soft control

The power of identification

Audience, audience, audience!

Credibility

Non-verbal communication

Winning words

   Profile: Carly Fiorina

   Profile: Jack Welch

Conclusion

For further exploration

Notes

# About the author

Caroline Hatcher, BA, BEd, MA (Hons), PhD

Dr Caroline Hatcher is MBA Director and a Senior Lecturer in the Graduate School of Business, Faculty of Business at the Queensland University of Technology. She has 15 years experience in tertiary teaching in the areas of speech communication, organisational communication and intercultural business communication.

Caroline is widely published and she regularly presents at international conferences. She is a co-author of *Speaking persuasively: the essential guide to giving dynamic presentations and speeches* (Allen & Unwin, 2002), now in its second edition in Australia and distributed in the UK and USA through international publisher Sage.

As President (2003–04) of the Australian and New Zealand Communication Association, Secretary-General of the World Communication Association, and a Director of the Society of Business Communicators (Qld), Caroline is actively involved in many aspects of communication research and practice.

She has lived and worked in the UK and Japan as well as in Australia. Caroline's consultancy work, to individuals and to organisations in the private and public sectors, involves providing advice on effective presentation skills and internal communication in organisations.

Caroline Hatcher can be contacted at <c.hatcher@qut.edu.au>.

# Executive summary

Every leader needs to be a good communicator. Unfortunately, all too often, we assume that the really good communicators are 'just naturals'. This chapter explores the reasons why, more than ever before, leaders—and managers more generally—need to win the hearts and minds of those they work with through persuasion, and to do so with integrity.

Modern organisations are full of people who want to be self-directed and in control of their destinies. Individualistic, autonomy-seeking employees demand both the opportunity to experience a challenging, engaging and stimulating workplace and the setting of clear boundaries and guidelines about the direction of the organisation. Consequently, persuasive communication, not authority, is now the critical link between leaders and their followers.

As a leader, you must ensure that others:
- understand your reasoning and your commitment to them and the organisation
- trust that you have the answers they need so they can commit to your goals
- clearly understand what you want them to do next, without the need for constant monitoring and direction.

This chapter offers some advice on the strategies that will help you achieve these outcomes, and some profiles of outstanding, persuasive communicators who put those strategies to work every day.

# Introduction

Leaders come in all shapes and sizes. However, one thing that successful leaders have in common is that they are easily recognisable for their passionate commitment to their goals and their unswerving determination to achieve them.

This type of passion was nominated as a 'unique form of sustainable competitive advantage' by ex-president of the International Association of Business Communicators, Kevin Thomson.[1] He claims a range of benefits for having passion at work—from excellence in customer service, enthusiasm for quality products and a spirit of innovation through to the capacity to motivate people to develop products that sell. This passion for success is often quite infectious and is exuded quite naturally by 'natural leaders'. Or is it?

Many managers are passionately committed to success, but they find themselves struggling to communicate their passion to their staff. Persuading staff to reach your organisation's goals and getting commitment is a significant challenge in contemporary times. It is for this reason that the capacity of a manager to persuasively communicate ideas and relationship-manage their staff is a significant dimension of leadership competency.[2]

The ability to communicate persuasively will enhance all of your other management skills, such as financial and human resource management, because it ensures that staff can:

- clearly understand your reasoning, and your commitment to the organisation and to them
- trust that you have the answers they need so they can commit to your goals and to make them their own
- understand what you want them to do next (perhaps the most important).

Carly Fiorina, CEO of Hewlett-Packard, recommends that the job of the leader should be 'to set the frame, to set the people free'.[3]

So this chapter provides an overview of the reasons why all contemporary managers need, now more than ever before, to be persuasive communicators. By considering some of the shifts in the social landscape and the changing power dynamics of organisations, this reasoning will become clear.

Having persuaded you of the value of committing to such a

goal, I will then outline some key elements of persuasive communication. The chapter will also provide you with examples of the way some inspiring leaders have used effective communication to mobilise their listeners. It is my hope that through this information you will gain some useful directions for developing your own persuasive skills.

## What is persuasion?

Persuasive leaders have most likely created their positive image with a great deal of hard work and strategic thinking. They are also experienced hands at doing so with integrity. After all, we put our trust in those we admire rather than in those who promise more than they can deliver.

Models of outstanding communication such as Jack Welch and Richard Branson are an inspiration to us all. Even a cursory reading of Jack Welch's autobiography, *Jack: what I've learned leading a great company and great people*,[4] or Richard Branson's *Losing my virginity*,[5] would highlight the highly conscious and conscientious attempts of both men to shape their communication in order to win the hearts and minds of their various stakeholders. Branson's account of his determination to stay true to his convictions, and to be successful while taking seriously his social responsibility, demonstrates it is possible to be successful and persuasive and to act with integrity. He is one of that rare breed of celebratory entrepreneurs whose motives are seldom questioned and who attracts staff who want to work for his company. *Being trustworthy pays dividends.*

But what does it mean to be persuasive? Although many people think of persuasion as a moment in time when someone tries to encourage another to do what they want, I want to propose a much broader way to think of persuasion.

> *Persuasion occurs when one or more people are involved in both one-off and ongoing activities or processes that create, modify, reinforce or change the beliefs, attitudes, intentions, motivations or behaviours of others.*

This process can be two-way, with modifications to the meaning of the interactions coming from the interaction itself.

And managers can increase their persuasive impact if their staff experience a heightened engagement within the interaction.

Being persuasive requires that a manager be rhetorically sophisticated. The concept of rhetoric, or the art of persuasion, is based on the notion that language can act as a symbolic means of inducing cooperation because people, by their nature, respond to symbols. Consequently, choosing a particular set of symbols, including words and images, creates the means for us to 'see' the world in a particular way. Rhetorical skill lies in finding the symbolic means to create a complementary view of an issue and, in doing so, resolve the differences in perspectives that others may feel. Thus, having the capacity for rhetorical sophistication allows us to create a *shared view* of a particular issue.

Although rhetoric has received a lot of bad press, it is important to recognise that rhetorical skill is not of itself ethical or unethical. Having rhetorical skill is just like having financial skill. How well you use these capacities will determine the outcomes, and there is the same onus on you to use this skill with integrity as there is with all of your other managerial skills. Nonetheless, because persuasive communication is often subtle and behaviour shaping, you have a particular responsibility to ensure that you consider the outcomes for all stakeholders and do not use your rhetorical sophistication to manipulate those around you.

An important part of persuasion occurs when managers and employees 'imagine' or envision together. The symbolic processes that occur in meetings and conversations create new ways to think and are integral parts of the persuasive process (in addition to the obvious processes such as modifying beliefs or changing people's behaviours).

Managers have a critical role in inventing and managing meaning in an organisation, and this process can play an important part in creating new and inspiring ways for employees to see what is going on around them.

Persuasion can be systematic, deliberate and thoughtful. If you are the target of such a deliberate message, you will no doubt recognise it. However, we can also be persuaded more indirectly, when meaning is channelled through heuristic cues. These heuristic cues are the rules that guide how we make sense of the world. All of us carry rules around in our heads that we have learned from childhood and that we develop through our experience. Most times, these decision rules or heuristic cues seem like natural things to do and become an automatic part of our thinking, so that we don't even notice we are using them. For example, while you are focusing on the content of a message and scrutinising the arguments systematically, a number of other activities are occurring. You might reflect that the source of the message is a very credible CEO, or that he or she has outlined six reasons to commit to the idea (you notice that it seems a very large number of reasons). You might respond positively to the opportunity offered by the CEO to 'imagine together', or find his or her message inspiring because she or he looks confident, warm and enthusiastic.

In other words, although the specifics of the messages are important, many of the *meta-messages*—the messages about how to understand a message—are critical also and are part of the persuasive process.

Another way to think about persuasion is to consider the 'sufficiency' principle;[6] that is, when making a decision, we usually strive to know as much as we need, but no more or less. There is enough support for this principle in literature on persuasion to assert that those who wish to persuade others seldom need to present a comprehensive, all-encompassing argument about an issue, because in most cases listeners make up their minds well before they reach the end of a long, detailed, comprehensive and potentially turgid overview.

All of this is a reminder that a rational argument, on its own, is often not enough to achieve commitment. Persuasion is a complex and multi-faceted process which often engages our hearts as well as our reason.

To begin, let's listen in on a familiar interaction at a local advertising company.

## Facing up or getting out

*The room is full of the sorts of people you have come to expect at a business meeting. There is the usual array of older, tired and overweight men and a large handful of handsome, well-dressed young bucks. Beside this younger group are two beautifully dressed, perfectly made up young women, and at the edge of* the group, two neatly and expensively dressed 50-year-old women who carry themselves well but with determination.

One of the older men, James Williams, is the managing director of the group and commands the attention of the room. Each of the managers in the room is focused attentively on the closing words of the meeting. Jim is speaking quietly but intensely.

We have had a great year. We have two major new clients, our established clients seem to be coasting along, and we have appointed some bright young graduates who have good ideas.

However, if we want to stay at the top, we need more than good ideas. I need each and every one of you to give me more! It's not enough to do a good job. I want you to care about what you do! I want you to ask yourselves this question: *Are you passionate about Denko Advertising?* If you are, the rest will follow! If you are not, then we are asking too much of you, and maybe Denko is not for you.

Is James Williams asking the right question?

## Persuasion and soft control

I'm sure *passion* is a word that all managers recognise from their professional readings, their conversations with other organisational members, and from the popular press. So why is the image of the 'passionate' manager so central to management success today?

There has been a significant shift in the way managers must relate to their staff. Hierarchical, authority-based relationships are being or have been replaced with matrix-style, team-based work. Although there are now strong accountability lines in organisations and greater imperatives for employees to meet task goals, there is also a democratic imperative and a growing preference for challenging work and competent management.

Richard Florida's thought provoking book, *The rise of the creative class*,[7] demonstrates through a range of large-scale surveys that challenge and responsibility are the most important drivers of job satisfaction in the contemporary workplace, and that working with talented peers is a critical dimension of what matters to employees. The notion of empowerment and individual autonomy is widespread, and what might be termed 'hard' control has been replaced with 'soft' control and self-discipline.

So, managers need 'unobtrusive' and indirect forms of control to do their job well.[8] This form of control is subtle but encompassing, and works because staff know the 'thinking' of the organisation; they understand what is going on and why the organisation is moving in a particular direction, and they choose to commit to that direction. If staff are to feel empowered to make decisions and act out the organisation's goals, they need to be absolutely clear about those goals.

Soft control is a form of self-regulation that comes from within, rather than from external controls—that's why it can be thought of as unobtrusive. Our society now values self-direction and individuals value being in charge of their own destinies, so members of organisations resent being constantly monitored and controlled, but will willingly regulate their behaviour if they understand and commit to the logic and passion of the organisation.

This subtle form of control requires that employees become connected, committed and inspired to do their best for their organisation and, in particular, for their manager. This is why effective and persuasive communication has become such a critical tool for all managers, not just those at the very top of the organisation.

Soft control may sound somehow devious or unethical, but it is important to acknowledge that societies have always relied on people to self-monitor and understand what is required of them without being told everything directly. Families and work groups are good examples of how members learn the rules and then act as they believe the family or work group wants them to. Organisations have just been a little slow to recognise that intrinsic motivation, harnessed through good, clear and persuasive communication, is far more engaging and productive than formal control.

## The power of identification

Setting the parameters for empowered action is a mighty task. It is less simple than in the past, when managers could give directions, threaten and cajole, and take authority for granted. The democratic imperative that permeates the personal lives of employees is increasingly apparent in organisational life and, as the drive for flatter organisations continues, the need for soft control will increase.

*Choosing to follow* replaces the *right to lead* in this equation. So, in the end, good management will become the capacity to engage staff sufficiently so that they choose to follow you. You don't need to look back, because the momentum is so powerful that the whole team is surging forward with you. Consequently, managers need to create a language of leadership that inspires, is emotionally intelligent and accessible to all staff, and at the same time possible to 'do' every day.

How staff become committed to their organisation and their manager is a complex process that many researchers have tried to understand in a variety of ways. One rather new way to think about this is to consider how an employee achieves *organisational identification*.[9] Put more simply, these are the mechanisms that lead employees to identify with their manager and their organisation. Researchers working in the field of corporate identity and reputation have been analysing the relationship between the communication employees receive and their development of supportive behaviours. As illustrated in Figure 2.1, the researchers have identified four key elements that determine this relationship and lead to positive employee identification:
- information availability
- personalised messaging
- communications quality
- emotional appeal.

Notice that the employees' positive response comes partly from having sufficient knowledge of what's going on, but also from the way they are made to feel about their manager and about themselves (including being given the chance to participate in the organisation's decisions, the level of personalised messaging they receive and their level of connection with the organisation).

Attempts to influence others in order to achieve a positive response have, of course, been the subject of attention for centuries, and were first explored by the ancient Greeks. Aristotle recognised that a mix of the various appeals must be used if listeners are to commit to the goals proposed by another. Aristotle taught that, when seeking to persuade, we should:
- seek to engage the rational thinking (*logos*) of our audience
- inspire a sense of belief and trust (*ethos*) in those with whom we communicate
- seek to engage our audience emotionally (*pathos*).

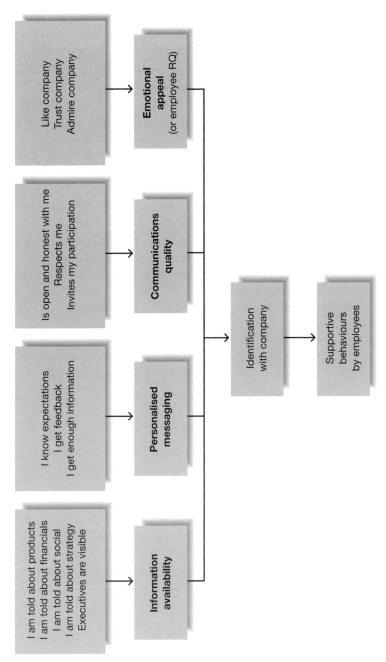

Figure 2.1 Measuring employee identification with the company[10]

This idea was further developed by US rhetorician Kenneth Burke, who explored the idea that identification was the important moment of connection between a speaker and a listener, when the listener identified their ways with those of the speaker.[11]

When employees identify with the organisation or an individual manager, the result is the positive achievement of psychological unity. It is here that James Williams, Managing Director of Denko Advertising, must turn his attention if he wishes to engage the passion of his staff. If his employees answer his question ('Are you passionate about Denko Advertising?') in the negative, then this is a reflection of his own communication skills rather than the limits of his employees. Why? Because achieving psychological unity is a significant and likely effect of high quality persuasive communication.

Kenneth Burke challenged us long ago to remember:

> *You persuade a man [or even a woman?] only in so far as you can talk his language, by speech, gesture, tonality, order, image, attitude, idea, identifying your ways with his.*[12]

Yet, many managers still frame their messages by starting with what they want to say. Listeners, on the other hand, start by asking: 'What's in it for me?'

## Audience, audience, audience!

Taking the audience as the starting point of any communication is hardly a revolutionary idea, but it is a surprisingly difficult task for most managers that I encounter.

The idea of framing a message from the point of view of the audience is an important start if you seek to win the hearts and minds of employees. If you wish to be truly influential, you need to be aware of the people you are talking to and adapt to their needs. Your target audience's frame of reference should always determine how you will approach them.

There are four golden rules about creating messages that are right for your audience and linked to the situation you are in and the characteristics of the people who will receive the message. This sounds like commonsense but is, unfortunately, a more complex task than most people recognise. The rules relate to:

1 situation
2 audience frame of mind
3 audience preference for type of communication
4 audience demographics.

## Situation

It is critical to assess the situation surrounding the delivery of your message. If you have to pitch a new idea to your team, it will really matter whether you are doing so after a long and heated debate about procedures and how some staff will ultimately be forced to change their behaviour, or whether you have just celebrated a successful sales period. Will you get five minutes to persuade your team? Will the item be at the end of an agenda or the beginning? Will the meeting be devoted entirely to the issue? The situation will be an important determinant of how you should approach an issue. You must be prepared to adjust your content accordingly.

## Audience frame of mind

You will need to consider whether your audience will oppose or agree with your ideas. You also need to consider their values and attitudes. The recent movie *What women want* with Mel Gibson explored just this idea. Gibson played a male chauvinist advertising agency star. He developed the ability to read women's minds following an accident. This new-found talent allowed Gibson to come up with advertisements that women loved. Why? He started with what women wanted rather than starting from his own perspective.

This facility of reaching into the mind of your audience might not be so simple outside life in the movies, but it does demonstrate that the real test of an effective message is not what the originator of the idea holds dear. Rather, understanding how the audience is thinking about an issue is critical, and respecting their perspective on things that will affect them will pay dividends.

## Audience's preferred type of communication

Audiences have preferences for certain types of communication. Peter Thompson, in his useful book, *Persuading Aristotle*,[13] created a simplified template for thinking about this issue. Most managers have, at some time, completed a Myers–Briggs assessment or other simple test to determine how they operate, and many managers can reel off their personal assessment. What Thompson did was to take this one step further by considering the adaptive communication strategies that are needed to suit differing personal styles (see Figure 2.2).

This model is useful because awareness of the communication needs of those listening to you gives you a map for what adaptations of your natural preferences will enhance your persuasive powers. For example, imagine that you are talking to an 'auditor' (the upper left quadrant of the figure). This person has a high preference for detail, careful outlining of the issues and proceeding slowly. You, on the other hand, like to talk 'big picture' and proceed quickly, searching out new directions as you go. When considering your listener's needs, you will do better to adapt to their pace, their information requirements, their tone and even their emotional state.

If you know that your audience has a variety of types in the group, the challenge is to build strategies to suit them. Your versatility will increase your likelihood of success.

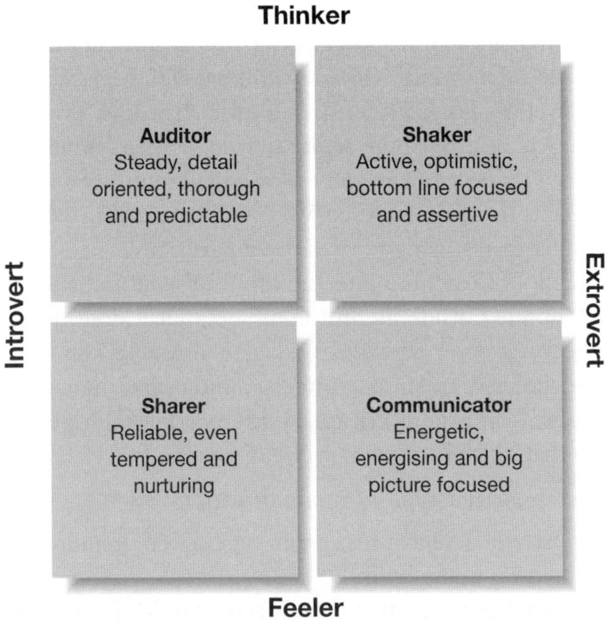

**Thinker**

| | |
|---|---|
| **Auditor**<br>Steady, detail oriented, thorough and predictable | **Shaker**<br>Active, optimistic, bottom line focused and assertive |
| **Sharer**<br>Reliable, even tempered and nurturing | **Communicator**<br>Energetic, energising and big picture focused |

**Introvert** — **Extrovert**

**Feeler**

Figure 2.2 Communicator style[14]

In a recent presentation, given to an extremely varied group of academic and professional staff about the significance of reputation to an organisation, I carefully incorporated a reference to the opinion of an economist who has identified the skewed distribution of rewards that accrue to good organisational performance. The presentation was directed to a generally highly motivated audience of sharers and communicators. However, there were a number of auditors in the room (whom I had identified as mainly economists). The economists were likely to find economic theory convincing here. I therefore commented that there is a disproportionately high return on a good reputation because of the human tendency to exaggerate small differences and to reward on the basis of *relative* importance rather than *absolute* importance. Thus, a good reputation can be a 'tipping point' giving a disproportionate share of visibility to an organisation. I then took this idea forward to propose the big picture idea that 'Reputational markets are winner-take-all events'.[15] By incorporating an auditor perspective and then, in a later phase, a communicator perspective, I maximised my chance to capture the listeners.

*Audience demographics*

Demographics are an important consideration when sizing-up your audience. Your audience's age, gender, educational experience, and socio-economic and cultural background will provide excellent signals about what matters, what does not, what 'hot buttons' listeners have, and what will be interesting to them.

Young employees will often have different priorities from older staff, and styles of communicating need to be shaped by these issues. Targeted illustrations of a particular point and the use of a more or less formal style of communication are possibilities. Richard Florida paints a very vivid picture here of the emerging preference amongst younger professionals for informality and what he calls the 'no collar workplace', with its new dress codes.

Or, as another example of differences, some Australians have what can be considered a relatively aggressive style of verbal interaction.[16] The cross-questioning that follows a pitch might be considered dynamic, engaged and searching by these staff members, but confrontational, negative and bordering on rude by those from cultural groups that value harmony and avoid conflict.

US leaders are able to use to good effect rhetoric that tugs at the heartstrings,[17] but Australian cynicism has traditionally required a more 'down to earth', egalitarian and pragmatic approach (although Richard Florida's research on the new workforce might suggest that there are new imperatives afloat).

The characteristics of the audience are as important as the content of your message. Recognising this is a critical step on the journey to becoming a successful persuasive communicator.

## Credibility

Just as you must consider audience characteristics when shaping your message, you are equally dependent on your audience to determine your credibility or *ethos*.

There are three primary dimensions that determine whether a listener considers you to be believable. Extensive communication research suggests that listeners make their judgment based on a combination of assessments of your *expertise*, *trustworthiness* and the goodwill or *sense of caring* that you generate.[18]

- *Expertise.* Attention to demonstrating expertise, or even the expertise of others on whom you rely to make your claims, is a critical pathway to achieving credibility with many audiences. Whether you seem informed, qualified, competent or experienced will shape how people hear the message.
- *Trustworthiness.* The listener's sense of your personal integrity may be generated over time rather than in the moment of encounter.
- *Sense of caring.* The listener's sense that you care, understand and have the interests of the listener at heart will play a critical role in the believability of the message.

Interestingly, it seems that your credibility will be of greater significance in an interaction where listeners are less involved in the issue being discussed than when they are deeply involved. In the case of listeners already or deeply involved, the strength of the arguments themselves is the most persuasive factor.[19]

In the workplace persuasion based on personal credibility requires considerable strategic focus on your part and is never a simple process. All those involved in the process need to recognise, over time, that you are trustworthy, knowledgeable and committed. You need to signal that moving forward together with your team is your desired outcome. Remember the model of employee identification presented earlier in the chapter.

## Non-verbal communication

A number of secondary dimensions also affect credibility. Much of your credibility is attained by how you communicate non-verbally. The levels of extroversion, composure and sociability of a communicator all contribute to the way an audience perceives the interaction. You can think about this as the level of 'immediacy' or the way that your non-verbal behaviour suggests warmth, closeness, friendliness and involvement with those with whom you are communicating. A large degree of separation between you and others could be either physical or psychological and either will determine the way your message is heard.

The way you use eye contact, the types and range of gestures you use, the vitality of your facial expression, the passion of your voice, the energy your body exudes, even the stillness which suggests that you are composed and relaxed in the discussion, are forms of code that allow others to make sense of your message.

A great communicator like Bill Clinton understands and uses this knowledge every time he interacts. The versatility of his facial expression, tone of voice, eye contact and vocal warmth provides an excellent model for those wishing to achieve communicative effectiveness. This is a secret code that everyone understands but which is nonetheless hard to master.

A good guiding rule on managing non-verbal behaviour in order to build rapport is to mirror the non-verbal behaviours of the audience.[20] Your upper body, in particular, is your expressive core, and adds powerfully to your communication. However, Anthony Robbins, that master of persuasion, noted in his best-selling novel, *Unlimited power*, that one good place to start to build rapport is with the voice. Robbins offers this advice:

*Mirror his tonality and phrasing, his pitch, how fast he talks, what sort of pauses he makes, his volume . . . People feel that they have found a soul mate, someone who totally understands . . . who is just like them.*[21]

There is ample research to suggest that human beings tend to believe the non-verbal rather than the verbal messages when there is a contradiction between the two. Nonetheless, as non-verbal communication specialist Edward Sapir suggested, non-verbal codes are both elaborate and secret. Because of this we can often detect—both consciously and unconsciously—subtle messages about the integrity of their meaning.[22]

If the speaker is insincere, we will often come away less convinced of the argument than if our reading of the non-verbal communication instils confidence in us. In sum, non-verbal strategies need to harmonise with the verbal message and support the relationship between the speaker and listener. Managing this harmonisation effectively must not be confused with manipulating it effectively.

Direct and sincere eye contact is also a critical part of persuasive behaviour. Many studies have demonstrated that those who engage in more eye contact, use pleasant facial expressions, and use gestures such as pointing, produce more compliance in their listeners than those who avert their gaze and use limited facial expression.

In summary, the broad repertoire of capabilities that managers should have to be persuasive includes:
- knowing what an audience needs to know
- finding ways to mirror the audience's thinking while leading them forward to imagine a new way to think, to change what they think or to reinforce a long-held belief
- giving a sense of direction so that employees carry with them the decision-making rules of the organisation.

As the model of positive employee behaviour that was proposed early in this chapter suggests, a mixture of appeals, both verbal and non-verbal, is needed to gain commitment.

There is, of course, an important word of warning to offer here. There is an increased danger that, if individuals are socially competent and highly persuasive, they can also be more successfully deceptive. For example, competent communicators who are attentive, friendly and precise can be more successful at deceiving others.[23] It is important to acknowledge that being able to bring the skills of the effective persuader to bear entails an added responsibility to use those skills with integrity.

# Winning words

Great communicators understand the power of language to shape the way an audience responds. Developing a heightened sensitivity to language choices is well worth the effort. The power of metaphors and analogies to stimulate new ideas and responses; the effect of repetition and rhythm to add clarity and focus; and the role of stories in making abstract concepts into real and meaningful experiences, are all useful tactics when building an argument. Whole books have been written on the effective use of language, but perhaps some illustrations of the strategies of good communicators can serve the purpose here of exploring effective language use.

## Profile: Carly Fiorina

One outstanding communicator who recognises the power of many of the strategies discussed earlier in this chapter is Carly Fiorina, CEO of Hewlett-Packard (HP). Fiorina has been presented in the media as a tough corporate warrior with the will to accomplish the almost impossible (as demonstrated by her ability to achieve a merger in 2002 between technology giants HP and Compaq).

Fiorina has an image as a charismatic leader and communicator. Jeff Christian, the headhunter who interviewed Fiorina for her position at HP, described her as 'incredibly captivating'[24] and one HP director claimed that Fiorina was seen as a 'very courageous leader' by employees[25] despite fear about the merger between HP and Compaq that she led.[26] She has been photographed and written about endlessly in newspapers, with Betty Spence, president of the US-based National Association of Female Executives, claiming that 'The Enron collapse is a story about Enron. The Hewlett-Packard story is about Fiorina'.[27]

Carly Fiorina has devoted a great deal of her energy to communicating with her various stakeholders. Throughout her time at HP, she has placed a high priority on talking to stakeholders, initially travelling to offices all over the world, then making endless presentations at industry conventions, to customers and to various stakeholders. Fiorina's perception of communication is worth noting. In 2000, she told Helen Trinca, a journalist for the *Australian Financial Review*:

> *Effective leadership requires an understanding that you don't own people, you can't control people. They must want to, they must choose to be in the company of others, oriented towards a particular mission. That means, in my view . . . using communication vehicles really creatively.*[28]

Fiorina promised to reinvent the company in three years, setting out to transform HP's slipping profits and worldwide image. Some of her employees and shareholders have disapproved of her strategies, and they have aroused the ire of Walter Hewlett, 57-year-old elder son of HP's late co-founder, Bill Hewlett. She took on the opposition to the merger with Compaq, arguing strongly with her detractors about the wisdom of this move and finally winning shareholder support. Showing an unanticipated tenacity against significant opposition, she defined a new direction for HP. By April 2002, she did what she had promised at the time of her appointment: she reinvented the firm by pulling off the acquisition of Compaq to create a US$87 billion dollar technology giant. In the second half of 2002, the company posted a quarterly net profit of US$390 million, a turnaround on the US$505 million loss in the same quarter of the previous year.[29]

One of Fiorina's key strategies has been to create strong images of what HP wishes to achieve, binding together dimensions of its past history and culture with a strong new image of a company that is inventing the future while being socially responsible. She regularly draws upon the powerful mythology of 'Bill and Dave' (Hewlett and Packard, respectively) in her internal communication, because these iconic and popular figures still matter to many of the staff at HP. This allows her to draw upon the strength of what has traditionally been called HP's 'garage culture'. The image of the old garage still appears around the organisation, eliciting images of spontaneity and natural backyard inventiveness.

However, Fiorina has taken another important step by projecting the idea of 'invention' forward, into the future. By leveraging the idea of invention for sustainability and for an improved world, she is creating a new way to see the fruits of technology.

In various speeches, Fiorina has coined some interesting phrases to capture her vision. She talks about 'the digital renaissance' and 'e-inclusion' as a way to think of the changes that technology is bringing to society. The clever use of these phrases is a strategy to counter the connotations of technology as something to fear. As a rebirth and a pathway to new development, a digital 'renaissance' puts a new and softer spin on the effects of technology. The idea of the 'renaissance man' also recalls a classical notion of human excellence and the changes that took the Western world into a new era of enlightenment. Choosing a metaphor with such a rich historical legacy engages listeners in the past and also leads them to the future, suggesting a parallel movement for good. The idea of 'e-inclusion' jumps off the term 'e-mail' but adds the idea of the people connection.

Many of Fiorina's speeches address the importance of leading change to improve society (the appeal to *pathos* is evident). However, her understanding of effective persuasion is demonstrated when she ensures that she weaves a strong and clear thread of logic through this seemingly emotive message. For example, when addressing an education and technology conference in 2002, she argued strongly that 'We (HP) must contribute—not just for our shareowners, not just for our customers, not just for our employees—but for our communities as well.'[30] She then moved quickly to point out that:

> This is, of course, an issue of enlightened self-interest, as much as it is about business or philanthropy. Education is the single most important lever for increasing economic prosperity. It is the single most effective lever, the most important lever for growing a diverse, highly skilled workforce.[31]

Alongside this careful weaving of *pathos* and *logos*, it is interesting to note Fiorina's use of repetition to reinforce the message in these examples.

In another example, this time in a speech about the importance of a strong brand, she argued: 'If you do the *right* things for the *right* reasons, then ultimately, the *right* outcomes can be achieved'. These simple examples demonstrate that good communicators pay attention to their language strategies as an essential part of building a persuasive case. A conscious and careful use of imaginative language and repetition can heighten the engagement of employees by helping them to see things in a different light.

Fiorina provides an outstanding role model with her clever, rich and engaging examples. Her speeches are available on the HP website.[32] Any manager wishing to find ways to develop their persuasive skills will be inspired by studying the structure, language choices and themes that she uses.

### Profile: Jack Welch

As one of the most celebrated CEOs of his era, Jack Welch is another great model of communication excellence. Welch has clear and well articulated advice on how to communicate with his stakeholders, just as he did on most things connected to GE and its operations during his time as CEO.

Welch, like Fiorina, believes in the power of language to make a difference. At GE, Welch was committed to what he called 'relentless consistency'. His advice was summed up by Robert Slater in his book, *Jack Welch on leadership*. Welch's tips are:

1  Present consistent messages about your business over the long haul.
2  Present consistent themes and strategies to every audience you address.
3  Articulate your messages, and then engage in a follow-up campaign to assure those messages are getting through.[33]

Notice the term 'campaign' here. Campaigns are often long and demanding and require strategy, energy and commitment. Welch's approach, like Fiorina's, demonstrates that persuading those around us to change, to commit and to excel is not a one-off hit (although each message is strategically important), but rather the building of a relationship that allows employees to think together with you—anticipating your direction and yet finding surprises, challenges and rewards in the freshness of the vision.

And this is, once again, where your choice of language plays such an important role in persuasion. Welch coined terms like 'boundarylessness' to help staff imagine a different way of operating at GE:

*We had to get rid of anything that was in the way of being informal, of being fast, of being boundaryless.*[34]

Welch's use of the term 'stretch' to think about goal setting was also powerful, and you have probably noticed the term creeping into your own vocabulary and goal-setting conversations. Why? Because it is accessible and an easy way to capture the difference between goal setting that simply restates what is easy to reach and what is really challenging. As Welch put it, 'If you do know how to get there, it's not a stretch target'.[35] This clever use of language is an important persuasive strategy. If you use catchy language well, its excitement is infectious, and you will hear others around you take up your idea because the way you expressed it captures their imagination. You will be a successful manager of meaning.

## Conclusion

There is little doubt that an effective manager needs to be an opinion leader to be successful in the contemporary workplace. This requires using the cognitive and behavioural skills of the persuasive communicator and also the heightened consciousness of the reflective practitioner who recognises the line between integrity and manipulation.

Managers who are rhetorically sophisticated have the all-important capacity to manage the meaning that is occurring in an organisation. Individualistic, autonomy-seeking employees demand both the opportunity to experience a challenging, engaging and stimulating workplace and the setting of clear boundaries and guidelines about the direction of the organisation. Clear, emotionally engaging and well reasoned arguments for the various commitments required of staff are critical elements for effective management.

For too long, the symbolic aspects of managing people have been seen as optional extras for the eccentric, and the 'soft' skills as the prerogative of HR departments. Managers must recognise that the social and cultural shifts largely brought about by increased affluence and educational levels are creating new organisational men and women who seek challenge, responsibility, creative expression and flexibility. These new employees require increasingly sophisticated managers, and to maintain their credibility, managers must take up the challenges that soft control brings. Being articulate, being able to sell ideas and engage the minds and hearts of employees are the new bottom line for managers.

One very important path to influencing others is through persuasive communication. However, the power of symbols such as language and images must be used with a strong commitment to ethical practice. If those in positions of leadership use their knowledge of the extraordinary capacities of language well, we can look forward to the growth of organisations that are fulfilling for their members and respectful of the diversity of views held about an issue, and where the creative instincts of all staff are heightened and explored.

## Tips for becoming persuasive

1. *Reflect on your current strategies for being persuasive. Now experiment!*
2. *Remember that an audience listens with one question in mind: 'What's in it for me?' So persuasion is all about audience! audience! audience!*
3. *Whether you are getting ready for a brief encounter or a formal presentation, think about your audience.*
4. *Adjust any communication to the communication style of your listener (consider the differences in Figure 2.2 each time you plan an encounter).*
5. *Take the time to watch (or read the text or case studies about) some good presentations, such as those of Carly Fiorina, to gain inspiration and gather a set of resources which you can adapt for your own presentations.*
6. *Always practise your presentations aloud in front of a mirror to heighten awareness of your non-verbal communication.*
7. *Remember that shaping effective, persuasive communication is fundamentally about strategic thinking. Aristotle called it the 'invention' or imagination stage of persuasion.*
8. *All persuasion should be built on integrity.*
9. *There is only short-term benefit in unethical persuasion. In the end, your credibility is your most valuable asset in persuading others to your point of view.*

## For further exploration

- D Goleman, R Boyatzis & A McKee, *The new leaders: transforming the art of leadership into the science of results*, Little Brown, London, 2002.
  
  Following on from Daniel Goleman's earlier book, *Emotional intelligence*, Goleman and his co-authors provide an excellent study of what they have identified as the repertoire of leadership styles that leaders can use. They stress how important versatility is in using these styles, and highlight the important role of persuasion in leadership.

- P McCarthy & C Hatcher, *Speaking persuasively: the essential guide to dynamic presentations and speeches*, Allen & Unwin, Sydney, 2002.
  
  My own book; it provides a practical guide to the development of persuasive skills. The book contains lots of case studies using Australian and international examples.

- K Thomson, *Passion at work*, Capstone, Oxford, 1998.
  
  Thomson takes the perspective that having passion at work is central to business success. The book takes the reader step-by-step through six secrets for personal success, suggesting that relationship management is just as important inside an organisation as it is with external clients.

- P Thompson, *Persuading Aristotle*, Allen & Unwin, Sydney, 1998.
  
  Australian journalist Peter Thompson offers a practical but thought provoking book about how to pitch ideas so that audiences will respond positively. It is worth reading just to reflect on your own style of communication and the communication preferences of others. Thompson's ideas about communicative styles inspired my comments on the subject for this chapter.

## Notes

**1** K Thomson, *Passion at work*, Capstone, Oxford, 1998.
**2** D Goleman, R Boyatzis & A McKee, *The new leaders: transforming the art of leadership into the science of results*, Little Brown, London, 2002.
**3** H Trinca, 'Her way', *AFR Boss*, March 2000, pp. 16–19.

**4** J Welch, *Jack: what I've learned leading a great company and great people*, Headline, London, 2001.
**5** R Branson, *Losing my virginity*, Random House Australia, Sydney, 2002.
**6** AH Eagly & S Chaiken, *The psychology of attitudes*, Harcourt, Brace Jovanovich, New York, 1993.
**7** R Florida, *The rise of the creative class*, Pluto Press, North Melbourne, 2003.
**8** P Tompkins & G Cheney, 'Communication and unobtrusive control in organisations' in R McPhee & P Tompkins (eds), *Organizational communication, traditional themes and new directions*, Sage, Newbury Park, CA, 1983.
**9** C Fombrum & C Van Riel, *Fame & fortune*, Prentice Hall, NJ, 2004.
**10** C Fombrum & C Van Riel, 2004, p. 100.
**11** K Burke, *A rhetoric of motives*, University of California, Berkeley, 1969.
**12** K Burke, 1969.
**13** P Thompson, *Persuading Aristotle*, Allen & Unwin, Sydney, 1998.
**14** Adapted from P Thompson, 1998, ch. 4.
**15** C Fombrum & C Van Riel, 2004 (see note 9).
**16** TA Avtgis & ASD Rancer, 'Aggressive communication across cultures: a comparison of aggressive communication among United States, New Zealand and Australia', *Journal of Intercultural Communication Research*, vol. 31, no. 3, 2002, pp. 191–200.
**17** K Parry, 'Better leadership? Ask the right questions' in C Barker (ed.), *The heart and soul of leadership*, McGraw-Hill, Sydney, 2002.
**18** J McCroskey & J Teven, 'A re-examination of the construct of goodwill and its measurement', *Communication Monographs*, vol. 66, no. 1, 1999, pp. 90–103.
**19** R Gass & J Seiter, *Persuasion, social influence and compliance gaining*, Allyn & Bacon, Sydney, 2003.
**20** R Gass & J Seiter, 2003.
**21** As in R Gass & J Seiter, 2003.
**22** As in P McCarthy & C Hatcher, *Speaking persuasively: the essential guide to dynamic presentations and speeches*, Allen & Unwin, Sydney, 2002.

23 R Gass & J Seiter, 2003 (see note 19).
24 'Glass ceiling warrior', *Australian*, 3 May 2002, p. 30.
25 B Pimental, P Sarkar & C Kirby, 'HP workers divided on merger', *San Francisco Chronicle*, 16 December 2001, p. G1.
26 J Swartz, 'Many HP employees oppose deal with Compaq', *USA Today*, 4 December 2001, p. 3B.
27 A Stanley, 'For women to soar is rare, to fall is human', *New York Times*, 4 December 2001, p. 1.
28 H Trinca, 2000, pp. 16–19 (see note 3).
29 D Crowe, 'More job cuts as HP slashes costs', *Australian Financial Review*, 22 November 2002, p. 71.
30 C Fiorina, 'Technology and education, a great partnership', National School Boards Association's 16th Annual Technology + Learning Conference, Dallas, Texas, 2002, viewed at <http//www.hp.com/hpinfo/execteam/speeches/fiorina/ceo/nsba02html>.
31 C Fiorina, 2002.
32 Hewlett-Packard website at <http://www.hp.com/hpinfo/execteam/speeches/fiorina>
33 R Slater, *Jack Welch on leadership*, McGraw-Hill, Sydney, 2004.
34 R Slater, 2004, p. 63.
35 R Slater, 2004, p. 103.

# CHARISMA AND INFLUENCE    3

Desmond Guilfoyle

Introduction

What is charisma?

'Doing' charisma

Referent power: meeting the perceiver's standards

Increasing your charisma

Charm

Conclusion

For further exploration

Notes

# About the author

Desmond Guilfoyle, BSc (Hons) (Psychology), MEd, Adv Dip Brdcst, Dip T&AS, CD, MAITD

Desmond Guilfoyle is an award winning author, broadcaster and performance enhancement specialist who has lectured and consulted throughout Australia, New Zealand, South Africa, Vietnam, Singapore and the USA.

As an adjunct to his position of National Learning Advisor for the ABC's radio division, he coaches executives and high visibility individuals in the art of public performance. The core of his work relates to the impact of self-perception on performance and behaviour. He has spent more than 20 years observing and researching how people build charismatic and power relationships with groups. His most recent book, *The charisma effect* (McGraw-Hill, 2002) has been translated into five languages and continues to sell strongly around the world.

Desmond has relationships with several Australian universities and is engaged in a number of joint research projects.

To find out more about Desmond Guilfoyle's work and to view selected articles, visit <http://www.mcgraw-hill.com.au/mhptr/books/guilfoyle_d_tce/f_book_1.html>.

Desmond Guilfoyle can be reached at <guilfoyle.desmond@abc.net.au>.

# Executive summary

Why are some people more personally attractive, popular, magnetic or influential than others? Is it genetic? Is it nurtured? Is there some secret surgical community that offers charisma implants to a chosen few? Contrary to widely held beliefs, charisma and personal attractiveness are not the outcome of some mysterious or indefinable 'X factor' in people—they are end result of some very special, but learnable, behaviours.

'Behavioural charisma' is the key to increasing personal magnetism, or what is known as *referent power*. Referent power, like charisma, is not something you have, but is the result of things you do: looking, behaving and speaking in a manner that creates a powerful 'click' with individuals and groups.

This chapter covers a range of easy-to-learn behaviours, attitudes and qualities that will enable you to increase your reservoir of referent power and improve your capacity to influence people.

## Introduction

In this chapter, I use social exchange models of interpersonal influence to describe influential and persuasive behaviour. These models identify particular types of interpersonal power that people employ to control and influence others. As you read this chapter you will brush against these concepts as you explore *referent power*, or in layperson's terms, personal magnetism or charisma.

Referent social power refers to an individual's ability to control people by tapping into their desire to identify with the source of that individual's power.[1] Referent power is all about attractiveness, but not necessarily physical attractiveness. It is the result of individuals and groups developing affection and admiration for the referent person as a consequence of that person manifesting certain 'special' qualities. For example, some theories suggest that we tend to develop perceived associations with individuals who mirror in their behaviour our own higher values and who manifest characteristics that we hold as desirable.[2]

People want to be like, or near, an individual with high referent power and are consequently influenced by him or her. When it comes to influence, high referent power is a significant advantage. Referent power creates 'internalisation' of influence because it is fuelled by inner feelings of attraction to, and identification with, the referent individual. As a result, referent power is often more durable than other forms of power, particularly reward and coercive power.[3]

The conscious and unconscious employment of referent power is an important feature of the comprehensive package we know as charisma. This chapter will focus on a number of crucial expressions of referent power that, if embraced, will allow you to increase your charisma quotient and improve your ability to influence others.

## What is charisma?

How is it that some liars, thieves and moral midgets are perceived at times as exemplars of probity and virtue?

Why is it that some people who really do possess the 'right stuff' are perceived as dishonest, untrustworthy and not up to scratch?

What is it about human perception that allows us to attribute good qualities to bad people on some occasions, and on other occasions to ascribe bad qualities to good people?

In the 1980s, when I was a current affairs interviewer with a certain amount of inside knowledge of the virtues and peccadillos of many of the political and corporate doyens of the time, I was fascinated to the point of obsession by those questions.

How could some 'Crooks in Dark Suits', as I came to know them, hold such enormous sway over the polity, over the investment community, and over the backroom boys and girls who often bankrolled their apogean journeys into the corporate, and sometimes political, mainstream? Conversely, why were many patently talented 'Honest Joes and Josephines' left out in the cold? Why did many perceive them to have suspect motives, negative qualities and unappealing personalities? Did they look, behave or talk differently?

Those questions started me on what was to be a 20-year search for some answers. Over that period I interviewed or modelled countless charismatic individuals—some 'dark', some 'luminous'—across a range of fields in a number of countries, in an attempt to understand some of the important variables that had to be present for 'charismatic clicks' to occur. (A charismatic click occurs when an individual meets the internal charisma standards of other individuals and groups—more of this later.)

I came to understand that you don't have to have the looks of the Hilton sisters or Brad Pitt to earn the charisma halo. Often we mistakenly equate high visibility and the attached fame with charisma. In truth, charisma associated with 'stardom' often wanes at a rate that is inversely related to the passage of time and the pull of gravity! It is subject to the fickleness of fashion and whim and is threatened by competition from an ever-moving assembly line of new names and faces. In the cutthroat world of modern entertainment and sport, today's celebrities can quickly become tomorrow's forgotten.

Charisma can also be situational. A high profile CEO can be the toast of the investment community until he presides over a financial setback or misreads his market. At that juncture his charismatic aura evaporates more quickly than a brief summer downpour.

I learned that charisma laurels can be awarded for acts of daring, feats of unusual strength or courage, and singular deeds of immense kindness or selflessness. In crises and times of threat, men and women may emerge who possesses the qualities, attributes and passion that are called for in dangerous or defining moments. On such occasions it is often the timing, the message and the mode of expression that click powerfully into the mind and mood of the masses. So it was with Winston Churchill who, on becoming prime minister in May 1940, promised:

> *Victory at all costs, victory in spite of all terror, victory however long and hard the road may be; for without victory there is no survival.*[4]

These were words of spine that a nation, which was in distress over events in Europe and fearing for its own future, was waiting to hear. Words made all the more powerful because the more spineless members of the British political establishment were squabbling about cutting losses, avoiding defeat and seeking accommodations with the Nazis. We see many less dramatic examples of this in corporate, political and, indeed, spiritual life: leaders and potential leaders who proclaim timely and passionate messages of healing, restoration, recovery and revival of past glories.

At the same time, I stumbled upon the charisma fast-food factory—a kind of loose global franchise of spin doctors and image peddlers who manufacture charismatic 'sensations' in much the same formulaic fashion as modern hamburgers are produced and marketed. These self-anointed image gurus transform their charges into stereotypical heroes, stars and saviours. Using the mass media as their platform, they craft scriptable elements into compelling storylines in which their characters play leading and defining roles.

The charisma halo, I discovered, is not a singular prize awarded only to those who have inherited the indefinable 'X factor'. It can illuminate the craniums of a diverse assortment of individuals for a variety of reasons, and in different situations and events.

It was, however, my comparative investigation of Crooks in Dark Suits and Honest (but uncharismatic) Joes and Josephines that led me to a working hypothesis of 'behavioural charisma'. This working hypothesis can be summed up in an old Grub Street ditty from the time of Samuel Johnson, brought to light by Allen Kurzweil.[5]

> *The viewer paints the picture,*
> *The reader writes the book,*
> *The glutton gives the tart its taste,*
> *And not the pastry cook.*

The subtext of this wonderfully lucid view of life is simple. As much as our individual natures may wish to deny it, the taste of the tart relies largely on the perceptions of those across whose palates the tart passes. For example, a book will appear dull or nonsensical when viewed through the filters of someone who is unappreciative of, or unfamiliar with, the symbols, storylines, style and plots it contains. But find some widely held or universal symbols, recycle a popular plot or narrative, or appeal to the national sweet tooth and you are almost guaranteed success. This, I discovered, was a common, but often unstated, assumption of those who had achieved mastery of the art of behavioural charisma.

This notion that you can appear, act and behave in certain ways to gain charismatic status flies in the face of the traditional and embedded view of charisma popularised by Max Weber, where the charismatic personality is set apart from ordinary humans and is regarded as somehow 'superhuman', or at least possessing highly exceptional powers and qualities not accessible to ordinary people.[6] Contrary to this received view of charisma, modern day charisma can be seen as significantly more than a conjunction of a privileged individual's history and future. People can be infinitely more than the sum of their pasts and can surpass their personal histories and circumstances to engineer new selves and new opportunities for visibility and followership.

## 'Doing' charisma

For the purposes of exploring behavioural charisma further, let's agree with the premise that people, generally, don't *have* charisma but *do* charisma—they exhibit a range of behaviours, look the part and communicate both verbally and non-verbally in a way that creates a charismatic click with individuals and groups. If we accept that principle, then we can begin to see charisma as a phenomenon that occurs in the minds of followers as a direct result of the above-mentioned triggers. Rather than a mystical quality embodied in the cream of the human crop, charisma can be seen as something that is awarded by individuals and groups to a person who does things that click with them in a very special way. So let's agree that people *attribute* charisma to individuals as opposed to those individuals having been blessed by the gods.

Attributions result from events that go on in our own heads, and Harvard psychology professor Ellen Langer observes that most of those judgments are mindless rather than mindful.[7] In other words, we don't put each and every person through an exhaustive process of analysis before we form an impression of him or her. We use what are known as processes of categorisation. Categorisation involves matching people against generally shared standards that lurk deep in our unconscious minds. We have ready-made schemata (complex networks of associations) for charisma that are surprisingly common in many sectors of our population.

Categorisation has two main functions when it comes to sizing up people:
- It gives you an expedient mental framework in which to test and check your impression of an individual against internal categories—call them standards if you like.
- It can sensitise you to any inconsistencies that may occur with your internal standards.

So, in a way, categorisation is a kind of internal marking system. When you meet someone, you automatically and unconsciously allocate ticks and crosses according to a set of 'correct' answers.

If much of the data you receive from the initial encounter fits a positive category or network of categories you have on file, you receive an all-clear signal, often in the form of a good feeling about the person. Subsequently, you will filter what the person says and does through the positive biases of that category. This is why you can meet someone and, in seconds, have positive feelings about him or her and conclude that they're a nice person. However, if the data doesn't fit your set of 'correct' answers, the contradiction will signal that this is a 'bad' person—an untrustworthy, dislikeable or unappealing individual. These negative signals are likely to dominate your ensuing mental processing of what is said and done.

If you didn't use categorisation as an unconscious mental shortcut, you could not exist as an organised and social being. Categories help us negotiate through life without having to deal with information overload. They are a blessing, but also a curse, because they facilitate a form of mindlessness (lack of attentive and conscious thinking) that can allow us to make judgments about people that can't be sustained.

Are you beginning to understand how the Crooks in Dark Suits often get the jump on the Honest Joes and Josephines? They have figured out, consciously or intuitively, that understanding categorisation is a key element of impression management.

## Referent power: meeting the perceiver's standards

Let's assume the perspective of some of those Crooks in Dark Suits for a moment. They have come to realise through experience that most people will make a judgment on a person without having had the opportunity to scrutinise the person in detail and depth. In fact, they rely upon it. They also understand that most of the time people will size up another person in a mindless way. The Crooks intuitively understand, or have learned, that just as people have internal standards for both nice and unpleasant people, they have internal standards for special kinds of people: people who have presence; people who radiate charm; people who exude power, passion, strength, mystery and other qualities that are scarce in the broader population.

Although the Crooks may not use the terminology of prototypes and categorisation, in numerous interviews I conducted these artful dodgers revealed a surprising unanimity of approach. In general, they:
- invested much time and effort in looking, sounding and 'doing' the part, thus enabling them to manage impressions of sincerity and credibility

- had gradually learned the art of charm and knew how to exude qualities of uniqueness and mystery
- held the view that, in order to have people follow, a leader must link their mission and message to the deeply held beliefs, hopes, aspirations, fears or prejudices of their potential followers
- understood the significant role that emotion plays in the choices people make
- had spent time learning how to seem curious about and interested in the people they wished to impress
- projected energy and passion when the moment required it
- learned how to do 'presence'
- learned how to be strong self-monitors and were often behaviourally flexible enough to fine-tune their actions and words midstream.

When I contrasted the approach of the Crooks with that of the many talented but unimpressive individuals I had the pleasure of coaching over the years, some profound differences became clear.

**1** Unexceptional individuals lacked the power to influence because they relied almost exclusively on content (reason, logic and 'truth') as the key component of their influencing strategies.

**2** The Crooks in Dark Suits paid much attention to identity. Generally, they recognised or intuited that honesty, magnetism, presence, confidence and so on are all in the eye of the beholder, and in order to have people follow them they had to meet their followers' standards or expectations.

**3** Unexceptional individuals expressed an almost obsessive preoccupation with 'being true to themselves' as an elemental aspect of being true to others.

**4** The Crooks appeared to have stumbled onto a way to 'respect' other people's models of the world by being 'true' to those whom they wished to influence.

Assume for a moment that honesty, integrity, confidence, charm, presence, likeability and other elements of personal magnetism and attractiveness are in the eye of the beholder, just as beauty is. Assume also that you cannot be perceived as sincere, likeable and genuine *if you fail to meet the perceiver's standards*. If that is the case, and you wish to influence or persuade a group of individuals on the merits of an honestly held position, how can you not consider meeting the standards of your listeners? If perceptions are governed as much by how a message is crafted and presented as by how messengers craft and present themselves to match the unconscious expectations (or standards) of listeners, how can you cling to specious notions of 'trueness to oneself' when you know that being true to others is a key to influence?

Why should thieves, liars and Crooks in Dark Suits have a monopoly of being true to other people's standards and categories? Surely, honourable persuaders can learn the same lessons and code their messages and selves to match the internal expectations, values and category biases of those they seek to influence.

## Increasing your charisma

If you would like to become an honourable persuader, then it's time to consider a charismatic makeover and to learn how to deliver against some of the near-universal standards that people use to determine who they will follow and who they will reject. Important factors that can increase or decrease referent power are:

1 eye contact
2 physiognomy
3 energy
4 smiling
5 expressing sentiment
6 body management
7 wearing the uniform.

These simple, workable behaviours, attitudes and approaches can make a very large difference to the way people embrace you and your message.

### Eye contact

In Western cultures, eye contact is a key factor in establishing and maintaining trust. The most effective way to make credible eye contact is to combine it with an external focus—a way of describing an experience that most of us have had of being 'out there' and fully engaged in a communication. If you make eye contact, but do so with an internal, self-conscious focus, your listeners will register unconsciously that your full attention is not directed on them.

Former US president Bill Clinton learned the techniques of external focus—along with how to walk like John. F Kennedy—from Anthony Robbins. Clinton combines, in a masterly way, fluid movement and external focus to galvanise the attention of all when he walks into a room.

- Practise, in non-threatening situations, putting all your focus and attention on both individuals and members of groups.
- Notice the difference between being 'out there' and 'going inside'. When you are internally focused you will notice a dialogue going on with yourself. You will notice that a lot of your valuable attention is being paid to you and not the subject/s of your communication.
- Engineer a state of mind that allows you to easily and effortlessly give 'soft' attention to those around you. Soft attention is not harsh and intimidating but is the result of you experiencing the dynamics of your environment and fully engaging with them.

Often people look at others with a wider-angled gaze, not directing their focus on those with whom they're communicating. This gives the appearance of looking 'through' people rather than looking at them. Here, the depth of field is beyond the person's head. Avoid the 'space cadet' gaze and set your focus directly on the person/people you are addressing.

The most effective form of eye contact is where you can establish a focus that takes in the eyes, lids, eyebrows and some of the musculature around the eyes, as shown in Figure 3.1 (see the area of the face that is circled).

## Physiognomy

The scientific exploration of facial expressions has a long history, beginning with Charles Darwin's tome, *The expression of the emotions in man and animals*.[8] There is wide agreement on the proposition that people first scan a person's face in search of information about the emotions of those they encounter. This has been shown to be a principal factor in the internal assessments people make of others.

Figure 3.1 Parameters of eye contact

We look to a person's face for information on their emotional state and in many cases for signs of who they are. Amateur face watchers will be pleased to know that the literature supports the theory that the older a person gets the greater the tendency for the face to set like concrete into his or her 'resting' state of mind. If your resting state is that of anger, seriousness, bitterness or gloom, rest assured it will begin to set that way after you turn forty. Gravity and the ravages of time may be partially responsible for the way our faces set in later life, but the evidence suggests that some of the lines and canyons are of our own making.

An ideal referent power posture is: head straight and erect but relaxed; face reflecting the emotional fingerprint of the content. This is *interpreted as*: confidence; self-assuredness; majesty; power; strength, courageousness, forthrightness.

Your facial 'mask' needs to send signals of openness and trustworthiness—pleasant, accessible and uncontrived. Your face must also match the depth, gravity or levity of the circumstances and be in agreement with your body—a confident and open head on a rigid body emits signals of gross incongruence. Your face, hands and body need to be in alignment and that is why the reflection of energy is most important.

## Energy

Earlier I mentioned Bill Clinton learning how to walk and act like John F Kennedy. When you observe Clinton doing his charismatic walk you sense that, apart from a strong level of engagement in his surroundings, he radiates a high and very affirmative quality of energy. It is not however crude or untrammelled energy, but is more like electricity being harnessed through a light bulb so as to ensure a constant emission of light. You sense the presence of great power and vigour, but it is contained and measured to meet the emotional temperature of the occasion.

Clinton's energetic presence is the result of a combination of internal state control, fluid movement, external focus, 'doing' confidence and one other very important variable—a willingness to be the centre of attention.

Most efforts at reflecting charismatic energy and movement begin as gawky, counterfeit imitations of the real thing. This is very much how Clinton began, but time and practice has ensured that new and powerful behaviours have become an habitual part of his personality.

In learning how to do Bill Clinton's charismatic walk be assured that you will not sink into a state of moral turpitude (although you may radically improve your prospects to do so if desired!).

First, however, you must make a decision that it's fine to be the centre of attention. Being the centre of attention does not require you to enter the space of an egoist or typical attention seeker, but the valid space every one of us has a right to occupy on occasions.

Sadly, many of us are not willing to be the centre of attention because of conditioning, inferiority complexes, false humility and sometimes for fear of being discovered to be the frauds that we may erroneously feel we are. Think back to a moment when all eyes were on you. Did the glare of the spotlight cause you to experience an uneasy self-consciousness and an urgent impulse to run into the shadows, or did you accept it and enjoy the opportunities it presented? If you experienced the former, perhaps you can consider finding ways to give yourself conditional permission to be the centre of attention in specific situations. Giving yourself permission to be the valid centre of attention is fundamental to a confident performance.

Having embraced the concept of attention, practise the following technique until it becomes second nature:
- Stand up, feel the connection between your feet and the surface on which you are standing. Imagine your spine is a jet of water,

firm but fluid. Imagine your head is a hollow ball riding on that jet of water. Feel the tension around your neck ease as you become used to the idea.
- Picture either male or female models walking down a catwalk. Notice how they race down the catwalk at breakneck speed. Begin walking at about half that speed, sensing a flow in your movement. Settle in to a beat of about sixty-five beats to the minute, the beat of baroque music. Keep your head comfortably on your shoulders; keep your head level and focus forward.
- Remember the Hollywood idols of the 1930s? They were taught how to slow down all of their movements so they could be captured properly on celluloid. That's why they often appeared like gods and goddesses. They used the same style of movement off the set as well. (John F Kennedy loved movies and copied the movements of his celluloid heroes.) Make all of your movements fluid and slower than you habitually move. Try drinking a glass of water, using a knife and fork, getting up out of a chair, changing body position, making a point and so on using slower and more fluid movement.
- When you talk with people, give them your full external focus; pay attention to your environment and fully engage yourself in the communication.
- Practise reflecting different energy levels in diverse settings.

This provides you with enough information to begin the process. Become a people watcher. Observe others who appear to move in a way that seems more harmonious with their environment. Copy them and notice the impact.

## Smiling

You are never fully attired until you put on a smile. Smiles are contagious. Real smiles that tap your inner reserves of good humour and congeniality are as important as eye contact. Real smiles set the scene for what follows after an initial introduction. Smiles also convey confidence and approachability and meet general prototypes that people have about charismatic personalities.

The best way to smile is to get in touch with your good humour and practise smiling at people. Try those you wouldn't ordinarily smile at, like surly shop attendants, bored waiters, the office cleaner, your workplace enemy and the unwelcome Sunday morning religious canvasser. Video yourself smiling and notice whether it's a smirk or a smile. A real smile—one that mirrors delight and good humour—can thaw the iciest of personalities.

## Expressing sentiment

One way charismatic people make enough of themselves available to be liked, embraced and followed is through their voice.

Rich, eargasmic sound is only one facet of the human voice and a minor one at that. An infinitely more important aspect of the human voice is its capacity to reflect the 'emotional fingerprint' of speech content. For it is through variations in loudness, pace and, most importantly, emphasis and pitch that paralinguistic cues are sent from speaker to listener to convey the meaning of, and commitment to, what is being said.

Think back to the last time you were slide-swiped by PowerPoint; where, in a dimly lit room, a silhouetted presenter clicked away more frequently than an ill-fitting set of dentures, accompanying the show with an insipid, monotonous commentary. Irrespective of the content, were you revved up and ready to embrace enthusiastically the ideas or propositions that were put to you? Or were you left drained, uncommitted and somewhat irritated over the impression the chair left on your backside?

Now recall a presentation by, or a two-way exchange with, someone who stirred or inspired you. What was different? Chances are his or her face, body and voice were in total alignment with the emotional fingerprint of what they were saying. Their delivery may have contained colour, energy and variations in pace; it may have included dramatic pauses; and it may have mirrored tonally a commitment to the substance of their content.

If you deny your listeners legitimate access to the energy and emotion associated with your content, the end result is often a clash between the content and the expression of the content. In most cases you will leave people uncommitted, disinterested, bored or confused.

The secret to using the voice as an instrument of influence is to allow it to be part of a 'full-bodied' communication of the content, harnessing its expressive power and supporting it with complementary body language.

Narrow tonal range, Easter Island expression, controlled body movement and neutral posture are often believed to be signs of stability, maturity and emotional balance—and so they are, at funerals. But in the competitive and sometimes cutthroat corporate atmosphere, such qualities fail dismally to win hearts and minds, build corporate cultures, garner support for new and novel solutions or line up people to support your ideas or propositions. For that you need to give a full-bodied commitment to the expression of your convictions.

- Reveal yourself vocally, as much as is needed to be liked and embraced.
- Self-containment prevents the matching of physical and tonal signals with the power of your words. Make sure that your body is in alignment with your words and vocal expression.
- Find the passion in what you do and express yourself so that it can be heard and seen.
- You have a right to make noise and to be the centre of attention. Accept the challenge.
- Practise vocalising a range of different emotions so as to add to your emotional–vocal inventory. You may sound corny at first, but over time you will integrate greater expressional breadth into your personality and you will sound natural.

*Body management*

We live in a highly body conscious society. At some level, people view the bodies of those they encounter as external representations of internal 'substance'.

Category bias (labelling) plays a large part in the impressions people form. Obesity, spare tyres and beer bellies are often viewed as a sign of weakness or a lack of self-control, and sometimes as a signal of avarice. Kim Beazley, for example, fought a constant battle to keep the size of his waistline under control because he knew that voters could make unconscious assessments involving managing his body and managing the country.

Although we can't escape the body blueprint in our genes, we can make the best of our appearance. We may be offended when people make judgments on how we maintain our bodies but the fact remains that people generally view our physical appearance as a metaphor for our personality and character.

The key to physical attractiveness is not so much to look like a god or goddess, but to look healthy. Healthy looking people send signals of self-control, strength, vigour, self-respect and of being on the ball. Notice how people characterise unhealthy looking public figures. People generally interpret excessively thin bodies and gaunt faces as signs of ill health, world-weariness, shrewishness and sometimes as a manifestation of creepiness, stinginess or evil. Mannequins with silhouettes that remind you of animated X-rays are an unfortunate exception.

Body movement, how you 'drive' your body, has a significant impact on the impressions you make. If your motion is stiff, jerky, slouched, laboured, lacking in vigour, or over- or under-animated, people will register that information unconsciously and possibly form a negative impression of you. For people to trust and like you, your physiology must be harmonious with the communication environment in which you find yourself.

*Wearing the uniform*

If you wanted to be accepted as a bona fide member of the Coffin Cheaters motorcycle gang you would be well advised to wear a leather jacket with the group's motif emblazoned on the back—a perfect accessory with which to match your tattoos! Similarly, if you wish to become an accepted member of a professional or management group you also need to wear 'club colours'. Uniforms are a way in which in-groups make membership distinctions, and they go to the heart of identification power. Dress is a primary medium of communication, often registering with people before all else, and if you wish to become an influential member of any group, your first task should be to observe and identify what is acceptable attire.
- What colours and styles are the alphas wearing?
- What footwear and accessories are considered tolerable?
- What level of grooming is considered the standard?

These questions are also important as you move away from your group and seek to influence other groups. When preparing your wardrobe to ensure you are communicating an appropriate image, ask yourself:

- What impression would be the most useful to convey, given the circumstances?
- Is it a formal or power setting?
- How will others be dressed—do I need to match that or up the ante?
- Do I wish to strategically reflect informality and accessibility?
- Do I need to wear the 'uniform' of the target group in order to convey an impression of being at one with them or do I need to wear a uniform that meets their expectations of what a person in my position should look like?

The key to effective dressing is to code your non-verbal signals (in this case your dress) in a style and manner consistent with the expectations of your target group. On rare occasions, and for strategic purposes, you may decide to dress up or down.

Your level of facial grooming is also important in making positive first impressions, because on first meeting people scan your face and eyes first. If your eyebrows resemble two caterpillars on the verge of turning into cabbage moths and your beard looks like a nesting place for rodents, rest assured it won't escape unnoticed.

For men, a clean-shaven appearance is preferable. Notice how few people at the top of their fields wear facial hair. If you must wear facial hair, ensure that it's neatly trimmed. Long sideburns are generally not advised, unless you are a record company executive or an Elvis impersonator.

For women, cosmetics should be applied subtly. Colours should be chosen to emphasise your best natural features and provide balance to your facial characteristics. Heavy makeup should be reserved for amateur theatrical productions—women who use it are often categorised as brassy or unsophisticated. Remember, wearing no makeup makes a statement in itself. Unless you have an unflawed complexion, it may be worthwhile considering at least a minimalist approach to makeup, remembering that referent power relates to the *perceiver's* standards and not your own.

# Charm

Charismatic people are almost always viewed as charming, and some have mastered the art so fully that they could charm a smile out of road kill. Once again, charm is not something you *have* but

something you *do*. Charm contains many variables, from an ethereal glint in an eye to the following essentials:
1 doing confidence as a behaviour
2 having a positive and resourceful state of mind
3 getting out of ego
4 demonstrating courtesy and respect
5 offering praise
6 being playful in a non-sexual way.

*'Doing' confidence*

As Goethe was said to have remarked, our behaviour is a mirror in which we show our self-image. Often it's our attitudes about ourselves that make us behave as though we are unworthy of notice. Recently, I was working with a talented and able woman on engineering a more positive and alluring persona. She lamented that, somewhere along the track, she 'lost confidence' and 'became invisible' and that one of her deepest wishes was to 'work towards having it again'. She was speaking as though confidence was something she carried around in her shoulder bag and it had somehow fallen out. Confidence was something that she 'got' when she achieved some objective or accomplished a task that had a certain degree of difficulty: a kind of tangible reward for persistence. She saw confidence as an object that gets embodied rather than something that one does, and she regarded visibility to be an effect rather than a cause.

Like happiness, we often see confidence as the prize at the end of an ordeal. My question to the woman was: 'Well, can you see yourself confidently going about rediscovering that confidence is something you have done and can do?' This was a watershed question for her, and after a few hours practising the following techniques she went into a career-defining meeting doing supreme confidence.

Confidence can be seen as a process and not something that happens after you have completed a process.
- Ask yourself the question: 'How do I *do* confidence?' When you are feeling and expressing your confidence, what is it you are doing?
- Recall a time when you were feeling confident. Register what it felt like, notice what you did, how your body was positioned, how you sounded and any other special qualities you experienced.

- Keep recalling, and as you do you can notice that it returns more quickly each time. When you reach the point where the experience is relatively strong, find a unique way of associating a 'trigger' with the experience. Your trigger could be the step forward to greet someone, movement towards a lectern, or standing up to address a meeting.
- Begin to practise triggering the feeling of confidence and maintaining an external focus, fully engaging in the moment or communication event. Soon you will notice that your behaviours reflect your state of mind and confidence becomes available to you when you need it.

*Positive and resourceful states of mind*

Resourceful states of mind are healthy mental attitudes that underpin achievement and add significantly to personal attractiveness. In a world where people are increasingly feeling isolated, powerless and vulnerable, individuals who manifest realistic and heartfelt positivity are as appealing as jam is to flies.

At some stage of their development, most charismatic personalities I have modelled have discovered the value of maintaining a positive frame of mind. Just as learned helplessness is a negative frame of mind borne out of perceptions of inadequacy and scarcity, 'learned self-helpfulness' is a frame of mind reflecting a belief that problems can be surmounted, that grey clouds can have silver linings, that the world is a place of abundance and that differences can be made.

Positive people avoid self-recrimination, eschew scapegoating and are more interested in finding solutions to problems than damning those who got it wrong. They have found a way to deal with the negative side of life and usually view negative experiences as opportunities for learning.

In explaining how he viewed his mistakes, one charismatic individual I deconstructed said that he felt he had never learned a thing in life through being successful. He viewed his biggest blunders as the wellspring of his wisdom. 'When I make a mistake, I take a close look at what I could have done differently and then I know I'm wiser today than I was yesterday.'

Systems theory argues that everything is feedback, and that there is no such thing as failure. Failure is a human concept invented to ensure compliance and control and I have rarely noticed it in the self-assessment vocabularies of charismatic individuals.

In my experience of 'unpacking' charismatic personalities, I have identified other key resourceful states of mind. Almost to a person, charismatic personalities practise the following states of mind:

- *Inner confidence.* 'I am a shareholder of this planet and I have both the resources and right to meet my potential. My inner confidence isn't affected by external events. Even in disasters of my own making, I can confidently go about learning from those situations. I am always certain of this.'
- *People ecology.* An acute awareness of the impact of one's actions and verbal and non-verbal behaviour on those around us. Emotional intelligence, self-monitoring and heightened awareness of how the individual impacts on others. An inner urge to 'connect' and have successful relationships. Recognising and supporting diversity of opinion. Understanding the uniqueness of each individual and seeking to help others find their unique way to self-actualisation.
- *Curiosity.* Often, questions form an important part of communing with individuals and groups. Effective questions result from an inner state of curiosity fired up by good listening technique. In my book, *The charisma effect*,[9] I outlined collaborative listening techniques I modelled from virtuosi in the art of listening. Curiosity, abetted by high level listening and information gathering techniques, is a quality I identified in most of the charismatic personalities I have studied.
- *Passion.* Charismatic people do what they do with passion, whether it is fulfilling a personal mission in life, believing passionately in something or being captivated and enriched by the process of being passionate.
- *Imagination.* This is about questioning why things are done and learning how to apply creative mindsets to issues, challenges and problems. Using the imagination to better wire oneself for the process of developing novel and unique options. Having an abundance mentality. Doing creativity.
- *Valour.* Having the courage of one's convictions. Never sacrificing one's personal mission or beliefs for an outcome or

result. Speaking up when one must, showing courage in the face of opposition, conforming to a strong code of morality and conduct and inherently knowing that working through risk (doing things that have never been done before) changes one's personal landscapes forever.
- *Integration*. Being the same person everywhere. Whether it's at work, home, or in sport or social environs, maintaining consistency in persona and approach. This relates as much to honesty and integrity (qualities that many people quarantine when at work) as it does to curiosity and empathy.

## *Getting out of ego*

Getting out of ego means forgetting about yourself and your status and giving 100% of your conscious attention to another person or people for a period of time. It describes the act of entering the territory of other people as a kind of tourist, focusing on points of interest—the history and interesting topographical and man-made formations, so to speak. It means experiencing delight at good news or accomplishment; it means being able to empathise genuinely; and it means making a conscious effort to map the territory of others as opposed to imposing your map on their territory.

If you are forever looking over your shoulder for a more important person with whom to connect, you will never master this essential charismatic, and indeed leadership, quality. Bill Clinton and the late Princess Diana are two contemporary charismatic sensations who did 'people focus' at the highest level. The occasions are too numerous to cite where people who met Clinton and Diana reported afterwards that they felt they were the 'most important person in the world' at the time. Both Clinton and Diana learned this behaviour, Diana having observed and learned it from her late mother, Frances Shand Kydd.

Getting out of ego gives you an emotional and intellectual green light to go about authentically making others feel important, expressing a genuine intensity of interest in their world. It is a state of mind that makes it easy for you to fully commune with others, to effortlessly summon up curiosity and to pay your respect to people as unique individuals. To achieve this state of mind and the resultant behaviour, consider the following:

- Start with external focus. Avoid taking inner readings of your own temperature and place your attention on those with whom you wish to communicate.
- Develop your attentive and collaborative listening skills.
- Practise viewing the world from the perspective of other individuals—put yourself in their shoes.
- Avoid judging people using your personal criteria—use theirs.
- Learn how to ask strategic open-ended and closed-end questions to elicit appropriate information.
- Practise eliciting information at different levels, from a surface level for chit-chat to deeper levels when you need specific or pertinent information.
- Respond fully to the other person. Listen to their content and react to it as though they were a precious friend.
- Give your fullest 'soft' attention.

*Courtesy*

Steven Covey, in his book *The 7 habits of highly effective people*,[10] observes that things that are extremely valuable to receive are often relatively cheap to give, and never were there truer words than when applied to common courtesy. Common courtesy costs very little and yet the dividends can be colossal.

In today's world, men and women are not expected to exude the gallant courtliness of medieval times when practising the civil virtues. However, in the post 'greed is good' era, there appears to be a re-examination of courtesy as it applies in the world of work and business.

Business 'etiquette' is a new buzzword that integrates the concepts of graciousness, courtesy and politeness, and it is beginning to be reflected both in customer and business relationships and in internal relationships in companies. Many companies have established codes of conduct that set benchmarks of personal conduct between customers, managers, staff, suppliers and so on. They are beginning to catch on to something that charismatic personalities have known through the ages.

You never get a second chance to make a good first impression, and heartless and corrosive 'me first' behaviours sour relationships before they even begin. Invest in the following benchmarks of courtesy and notice the personal credits begin to accumulate:

- Get out of ego.
- Express a congenial and receptive mood (express your moodiness with a punching bag at the local health club).
- Give people the gift of a genuine smile.
- Reflect in your facial expressions the emotional fingerprint of the other person's content.
- Use please, thank you and the subject's name at appropriate junctures.
- Map out other people's territory first and seek to understand their needs and values before inviting them to visit your territory.
- Validate people by acknowledging their opinions. A simple example: if someone says: 'Boy, it's hot' say something like: 'So you're feeling the heat' rather than remarking that you think the temperature is just perfect.
- Always attend to others' needs before your own. Put yourself at the disposal of people, both superiors and subordinates. Don't be a doormat, but be aware of their comfort, access, sensibilities, needs and concerns.
- Find some personal way to mark your contact with people. For example, a follow-up email or phone call.

*Praise*

Some people are loath to offer praise because they feel that every compliment they give takes the limelight away from where it should rightly be (on them!). Others avoid giving compliments because they don't want to be viewed as sycophants or false flatterers. There are even some who refuse to praise others because their worldview has become so malignantly bitter that giving a compliment is like giving succour to the enemy. And yet, we know from our own experiences that there is practically no limit to the amount of genuine praise that we can swallow, because praise and flattery feed into our desires to be appreciated and valued.

    I once unpacked a charismatic senior executive who fervently believed that boring people did not exist on this planet. She operated from the assumption that everyone had a story to tell. She said it was through stories that she learned so much about human nature and how to harness it. She found no difficulty in complimenting people because, just as she had the capacity to draw out stories from people, she also had a talent for observing or discovering things about them that were special, unique or attractive.

While I was eliciting the story of her particular charismatic genius, she was coaxing gently from me stories that I had never heard myself tell before. On parting, I thanked her and later wrote a letter expressing my gratitude for the gracious way in which she submitted to my questioning. But, before I had time to put a stamp on my envelope, I received a card from her, the card expressing in a whimsical but understanding way the content of a personal experience I had recounted. Her written message continued with the theme, ending in a compliment that involved an observation about what she believed I had become as a result of that experience. I was profoundly moved and, even now, when I recall the event I continue to have warm feelings towards her. Hers was the quintessential compliment.

I later did some research on compliments and identified the following guidelines in giving praise:

- Compliment people for their accomplishments in areas that you know are important to them.
- It is best when you don't put a value on a compliment. Comments like 'That was good', 'You were great' and 'That was excellent work' tend to establish an uneven power relationship. Focus on content, as illustrated in the following examples. The best compliments appear to be where the power relationship is one of equality and where the compliment giver focuses plausibly on the details of the compliment. For example:

   'I noticed how you kept your message to three major points and that really had an impact on those present. You won the day.'

   'I read your report, and the points were so easy for me to embrace. The arguments were set out very clearly and it seemed natural for me to agree with your conclusions.'

- Personal compliments are best given in a similar way to those in the previous example, because this eliminates the sleaze factor (unless of course you wish it to be present):

   'Your new hairstyle frames your features perfectly, particularly your cheekbones.'

'Gee, I wish I'd found that outfit first! It is just the right combination of style and formality and looks like it came from the Via Veneto.'

Remember, one of the most powerful forms of flattery you can offer anyone is to fully engage in listening to them without making premature interpretations or judgments.

*Playfulness*

Playfulness is a word not usually associated with adult behaviour outside of mating rituals. However, it is entirely possible for adults to be playful with members of either sex without there being any sexual undertones.

Playfulness is a quality I have noticed in many of the charismatic personalities I have deconstructed. The playfulness I refer to is a sophisticated form of asexual flirtation or social exchange where the charismatic individual encourages a subject or subjects to enter a playful state. The best way I can describe it is to offer some examples.

You can often see this state of playfulness being acted out when a group of lads, no matter what their age, 'hoon about' together. You also notice the female equivalent when a group of women engage in a ritual of play in which there are no victims and each participant adds her contribution to an event of pure fun-making. In one way I see it as individuals giving birth to states of mirth or joy, because that is often the outcome.

Perhaps the best way to understand playfulness is to visit a local preschool or primary school and observe playfulness among children. With children, play often facilitates the acting out of solutions to conflicts, allows them to try out ways of dealing with particular challenges and issues, and helps them develop interesting and novel ways of relating to others.

Playfulness, however, extends far beyond the schoolyard. With charismatic adults I have modelled it represents a slant or approach to life. Adult playfulness helps them transcend the formal boundaries and structures that often make being an adult so burdensome. Playful minds are fertile minds and can help stimulate original thinking, can break down barriers of all kinds and can often iron out social differences. Adult playfulness, as I have observed it in its better forms, involves a kind of indomitable friskiness or cheekiness that charms new acquaintances, lubricates friendship and often establishes the necessary pre-conditions for adults to enter an agreement frame of mind. In my experience, charismatic personalities instinctively know that if people associate pleasure and stimulation with them they have overcome a key barrier to influence and persuasion.

## Conclusion

Much interpersonal behaviour is manipulative, particularly when it involves the use of personal power to influence how other people think and behave. Manipulation in, and of, itself is neither 'good' nor 'bad'—it just *is*. The word derives from the Latin *manipulatio*, meaning to shape or mould. Therefore, manipulation can be seen as an attempt to mould or shape the thoughts and behaviours of others, and there's nothing wrong with that. Inevitably, however, when we engage in manipulative acts we arrive at a moral crossroads. So here are two relatively simple navigation rules to help you choose your direction. Ask yourself if the manipulation will:

**1** empower rather than enslave others
**2** achieve a mutual rather than self-serving end and help others fulfil their needs and goals.

In my experience of studying both Crooks in Dark Suits and Honourable Persuaders, the general lesson appears to be that those who elevate and empower people through their manipulations succeed a lot better in both life and work. Those who use their power to subjugate others and to realise their own ambitions at the expense of others tend ultimately to crash and burn, and often take many innocents with them. I believe that the immutable rule is:

> *You cannot sustain high and enduring referent power without a commitment to an ethical approach.*

In this chapter I have only scratched the surface of charisma and referent power by exploring how certain attributes and behaviours can increase personal attractiveness and contribute to your ability to influence the thoughts and actions of others. There is much more to learn—use your powers of observation.

A central theme running through this chapter is that most expressions of referent power are the result of specific and learnable behaviours. There is nothing mystical or magical about personal magnetism, just as there is little mystery about doing charisma. The secret is to recognise that charismatic behaviours can be learned over time. The only obstacle is deciding when and how to start.

### Tips for increasing referent power (personal magnetism/charisma)

1. *Recognise that personal magnetism is the result of looking, behaving and speaking the part.*
   By arriving at the conclusion that you 'do' personal magnetism rather than 'have' it, you are mentally preparing yourself for action.

2. *Make a habit of cataloguing and understanding the standards of those whom you wish to influence or persuade (the perceiver's standards).*
   Ask, observe, become a people watcher and map out the territories of those you wish to influence before you deliver your message. Be 'true' to the standards of those you wish to impress.

3. *Reveal enough of yourself (the attractive elements of your personality) to be liked and embraced.*
   Reflect the 'energy' of your content and respond to the energy of others. Allow yourself to show passion and reveal the courage of your convictions through your voice and movement. Make your movement fluid.

4. *Wear the uniform.*
   Dress and groom yourself to meet the expectations of your audience.

5. *Get out of ego and get out there.*
   Focus 'externally' on others and give people your fullest attention. Let them know that they are the most important people in the world at a given moment.

6. *Become an expert empathic listener.*
   Become a collaborative listener and tap into your natural curiosity about people. Send signals to people that you are vitally interested in them.

7. *Develop resourceful states of mind.*
   Be positive and solution focused. With all the doomsayers in the world, a positive and optimistic attitude is a magnet for those in need of hope and a salve for the battle weary.

8. *Perfect the art of praise.*
   Develop your talent for observing and discovering things about people that are praiseworthy. Offer plausible compliments that specify how people are special or unique

> 9 *Become a master of the civil virtues.*
> Drop 'me first' habits and demonstrate courtesy, ethics and grace.
>
> 10 *Learn to be more playful*
> Find the fun in moments at appropriate times. Learn asexual flirtation and creative moments of levity to lubricate interpersonal communications.

## For further exploration

- DA Benton, *Executive charisma: six steps to mastering the art of leadership*, McGraw-Hill, New York, 2003.
  An informative read that covers some of the important basics of improving one's power to influence.
- A Blatner & A Blatner, *The art of play: helping adults reclaim imagination and spontaneity*, Bruner/Mazel, New York, 1997.
  Provides a solid theoretical background and useful ideas about loosening up and exploring opportunities for more rewarding human interaction.
- RB Cialdini, *Influence: the psychology of persuasion*, William Morrow, New York, 1993.
  Essential reading for any executive. A groundbreaking book that deals with key categories of influence and persuasion.
- D Guilfoyle, *The charisma effect*, McGraw-Hill, Sydney, 2002.
  My own book, which focuses on the 'how to' of various forms of social power and influence with significant information on identity engineering.
- AR Pratkanis & A Aronson, *Age of propaganda: the everyday use and abuse of persuasion*, WH Freeman & Co, New York, 2001.
  An important and scholarly work that outlines the misuses and abuses of various forms of social power.

## Notes

1 JRP French & BH Raven, 'The bases of social power', in D Cartwright (ed.), *Studies in social power*, Institute for Social Research, Ann Arbor, 1959.

2 RE Clarke, *Reference group theory and delinquency*, Behavioural Publications, New York, 1972; T Shibutani, *Society and personality*, Prentice-Hall, New Jersey, 1961.

3 LL Carli, 'Nonverbal behaviour, gender and influence', *Journal of Personality and Social Psychology*, vol. 68, 1985; LA Rudman, 'Self-promotion as a risk factor for women: the costs and benefits of counter-stereotypical impression management', *Journal of Personality and Social Psychology*, vol. 74, 1998.
4 *Churchill: the chronological dictionary of quotations*, Bloomsbury Publications, London, 1988.
5 A Kurzweil, *The grand complication*, Arrow Books, London, 2001.
6 M Weber, *The theory of social and economic organisation*, The Free Press, New York, 1974.
7 E Langer, *Mindfulness*, Perseus Books, Reading, Mass., 1989.
8 C Darwin, P Ekman & P Prodger, *The expression of the emotions in man and animals*, Oxford Press, Oxford, 2002.
9 D Guilfoyle, *The charisma effect*, McGraw-Hill, Sydney, 2002.
10 S Covey, *The 7 habits of highly successful people*, Simon & Schuster, New York, 1989.

# THE POWER OF POSITIVE SPIN    4

Thomas Murrell

Introduction

The power of spin
  Case study: may I have a Nudie please?

The rise of integrity marketing

Can spin and ethics coexist?
  Case study: a hammer thrower's story

A new take on spin: the *brand trajectory model*

Harnessing the power of positive spin
  Winning the media game
  What is news?

Moving people to action
  Case study: up close and personal with Bill Clinton

Influencing in times of crisis
  Improving your media performance during a crisis
  Case study: Western Power's 'Black Wednesday'

Integrity marketing: the six stages of influence

Conclusion

For further exploration

Acknowledgments

Notes

# About the author

Thomas Murrell, BAgSc (Hons) (Adel), DipAgEcon (UNE), MBA (UWA), CSP

Thomas Murrell is a speaker on the international business circuit and the Managing Director of 8M Media & Communications, an integrated media, marketing and management consulting company.

Described by *BRW Magazine* as 'committed to using creativity as a competitive edge', Thomas is recognised as an expert on how to be media and marketing savvy. His *Integrity marketing*, *Brand building* and *Winning the media game* seminars are full of real-life experiences and practical advice.

In a former life he was a TV and radio personality, executive producer and senior media executive and describes his 12 years at the Australian Broadcasting Corporation as 'an apprenticeship'.

Thomas is the author of *Media fundamentals: how to turn your big marketing idea into a competitive advantage* (8M Media & Communications, 2001) and *Web marketing essentials* (8M Media & Communications, 2002). He has just released his signature *Media & Marketing Masterclass*™ series on six interactive CD-ROMs.

He uses metaphors from his experience as a National Junior Hammer Throw Champion to demonstrate the 'power of positive spin'; and a Vincent Fairfax Fellowship (at the St James Ethics Centre) helped him to formulate his ideas on the relationship between positive spin and ethical leadership.

You can find out more about Thomas Murrell and his work through *Media motivators*, his regular electronic magazine that is read by 7000 marketing and PR professionals in fifteen different countries. You can subscribe by visiting <www.8mmedia.com>.

Thomas Murrell can be contacted at <tom@8mmedia.com>.

# Executive summary

Australians are recognised as the best storytellers in the world, yet they fail to turn this strength into loyal, profitable customers.

There is a new breed of manager, however, who realises that many leadership functions, including those of influence and persuasion, involve a degree of 'spin'. This may involve putting a *positive spin* on things to minimise negative perceptions about a product, service or organisation.

This chapter introduces aspiring leaders to the new concept of *integrity marketing*. This marketing style is based on the premise that, in today's crowded, noisy and brand saturated marketplace, managers and leaders need to look at new ways of influencing key stakeholders.

The chapter also introduces the *brand trajectory model*, which is a framework for creating high-level trust with prospects, customers and clients. This model makes it clear that, if leaders/managers are to attract, win and retain profitable customers, they must be better at managing the message. In this way they can build credibility, authenticity and value in their corporate or personal brands.

Traditional communications thinking is often based on expensive and ineffective advertising strategies designed to reach consumers. This new approach is based on the leader's role in aligning the values of an organisation with those of its staff and customers. Central to this concept is the ability to generate *positive spin* to create momentum, leverage and torque.

# Introduction

Imagine you are the CEO of a new start-up company. This business operates in the most competitive industry in the world. Globally, the industry sector has lost billions of dollars and shed millions of staff over the past three years. It has been hit by what industry leaders call 'the four horsemen of the apocalypse': September 11, the world economic downturn, SARS and the war against Iraq.

Your major competitor spends more on producing one television commercial than your whole annual marketing budget. Yet, in less than three years you have gone from zero market share to capturing nearly 30% of the market. Annual revenues have grown from zero to more than $100 million.

Your company, which started with less than $15 million, is now worth around $2.4 billion. In fact, if you had invested just one dollar with the company 18 months ago, it would now be worth around five dollars.

Sound far-fetched and fanciful? What business am I talking about? Well, it is the story of Virgin Blue, the most successful start-up in aviation history—an idea hatched on the back of a beer coaster in a UK pub.

The premise of this chapter is that you can learn from people like Sir Richard Branson, of Virgin fame, to be a better leader, a more effective communicator and an ethical influencer by harnessing the *power of positive spin*.

## The power of spin

'Spin' is an ambiguous term with a variety of meanings. It is typically viewed with scepticism by many leaders.

Yet there is a new breed of manager who realises that many leadership functions, including those of influence and persuasion, involve a degree of spin. This may involve putting a *positive spin* on things to minimise negative perceptions about a product, service or organisation. Here a leader's choice of words is critical because:

> . . . language is the operating system of the mind. No word is ever accepted on its own merit. Every sound, every syllable, carries its own baggage, which is sometimes positive, sometimes negative, sometimes

*neutral. If you want to create a favourable impression in the mind, you have to use words that reflect the perception you are trying to create.*

A Reis and L Reis[1]

What is the role of spin in the context of business and organisational leadership? It is all about managing meaning. Spin is the angle, the take, the hook or the emphasis given to a certain message. This can be both selective and subjective. Positive spin is achieved when the most convincing, memorable or motivating meaning of a message is delivered to achieve a desired communication objective.

Spin—the management of meaning and communications—can operate at three levels: contextual, strategic and personal. Effective leaders work all three levels.

*Contextual level spin* involves looking at the bigger picture, and managing the message within a wider perspective. In a leadership context this may involve such tasks as developing and communicating a global vision for an organisation. Here, the words chosen or spin taken are critical for achieving such a task. Messages taken out of context are dangerous and should be avoided, especially if dealing with the media to communicate to the wider public. Skilled leaders understand how the media operate, with a focus on the 7-second 'sound bite', and work within these contextual constraints to manage their message.

*Strategic level spin* looks at how the messages conveyed by a leader help to achieve organisational objectives. The most powerful messages are those where the meaning is clear and congruent with the vision, mission and brand values of the organisation. Examples may include a leader's role in turning a vision and ideas into effective business strategies, or in sharing knowledge throughout an organisation.

*Personal level spin* focuses on one-to-one communication and how a leader's message can be used to motivate and inspire others. Examples may be a leader's role in encouraging innovation and risk-taking, leading transformational change or improving customer service.

The idea of leaders using positive spin as a source of motivation for themselves or others is not new. The US author and speaker,

Dr David Schwartz, has been pushing these concepts to eager readers of *The magic of thinking big*, since it was first published way back in 1959. He argued:

> *Belief, the 'I'm-positive-I-can' attitude, generates the power, skill and energy needed to do. When you believe I-can-do-it, the how-to develops.*[2]

Spin used in this way helps to put things in context. It can also be used to allow teams or individuals to see and set alternative priorities.

Let me give you a practical example of positive spin in action.

### Case study: may I have a Nudie please?

It was 5.30 am on a typical Saturday morning after a long, hard week at work. I was woken by my 5-year-old daughter and wished I hadn't stayed up late the night before watching football.

She prodded me, innocently asking: 'Dad, can we go to Kings Park to get a Nudie?'

'What did you say?' I asked back in a half daze.

'We went to Kings Park this week and had a Nudie drink,' she piped up, peering into my bleary eyes.

By now our 3-year-old son had joined in as the support act. 'Can we, Dad, pleeeese!' he pleaded as he leapt from the end of the bed onto my prostrate body.

So what happened next? Well, like hundreds of other parents around the western suburbs surrounding beautiful Kings Park in Perth, we gave in, got dressed, and headed up to Sticky Beaks café. As the first there, we immediately went to the counter and ordered two Nudies, feeling somewhat embarrassed. They came in funny-shaped bottles, were half the size of normal fruit juice drinks and cost twice as much. After one taste, we were hooked—and it hadn't cost the company a cent.

So what is the point of telling this story? Well, it demonstrates the power of word-of-mouth marketing, a memorable name and the 'gravity effect' of a strong brand.

'The idea of having a juice company name that doesn't sound like a juice company name is fairly unique,' is just one of thirty-four reasons listed on the Nudie website to explain the imaginative name.

'Going into a store and asking for a Nudie is a great way to break the ice' and 'It was about time the web address www.nudie.com.au was put to good use' are listed as other reasons.

Writing in the *Australian* recently, Simon Canning said: 'Nudie has become the latest incarnation of what ad experts call a "disruptive brand", eschewing traditional advertising and striking up a direct conversation with its customers.'[3]

## The rise of integrity marketing

As a leader, the benefit of using the power of positive spin is that you quickly and cost effectively build trust, credibility and strong brand awareness among consumers.

Australians, as Rupert Murdoch maintains, are the world's best storytellers. Yet few Australian businesses are able to harness the power of storytelling to influence clients and customers and create more demand for their products or services. Many leaders are failing to make the most of this talent.

There are simply too few people following the lead of Sir Richard Branson and using media creativity, innovation and storytelling to build brands that can quickly dominate the competition. Successful leaders rely on a media savvy approach to turn their ideas and ingenuity into creative and practical ways to attract, win and retain even more profitable customers.

Speaking frankly about Virgin Blue's approach, CEO Brett Godfrey says: 'We have a simple philosophy—our major marketing tool is our PR department. It's the major focus of what we do. Richard Branson is our walking, talking billboard. We believe that every employee has a responsibility to promote the airline.'[4]

Research shows that consumers in major capital cities in the USA are bombarded with between 1500 and 3000 marketing messages a day; and by the time US teenagers are 18 they have been exposed to more than ten million discreet advertising messages.[5] Most of these interruptions have little impact because consumers are now better educated and better informed.

Traditional marketing has a low credibility factor—it just isn't working as effectively. So in today's era of increasing cynicism, brand saturation and information overload it is critical to take a *values-based* approach to marketing. This new and innovative approach is about building trust with consumers and ensuring that the core values of an organisation match those of its employees and the consumers it is trying to reach.

In my speeches to audiences around Australia and overseas, I'm calling this new approach *integrity marketing*. Integrity marketing is about creating brands that people trust and will seek out rather than the traditional and expensive strategy of reaching out to consumers.

The values of an organisation need to be communicated clearly to everyone in the organisation at all levels—from senior management down to the front receptionist. Staff are often the major contact point between an organisation and its customers and they must convey the values of the organisation to those customers. The greater the alignment of an organisation's values with those of its staff and customers, the stronger the brand and the greater its influence.

Good leaders use stories and the power of positive spin to communicate their values. In effect, the brand 'comes from within' as everyone within the organisation becomes an advocate for the brand and the values it represents. Managing meaning and good communication is essential to this process.

## Can spin and ethics coexist?

Spin is an emotive topic. It seems everyone has an opinion on spin, influenced by their background, values and beliefs. Those who work as professionals in the area of public relations and communications often have a love–hate relationship with the media. The view of journalists that so-called 'spin doctors' provide weapons of 'mass distraction' is common.[6]

Although storytelling and the classic Australian art of 'spinning a yarn' are critical for communicating directly with customers and for influencing others, spin can have a negative or dark side—it can be used to hide, confuse or hype-up a situation. When considering whether to use spin in a particular situation, in what context or to what degree to use it, the important question to ask is: *Is it fair?* This is different from: Is it legal?

If you are honest people will trust you. If you try to pretend you will be gone. The best way to test your actions in using spin is by applying the 'sunlight test'. Would you be proud of your actions if, in the cold hard light of day, they were revealed to everyone on the front page of a major daily newspaper?

Ultimately doing 'the right thing' is at the heart of good ethical leadership, including the use of spin. Strong leaders believe that 'truth is more important than good news'. So when the use of spin would be unethical, leaders should reflect on their own values and those of the people around them . . . is this really the way they want to do business?

Much of my thinking in this area has been shaped by the remarkable and life changing experience I gained through the Vincent Fairfax Fellowship. This 2-year program, run by the Sydney-based St James Ethics Centre, provides young Australians with an opportunity to develop practices and habits of ethical leadership. According to John van Geldermalsen, the centre's Director of Leadership:

> *Quality of leadership is critical to any endeavour. We expect that graduates of this program will not only significantly and positively impact on that quality in particular areas of society that they influence, but will also have a material effect on the quality of leadership across society as a whole.*[7]

Undertaking the Vincent Fairfax Fellowship certainly helped me to ask the tough question about whether marketing, spin and ethics can coexist. The program taught me the importance of self-reflection and how our own values shape our actions.

## Case study: a hammer thrower's story

Our values are shaped by significant events in our lives. Patterns of behaviour learned early in life shape later success or failure. For me, being involved in sport, in particular athletics, helped create a pattern of success that has helped me throughout my personal and professional life.

As a fresh-faced, curly-haired young man with big strong thighs, I had a passion for the quirky and highly technical sport of 'hammer throwing'.

And yes, I've heard and probably told most of the gags surrounding this unusual athletic pursuit. Like: 'What's the hardest thing about hammer throwing? Hitting the nail on the head at 70 metres!' 'In fact, hammer throwing had such a low profile as an Olympic sport that it was known as track, field and . . .

carpark!' And, 'Did you hear the story about the cross-eyed hammer thrower? He didn't win the competition, but he certainly kept the crowd on their toes!'

For those unsure of what hammer throwing involves, you take a 7.26 kg (16 lb) steel ball with a swivel on the end of high-tensile wire, wear a glove and spin around three or four times in a 7.5 ft concrete circle and then let go.

The name hammer throw is actually derived from older competitions where an actual hammer was thrown.[8] Such competitions are still part of the Scottish Highland Games and I've been known to throw the fixed handle hammer wearing a kilt!

Seriously, hammer throwing taught me some important lessons in life.

I was a state schoolboy discus champion—but when I was 17 years old I stopped growing. Discus is based on the 'slingshot' principle and the longer your arms, the greater the sling and the greater the distance you will throw. I just wasn't tall and lanky enough to go from being a good discus thrower to a great one. So I took up the hammer—it was more suited to my body shape and lower centre of gravity!

Hammer throwing is based on the physics of a 'spinning top'. The faster you spin around, the faster the speed of the hammer head, the greater its velocity and the further it will go when you release it. It is also a highly technical event, requiring great timing as well as balance, speed and power. This taught me my first lesson: you must be flexible *and* focus on your strengths.

Second, I discovered the power of goal setting. In 1981, I narrowly qualified for the national championships as a hammer thrower in the South Australian Track and Field Team. They were held in my home town of Adelaide, so there was no cost to include me in the team as an 'extra'! I finished seventh, about half way down the field of fifteen. But I worked out that five of the people who had finished ahead of me were turning senior next year and wouldn't be competing again in this group. I said to myself: 'I can do this, I can win this next year'.

It is great to dream to win—but you need the desire to back it up. With desire comes discipline and dedication. So I gave up playing Australian Rules Football, got a coach and spent a whole winter working on my technique, timing and strength. The desire provided a sense of direction and purpose.

The next year, I won the National Championship, throwing a personal best, setting a new State record and gaining selection in the 1982 Commonwealth Games Track and Field training squad.

Hammer throwing taught me a lot about life and the importance of setting *goals to achieve your dreams. This pattern of success has been a great source of personal inspiration and motivation and I now share it with others.*

*My message is simple: dream it . . . desire it . . . then do it.*

## A new take on spin: the *brand trajectory model*

The hammer throw competition is decided by who can throw the ball the furthest. You gain maximum distance by swinging the hammer twice around your head while stationary, and then rotating very quickly with a 'heel toe' turn three or four times before a final release at the front of the throwing circle.

The men's hammer throw has been in the Olympic Games since 1900 and the women's hammer throw was first included at the Sydney 2000 Olympics, following inclusion in the World Championships a year earlier.

Despite this it has a long history:

> *Legends trace it to the Tailteann games held in Tara, Ireland, about 2000BC, and tell of the Celtic hero, Cuchulainn, who gripped a chariot wheel by its axle, whirled it around his head, and threw it further than did any other mortal. Wheel hurling was later replaced by throwing a boulder attached to the end of a wooden handle. Among the ancient Teutonic tribes forms of hammer throwing were practiced at religious festivals honoring the God Thor.*[9]

Figure 4.1 illustrates the dynamics and trajectory of the hammer during each turn or spin by the athlete.

The principles of hammer throwing have allowed me to develop a powerful concept for *breaking through brick walls* in business. These 'brick walls' usually occur at some time during the life cycle of a product or service—or an organisation or a leader's career.

Brick walls can happen even to the largest of companies. Richard Gluyas, writing in the *Australian* on the impact of corporate culture on a company's success, quoted a McKinsey & Co study of US management consulting companies. The study found that only seventy-four of the companies on the 'top 500' list in 1957 were still on the list 40 years later in 1997.[10] The remaining companies, in a range of industries across all sectors,

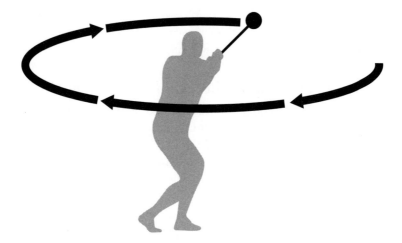

Figure 4.1 The hammer throw

had hit 'brick walls' or barriers and were unable to grow in a sustainable way over a long period of time.

Typically, failure occurs after the initial enthusiasm for a new product, service or management fad wanes. In marketing terms this is known as the maturity stage of a product's life cycle.

How do you overcome this waning enthusiasm? The *brand trajectory model* provides a framework for breaking through barriers. Brands help keep products or services fresh in the minds of consumers—and good marketers and influencers are able to identify what is at the core of a brand. These core elements are not static—they change over time.

You have to first develop and then nurture a brand if you wish to build up its value, or velocity. Just like hammer throwing, 'a brand is a dynamic and complex network of association built up through past experience'.[11]

Like hammer throwers, good leaders can't change the location where their throws have to land, but they can adjust their trajectory. This has a big impact on the final outcome and can be the difference between winning and losing. 'The contributory factors that determine the distance of the hammer throw and the tangential velocity of the hammer head at the moment of release, will be determined by the increase in speed of each turn, a rate of increase that is individual for each thrower.'[12]

Similarly, brands build momentum over time and the trajectory they travel along is very important to their overall success.

Here are the major components of the brand trajectory model.

- *Brand features.* At the furthest point from the hammer thrower's body is the hammer head. This represents the tangible and most visible aspects of the brand. This is where the most velocity is created. It represents the brand's unique features, qualities or attributes, similar to the outer layer of a 'brand onion' or 'brand pearl'.[13]
- *Self-motivators.* Next is the swivel. This provides a fluidity, grace and rhythm around which the hammer's head can rotate. As hammer throwers will know, you can accomplish a lot more and throw a lot further with the swivel head hammer than with the traditional fixed head hammer of the Highland Games. The swivel represents the 'self-motivators' or lubricant of the brand that allows the benefits of the product to be easily articulated by the organisation and recognised by the customer. This is a small but powerful part of the brand trajectory.
- *Brand values.* The high-tensile wire represents the values or beliefs communicated by the brand. These often create tension and conflict, but allow the brand to extend out to consumers. The wire allows momentum to be created through the earth's gravity, combined with the forces of the spinning athlete and the torque created between the hammer's head and thrower's body. This provides leverage and flexibility. Good brands have both of these qualities.
- *Brand presence.* The handle represents the personality or lifestyle of the brand and provides 'presence'. This can be either enhanced or sometimes hidden by the glove the thrower wears to protect his or her fingertips from being crushed by the huge centrifugal forces coming through the handle. Brands that are hidden are not very strong. Powerful brands let their lifestyle shine through.
- *Brand core.* At the centre of the model is the brand's 'core'. In hammer throwing, this is the torso of the athlete, where all the energy and power is generated. This is the core of the brand. The body creates the brand's power, momentum and torque.

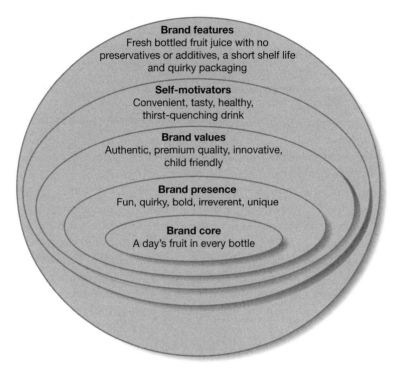

Figure 4.2 Brand trajectory for the Nudie juice brand[14]

Figure 4.2 illustrates the brand trajectory model for Nudie juice. This model can be applied to both corporate and personal brands. Here are some tips on how to do this.

*Five tips for applying the brand trajectory model to your own situation*

1 Create a name that is memorable and distinctive.
2 Tell a story behind the name that will capture the imagination of potential customers.
3 Use word-of-mouth marketing and be media savvy by seeking out free publicity.
4 Align your company's core values with those of your staff, suppliers and customers.
5 Create brand champions inside and outside your company to help tell the story.

# Harnessing the power of positive spin

Have you ever wondered why some organisations seem to continually receive positive media attention and publicity? The answer is really quite simple: these organisations *understand how the media work*. They have learned to harness the power of positive spin by being skilled media communicators and through effective media relations.

## Winning the media game

Organisations that have harnessed the power of positive spin work *with* the media rather than against them. Like Branson, Dick Smith and others, they are skilful at winning the media game by gaining the attention of editors and journalists, and as a result they gain thousands of dollars of media coverage for free.

How do they do this? Well, first they understand the considerable differences between the various media. They realise that different media have diverse but specific requirements for their 'news'. In short, they know how the media operate. For instance, newspapers and magazines do not necessarily require a photograph to accompany a story, whereas television journalists will not even consider a story unless they can obtain interesting footage to accompany it. (Branson has been a genius at providing the media with visually appealing stories, such as footage and shots of him being suspended by a cable below a helicopter while flying over Sydney Harbour.) A radio station, on the other hand, is interested only in quotes they can use as sound grabs.

They also understand how to present a story to the media so that it grabs their attention. The most effective way to pitch a story is through a *media release*—a highly stylised piece of writing presented in a relatively universal format. There is often very little difference between a well-written media release and a published story.

Before preparing your media release, you must first clarify your communication objectives. This means that you have to determine what you want to achieve. Are you trying to provide information, influence public opinion, build a profile for your organisation or product, implement marketing strategies or launch something? You have to clearly define what you want to do, what you want to say and how you want to say it.

The next step is to determine your target audience. Are they customers, suppliers, competitors or the general public? Once you have determined this, you have to evaluate the demographics of this audience. What age are they, what is their level of education, their geographic location, their beliefs and values?

You must also consider how they access information. What media do they usually use? What newspapers and magazines are they reading? What television programs are they watching and what radio stations are they listening to? What websites are they visiting and which ones are they bookmarking as favourites? The market intelligence you gather about your target audience will assist in determining what channels of communication you will use to convey your message.

In hammer throwing, you can have the furthest throw but still not win the competition. Unless it lands in the sector marked out on the field it is not a legal throw. Marketing and media relations are a lot like this. Unless you identify your target audience and land your best throws inside the sector, you can waste a lot of time, effort and energy with little reward.

### What is news?

One of the keys to getting media coverage from a media release is to stand out from the crowd. In the media industry this is known as 'the hook'. Media institutions often receive hundreds of media releases a day, so if your media release does not stand out then it is less likely to be published. Your message has to have strong news value.

In general, news value or newsworthiness can be divided into seven categories, which often overlap:

**1** *Immediacy*. The more immediate a story, the greater the interest it will generate.
**2** *Consequence*. The more people a story affects, the greater its newsworthiness.
**3** *Topicality*. If a story is highly topical or on the cutting edge, it is more likely to gain media coverage.
**4** *Drama*. The more dramatic a story is, the greater the media attention.
**5** *Proximity*. The closer it is to your audience's centre of influence, the higher the news value.

6 *Relevance.* The greater the relevance to the target audience, the more likely it is that the media will run your story.
7 *Human interest.* The more quirky or unusual it is, the more likely it will be to grab the attention of the media. Dog bites man is not a story, but man bites dog is!

There are many ways that you can stand out from the crowd and gain news value to build your brand. Some of the most effective are:

- *Become an expert.* Position yourself as a leading authority or expert in the particular area that you are trying to publicise.
- *Have a gimmick.* Create an angle, something quirky or unusual, or a message with human-interest appeal. Who can forget Dick Smith towing an iceberg into Sydney harbour or his 'Dickheads' line of matches.
- *Stand for 'something'.* Take a stance on a particular topic or issue.
- *Release a new product.* Something new and innovative is almost guaranteed to receive media coverage.
- *Be controversial.* Controversy attracts the media (but beware of being too controversial, as it may backfire and you could wind up getting bad publicity).

Here is a great example. Krispy Kreme, a start-up US chain of doughnut stores, built their brand and sales in Australia with no advertising. How did they do it? They gave away more than 30 000 free doughnuts and, importantly, each media release they sent was accompanied by about four dozen fresh doughnuts. This certainly grabbed the attention of the media.

'In the year since Krispy Kreme delivered its first press release to a newsroom—accompanied by what would become a ubiquitous box of doughnuts—the brand has been mentioned in one form or another in Australian media nearly 1000 times, according to Media Monitors tracking,' reports Simon Canning from the *Australian*, who also fessed up in the article to receiving and eating his fair share of doughnuts.[15]

Media savvy leaders develop and maintain a long-term relationship with the media. Media coverage generates credibility through third party endorsement and provides social proof that traditional advertising can't match. This creates momentum, torque and leverage.

The downside is that you have reduced control, which is why I recommend media training for all aspiring leaders, and the use of media releases to control your message.

## Moving people to action

Storytelling and speaking in public can be a powerful platform from which to generate positive spin. They can help to raise the profile of your business, generate new leads, create greater profits, or they can help boost your career. This is also one of the quickest ways to create a positive reputation and influence people.

Your objective in every speech should be to move people to action. However, speaking in public can be nerve-wracking and seriously stressful for first timers. Writing a speech can also be a major challenge, especially as you have to write for the ear.

Former US president Bill Clinton is arguably one of the most influential communicators of his generation. His ideas and ideals have made a significant impact on millions of people around the world. How did he do this? Is his famous charisma real, managed or fake? Is it an innate or learned skill? What role does spin play?

### Case study: up close and personal with Bill Clinton

*We can all learn from watching other speakers, especially good ones. I recently achieved a long held ambition to hear Bill Clinton speak in person. The event I attended in Perth was a $1500 per head black-tie dinner to raise money for sick children.*

*What was my motivation for spending an evening with former president Clinton? Anyone who reportedly earns $300 000 for a 50-minute keynote presentation must be good. As a professional speaker myself, I wanted to see Clinton in action. I wanted not only to hear what he said, but how he said it.*

*Here's what I learned from hearing Bill Clinton in person and analysing how he was presented. As a leader, you should be able to adapt at least some of these points to fit your own circumstances.*

1 The marketing strategy. *In previous years, a big advertising blitz had brought audiences to see speakers such as former Soviet leader Gorbachov and others. The marketing approach of the promoters was very commercially focused, and included a massive advertising budget. By contrast, the Clinton event had a more humanitarian angle, with funds being raised for a good cause—sick kids—through the Princess Margaret Hospital for Children*

Foundation. *This was a great match with two of Clinton's core values: building community; and empathy with the concerns of ordinary people. The marketing campaign relied heavily on positive spin through media coverage to create awareness of the event.*

2 A memorable entry. *Clinton's entry to the ballroom was brilliantly stage-managed. Everyone was asked to stand and then he walked into the room to his US presidential election theme song, 'Happy days are here again'. The atmosphere in the room was electric and made the hairs on the back of my neck stand up!*

3 Personal presentation. *His dress and presentation were absolutely immaculate. (Maybe the $500 haircuts help!) Many women at my table commented that Clinton was far better looking in the flesh than on TV.*

4 The power of presence. *There was a buzz about being in the same room as former president Clinton. His body language, smile and confident handshake embodied charisma. His considerable charm reminded me of that high school science experiment when you tip iron filings onto a white sheet of paper covering a strong magnet. People were attracted to Clinton like metal filings to a powerful magnet.*

5 Warm-up. *Alan Jones was MC and the warm-up included a short film that took a lighthearted look at Clinton's last days in office. Scenes included Clinton washing the presidential car, clipping the hedges and playing switchboard operator in the Oval Room. A great scene from a press conference showed Clinton talking to a single sleeping journalist.*

6 Introduction. *A well-constructed introduction helped build empathy and highlighted that Clinton's life had not all been plain sailing. The facts that his father died when he was young, his mother was a nursing assistant and he was born in Hope, a town of 6000 people, helped put his success and achievements in context.*

7 Building on a sense of destiny. *A strong personal brand is built on stories. The story of Clinton, then a fresh-faced 17-year-old, meeting President John F Kennedy at a youth leadership camp, was used to great effect. It was mentioned in the introduction, and the now famous photo of Clinton shaking JFK's hand in the Rose Garden of the White House on 24 July 1963 was also used in the commemorative brochure given to each guest at the Perth dinner. In his memoirs, Clinton tells the story of how, on his first day as President, he took his mother down to the Rose Garden to show her exactly where he had stood to shake JFK's hand nearly 30 years previously.*[16] *Other brand building*

shots included an intimate moment with Hillary, a shot of him playing the saxophone, a jogging photo, one with his daughter Chelsea and one featuring Clinton lined up with three past presidents. They all helped to define 'Clinton, the man'.

8 Customising the message. *Clinton's speech in Perth was customised to include stories relevant to a Perth market, including the 'City of Lights' story.* Here he recounted memories of Perth switching on its lights at night for US astronaut Colonel John Glenn as the first Mercury spacecraft passed over the city in 1962. Most of the audience were baby boomers and he created a positive and powerful emotional connection with them—many recounted their warm memories of running out into the back garden with young children and shining torches up into white sheets hung on Hills Hoist clotheslines to create a blaze of light. They remembered Perth as a much safer, friendlier place. I'm often asked: Did Clinton research and write the speech himself to include this story? I will never know, but as he is one of the busiest men on the planet, I'm convinced he didn't. Did he tell this story to other audiences he was speaking to around Australia and in Asia? No, he customised it for Perth, and by building in emotion he created a powerful rapport with the audience. You, too, can do this in your own speeches by including local stories relevant to your audience. By using this technique, you can be a more influential communicator.

9 Using humour. *Clinton had some great lines about how he could have helped previous presidents in dealing with the media in tricky situations.* Humour is an effective strategy because it relaxes people. A whole range of positive drugs are released in our bodies when we laugh. We feel better and learn more. Humour also helps a speaker appear more authentic and human.

10 Memorable one-liners using opposites. *This can be very effective.* For example, when talking about possible solutions to the war against terrorism, Clinton said 'most of the big things in life are simple'.

11 Repetition. Clinton used this proven speechwriting technique to great effect.

12 Using metaphors. *Clinton used the metaphor of the gap between the invention of the club and the shield to describe the present situation in the war against terrorism. He said: 'This gap needs to be closed'.* Metaphors can give intangible concepts more impact with an audience.

13 Developing empathy with the audience. *Clinton told the story of how he was in Australia at Port Douglas on September 11, and how his daughter Chelsea was in downtown New York. He connected with every parent in the room*

> when he talked about his feelings when he couldn't contact his daughter for three hours on that day.
> 14 A call to action. The aim of the event was to raise money for a children's hospital. Clinton's final words were: 'I want you to help'. Simple, direct and powerful.

I certainly learned a lot by seeing one of the world's great communicators in action.

Whatever your views on Clinton, his personal warmth, ability to connect with an audience and presentation skills are outstanding. Everything Clinton did that night created momentum, leverage and torque.

## Influencing in times of crisis

Hammer throwers can spin out of control and so can leaders.

How do we know when a crisis is a crisis? One answer, according to *The dictionary of media and communication studies*, is when the media tell us it is![17] The media's capacity for agenda setting and making editorial decisions on front page headlines or lead stories can influence the notion of a crisis in the mind of the public. Once a crisis story gains momentum in the media it is difficult to stop and organisations can be forced into crisis management mode.

So why is it that so few leaders have a plan for dealing with the media during a crisis or a high-risk event? Many Australian businesses and local councils have no contingency plans to cope with an emergency or crisis event. Of those that do have plans, I wonder how many have an effective strategy for dealing with the media? Why? Because when a crisis strikes, the media are often the first ones to call.

During a crisis, the media can play an important role—informing the community of what's going on and what you are trying to achieve. However, you can throw even the most thorough risk management plan into chaos if you do not maintain good relations with the media and do not have a strategy to deal with them.

In the emergency and crisis media management workshops I

run, I give the following two examples to highlight why a plan to deal with the media should be an integral part of any risk management plan.
- A fatal accident occurs at a work site and, before the organisation can contact relatives, a well-meaning colleague is ringing the local radio station dedicating a song and naming the recently deceased workmate.

   This illustrates the importance of having a media crisis plan, and then communicating this plan to all employees. It must be made clear that during a crisis all contact with the media should be through one or two official spokespersons.
- A sick infant is brought into the emergency ward of a busy hospital. The infant is given an incorrect dose of a drug, relapses and subsequently dies. A nurse working at the emergency ward that night is studying journalism part time. She tells a fellow student of the incident. The fellow student works at a major daily newspaper and tells the editor. Next day it's front page news.

   This example illustrates how information often flows to the media through informal channels.

So how do you stay ahead of potential disaster in circumstances like these? The most important tactic is to have a media plan and to understand the requirements of different media during a crisis or high-risk event.

In an emergency or crisis situation there is a range of influencing tools available to a leader. Often the best way of getting your message across to the broader community is to use those media that reach the widest possible audience. The most immediate is radio news bulletins, followed by TV news and then daily newspapers.

If you are in a crisis situation, it is likely that your story will have strong news value. The challenge will be not so much getting media coverage, but managing both the media and the message.

Also, in a crisis situation, the story may develop and be ongoing. Journalists will be looking for new angles and developments to 'keep the story alive'. Here the challenge is to keep providing accurate and timely information.

## Improving your media performance during a crisis

When a story breaks it is important to develop good relations with the media and to manage the way the message is communicated.

The dangers of appearing before the media unprepared were highlighted by the Nine Network's *60 minutes* coverage of the Australian mining company at the centre of the major cyanide spill in Eastern Europe in 2001. The visual images were powerful—huge fish belly-up in the river being pulled out by locals with pitchforks. Such emotive images are difficult to combat.

Unfortunately, the company was not very smart in thinking about and managing the way in which it wished to be seen. The mining CEO was interviewed in a 5-star hotel room and was dressed immaculately in a suit and tie. Even if you didn't hear what he was saying, the visual message was of someone aloof, uncaring and remote. The company had missed a golden opportunity to do the interview at the site of the spill, sleeves rolled up and giving the impression of doing something about the situation and being in control. In fact, the image the CEO conveyed reinforced community perceptions of the mining industry reaping huge profits, while being dirty, dangerous and environmentally unsound.

The keys to performing well in such a situation are:

- *Plan and prepare.* When a crisis occurs know the exact status of it and every fact available. For example, who are the people involved, what are the circumstances and what is the latest information?
- *Act decisively.* A crisis is no time to dither. Get as much information to the media as you can, as quickly as possible. If you don't take control of the information, the media will look for other sources to provide a 'sound bite' or 'news grab' and these may not be accurate or reliable sources.
- *Update constantly.* Often in a crisis, rumour, emotion and incorrect information can quickly fill the information void. Continually update the media as information comes to hand.
- *Focus with laser-like precision on the needs and emotions of those affected.* When presenting and planning your media response,

think of the target audience and the words that will reassure them.
- *Show empathy with those affected.* Be involved and take a hands-on approach. Do television interviews on location rather than in a comfortable office remote from the crisis and audience.
- *Choose your words carefully and keep on message.* Spend time formulating 'control phrases'; that is, phrases or short, sharp sentences that sum up your key message. Use them to introduce your agenda and repeat them as necessary to ensure your message is clearly heard.
- *Keep cool, calm and collected.* Be diplomatic and confident and refrain from becoming angry with journalists.

Winning over the public's trust and confidence can be a difficult task. Just ask the outgoing chairman and managing director of Western Australia's major electricity utility, Western Power.

### Case study: Western Power's 'Black Wednesday'

The handling of a power crisis on a hot, sticky day in Western Australia, in February 2003, is a classic case of what can go wrong when a public utility fails to communicate with the community.

It doesn't take Einstein to work out that Perth gets hot in February and that this puts pressure on the power grid. On that day, the power utility couldn't cope with the electricity demands associated with a typical Western Australian summer. This caused widespread and long lasting blackouts, wreaking havoc in homes and businesses.

This became known as 'Black Wednesday'—and the problems started at the top.

Unlike their colleagues over at the Water Corporation, who over the years had developed the fine art of desensitising the public to bad news such as water restrictions, Western Power failed miserably at the task in February 2003.

While the senior Western Power executives enjoyed the comfort of their corporate offices, Perth residents and businesses were asked to swelter in 40-plus degree heat without their airconditioners and fridges, or risk fines of up to $10 000.

So what went so horribly wrong for managing director Stephen van der Mye and chairman Malcolm MacPherson? Clearly, it came down to their inability to communicate with the public and inform people of just what was going on. The then managing director appeared to lack either the skills or the will to deal with *the media and thus adequately inform the community about the crisis. His failure to appear on camera earlier in his tenure confirms this.*

*Alarm bells should have started ringing when cynical local media demanded to know why Stephen van der Mye continued to commute from Melbourne every week to earn his reported $400 000-plus annual salary. The new concept of highly paid 'fly-in-fly-out' public servants was not well received by a parochial Perth public.*

*The situation then went from bad to worse with the failure of Western Power's management to provide an adequate explanation of who was responsible for a faulty Western Power line that allegedly started a bushfire, causing the deaths of two locals in the Great Southern region of Western Australia.*

How do you stay ahead of potential disaster in such circumstances? Simple: have a plan, road test and refine the plan with a hypothetical scenario, and then execute the strategy when the real crisis occurs.

The least Western Power could have done was to pre-warn the public of an impending crisis situation and then put in a process of ongoing, two-way communication with the people who matter—the residents of Perth.

The ability to build public goodwill towards an organisation should be a critical skill of any CEO, especially one brought in as an agent of change. Leadership starts at the top and it is not surprising Stephen van der Mye and Malcolm MacPherson resigned.

Western Power has apologised for its 'inadequate and incomplete communication' over the power crisis, but it will take a long time to rebuild its reputation, and to restore the trust and goodwill of the Perth community.

So what can be learned from the events of Black Wednesday 2003? Here are some lessons all leaders should be aware of when dealing with the community over a public issue.

*Five ways to manage a crisis*
1 Plan for a crisis in advance.
2 Clarify your communication objectives.
3 Determine your spokesperson and road test their skills prior to a crisis.

**4** Stick to the facts. Show empathy with those affected.
**5** Develop an open and honest relationship with the media. Avoid 'No comment' and be proactive.

## Integrity marketing: the six stages of influence

Central to my premise of integrity marketing is the ability to align the values of an *organisation* with those of its *staff* and its *customers*. I call these the three power rings of influence.

An organisation goes through six stages in order to align its values with those of its staff and its customers:

**1** The values of organisation, staff and customers are equal but separate.
**2** The values of the organisation are dominant over those of staff and customers.
**3** The values of the staff are dominant over those of organisation and customers.
**4** The values of the customers are dominant over those of organisation and staff.
**5** There are some shared values between organisation, staff and customers.
**6** There is total overlap and congruency in values of organisation, staff and customers.

Phillip Kotler's models explaining the difference between marketing and public relations shaped much of my thinking in this area.[18] I've also built on the values-based model presented by fellow professional speaker, David Penglase, in *What's ethical about selling*.[19]

Better alignment of values means better branding and more influence and, of course, creates more momentum, torque and leverage.

*Stage 1: the values of organisation, staff and customers are equal but separate*

Leaders and organisations at this stage typically have poor communication and are inefficient. The values of each group are not clearly articulated. Organisations are not very profitable and have mid-level market share.

They have *low influence*.

Examples include large government departments and agencies.

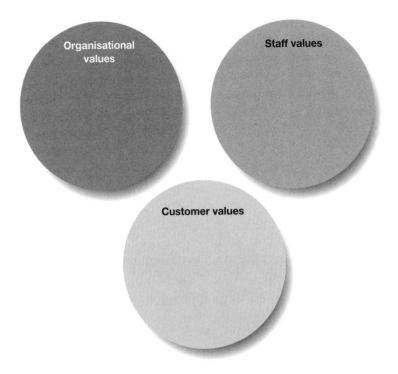

Figure 4.3 Stage 1: incongruent values of organisation, staff and customers

*Stage 2: the values of the organisation are dominant over those of staff and customers*

Leaders and organisations in this stage typically have formal, hierarchical structures. They are slow at decision making and not very media or marketing savvy. They are stable but lack innovation. Often they are described as inflexible. Morale can be low, with the self-esteem and individual creativity of staff crushed. This results in high staff turnover and poor customer loyalty. Organisations in this stage can be profitable and have often come from a protected market monopoly situation.

Their *influence is waning* and is now limited.

Examples include large, once dominant private companies or government organisations that have been privatised. They could be in the banking, aviation or telecommunications sector.

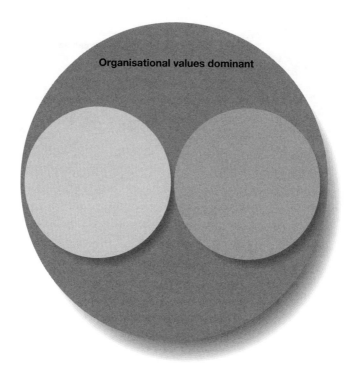

Figure 4.4 Stage 2: the ring representing the values of the organisation is dominant

## Stage 3: the values of the staff are dominant over those of organisation and customers

Leaders and organisations in this stage are typically inefficient, indulgent and low-profit or loss making. They are dominated by 'the loudest'. Decision making is poor and often ad hoc. There is poor communication, a lack of commitment by staff and a high turnover of leaders. Leadership is political rather than strategic. There are cliques, power plays and strong egos involved. Many are motivated by self-interest.

Their *influence is limited and spasmodic.*

Examples include some organisations in the community or not-for-profit sector and Parliament House at a State or federal level.

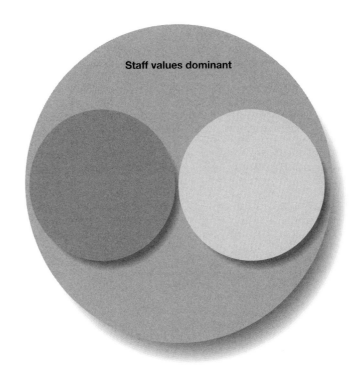

Figure 4.5 Stage 3: the ring representing the values of the staff is dominant

*Stage 4: the values of the customers are dominant over those of organisation and staff*

Leaders and organisations in this stage are typically inefficient, unstable and financially poor. There is a lot of in-fighting, with poor communication dominated by internal politics. There is often a lack of structure and professional leadership skills. There are few formal structures and decision making is ad hoc rather than strategic.

Their *influence is inconsistent* and is constantly changing depending on who is in charge.

Examples include organisations such as industry associations, sporting clubs, unions and other groups in the education and health sectors. They even include consultants, printing companies, retail travel agencies, nursing homes and pharmacies.

Figure 4.6 Stage 4: the ring representing the values of the customer is dominant

*Stage 5: there are some shared values between organisation, staff and customers*

Leaders and organisations in this stage are working well but not at their full potential. They may be in a start-up phase or undergoing change and there is a degree of chaos and confusion. Decision making is fast, flexible and done on the run.

Their *influence is growing* and often they are taking market share from more traditional organisations.

Examples include emerging or fast-growth companies or government agencies going through change.

*Stage 6: total overlap and congruency in values between organisation, staff and customers*

This stage represents *integrity marketing* at work.

Leaders and organisations in this stage have reached their full

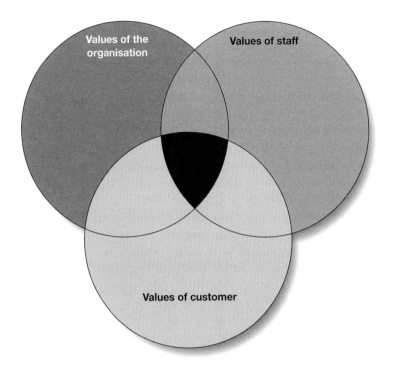

Figure 4.7 Stage 5: the three rings start to overlap, with values starting to become congruent

potential. They have high repeat business and customer loyalty. They are market dominant in their niche, with high profits and levels of customer satisfaction. They have a talented and motivated staff. They attract and retain the best staff. Leadership skills are high and morale is good. They are media and marketing savvy.

They are *very influential*.

Examples are found in all sectors and include many of the companies and individuals I have mentioned in this chapter.

The integrity marketing model illustrates the link between leadership and influence. The value of each of the three power rings can be measured. And the good thing is—as a leader you can influence all three.

Remember, more alignment means better branding, which

creates more momentum, torque and leverage and, therefore, more influence.

## Conclusion

The abilities to lead, persuade and influence are essential for aspiring leaders. Being able to tell a story that inspires, motivates and informs is also important, as is the ability to break down brick walls. Consequently, media management has become one of the strategic tools for use by managers and leaders to drive marketing opportunities, communicate key messages, achieve social change or influence government.

In an age of convergence in the media and increased scepticism over traditional communication methods, a new breed of leader is emerging that sees the media as an opportunity and not a threat. Such leaders use the media to build their organisation's image, reputation and identity.

This is the true power of positive spin.

## Ways to harness the power of positive spin

Here are ten tips that will help leaders to influence others by creating momentum, torque and leverage through the media.

1. *Know your strengths*
   What is your specialised area of expertise? What unique services or information can you offer? Position yourself as the expert.

2. *Clarify your communication objectives*
   What do you want to achieve? Do you want to inform or entertain? Provide information? Build a profile? Influence public opinion? Conduct personal marketing? Market or launch a new product or service?

3. *Be laser-sharp in targeting your audience*
   Who is your target audience? General public? Customers? Competitors? Suppliers? What is their age range and level of education? What are their beliefs and values and geographical location? How do they use the media?

4. *Understand the best way to reach your target audience*
   What do they read, watch, listen to and surf? TV, radio, Internet, newspapers—local or State-wide, specialist or general, industry publications, community newsletters?

5. *Know your key message*
   Distil what you want to say into three key points. Work out the best time to deliver this message and who will deliver it.

6. *Build your case*
   What are the features, advantages and benefits of your message for your target audience? What evidence do you have to prove your claims?

7. *Use a hook*
   What will make your message stand out from the rest? Be creative. Use a press release to control the information flow.

8. *Develop relationships*
   Visit and meet members of the media face to face. Network and get to know them.

> 9  Use the three golden rules
>    To perform at your best: know your topic; be prepared; relax.
>
> 10  Seek help
>     For maximum impact, effectiveness and value, seek the advice of a media and communications professional.

## For further exploration

- A Reis & L Reis, *The fall of advertising and rise of PR*, Harper Collins, New York, 2002.
  I think this book, written by Al Reis and his daughter Laura, is one of the most influential regarding the role of PR in brand building.
- R Cialdini, *Influence: the psychology of persuasion*, William Morrow, New York, 1993.
  This book provides many insights into influence.
- A Robbins, *Unlimited power: the new science of personal achievement*, Simon & Schuster, New York, 1986.
  This is an inspirational classic, worth reading and re-reading.
- N Hill, *Think and grow rich*, Random House, New York, 1960.
  This book by Napoleon Hill has been reprinted many times. It is a 'must have' for anyone interested in success.
- S Godin, *Permission marketing: turning strangers into friends, and friends into customers*, Simon & Schuster, New York, 1999.
  This book defines the new rules for marketing in the Internet age.
- If you are aged between your late 20s and late 30s, and are interested in ethical leadership, I would encourage you to apply for a Vincent Fairfax Fellowship. Details are available at <www.ethics.org.au>.
- TAC Murrell, *Media fundamentals: 8M's essential media guide*, 8M Media & Communications, Perth, 2001.
  This is my own book. I'm often asked by small companies and not-for-profits with no marketing budgets how they can implement many of these concepts in a practical way. This book provides a step-by-step guide on how to harness the power of the media. It contains case studies and templates you can adapt to your own situation.

- Media & Marketing Masterclass™, available at <www.8mmedia.com>. My own product, this is a set of six interactive CD-ROMs, all with video, PowerPoint slides and supporting learning materials in an easy to use format. It is full of practical, 'how to' marketing and media ideas.

## Acknowledgements

I want to thank Sir James Cruthers, Chairman of the *Sunday Times,* for his comments on my first draft. As he said: 'As an old sub I always enjoy hacking things around'. Angus Carter and Serene Lim of Hong Bao Media in Singapore provided positive feedback on my *six stages of influence* model.

Earlier versions of some of the material in this chapter appeared in:
- TAC Murrell, 'Don't forget your media plan', *Corporate Risk*, November 2000, p. 76.
- TAC Murrell, 'Winning the media game', Annual Journal of the Graduate Management Association of the University of Western Australia, 2001, p. 12.
- TAC Murrell, 'Integrity marketing', *Franchising*, vol. 14, no. 6, November/December 2001.
- TAC Murrell, 'The communicator in action', *National Accountant*, October/November 2002, p. 42.
- TAC Murrell, 'The lessons in crash and burn', *Western Suburbs Weekly*, 24 February 2004, p. 9.
- TAC Murrell, 'Effective advertising', *Western Suburbs Weekly*, 22 June 2004, p. 9.

## Notes

**1** A Reis & L Reis, *The fall of advertising and rise of PR*, Harper Collins, New York, 2002, p. 186.

**2** DJ Schwartz, *The magic of thinking big*, Simon & Schuster, New York, 1987, p. 13.

**3** S Canning, 'Nudie juice boss reveals all', *Australian*, 10 June 2004, p. 19.

**4** R Burbury, 'Marketing 2002', *AFR BOSS Magazine*, May 2002, p. 9.

5 S Canning, 'Coolhunters armed and dangerous', *Australian*, 25 September–1 October 2003, media section, p. 22.
6 B Crawford, 'Editors battle the twin sins of secrecy and spin', *Australian*, 24 October 2004, p. 19.
7 J van Geldermalsen, 'Ethical leadership', *Living Ethics*, issue 56, Winter 2004, p. 1.
8 *Wikpedia free encyclopedia* at <http://www.fact-index.com/h/ha/hammer_throw.html>.
9 H Connolly, *Hammer throwing history* at <http://www.hammerthrow.com/technique/articles/default.asp>.
10 R Gluyas, 'A world of cash and burn', *Australian*, 8 July 2004, p. 29.
11 S Brook, 'Tapping into the brain to give brands a buzz', *Australian*, 10–16 March 2002, media section, p. 20.
12 M Gutierrez, VM Soto & FJ Rojas, 'A biomechanical analysis of the individual techniques of the hammer throw finalists in the Seville Athletics World Championship 1999' at <www.xs4all.nl/~mwijand/Hammer/Seville99Hammer.html>.
13 Presentation given to my media planning students at the University of Notre Dame, Western Australia, by Janelle Swinney, the marketing manager of Kailis Australian Pearls, 21 June 2003.
14 Nudie juice case study presentation given by media planning students at the University of Notre Dame, Western Australia, 10 July 2004.
15 S Canning, 'Tried and tasted strategy', *Australian*, 25 March 2004, p. 21.
16 WJ Clinton, *My life*, Hutchinson, London, 2004, p. 480.
17 J Watson & A Hill, *The dictionary of media and communication studies*, 5th edn, Arnold, London, 2000, p. 71.
18 P Kotler & W Mindak, 'Marketing and public relations: should they be partners or rivals?', *Journal of Marketing*, vol. 42, no. 4, 1978, pp. 13–20.
19 D Penglase, *What's ethical about selling*, Strike Zone, Sydney, 2002, p. 26.

# THE POWER OF NETWORKING 5

Robyn Henderson

Introduction

The power of networking

Networking with integrity

    Networks aren't for sale!

Lessons in influence from master networkers

    Communicating and connecting

    Giving recognition

    Empowering others

    Role modelling

    Strategic alliances

    Mastermind groups

Conclusion

For further exploration

Notes

# About the author
Robyn Henderson, CSP

Robyn Henderson is regarded as a global networking specialist. She has spoken in eleven countries, presents over 150 times each year and has never advertised. All her work comes from networking, referrals and her website.

Robyn's career includes over 12 years as a professional speaker, 9 years in sales and telemarketing management and 13 years in hospitality. She successfully ran a women's business network for 6 years in the 1990s. She is a CSP—a certified speaking professional with the National Speakers Association of Australia; an accreditation shared by fewer than 500 people internationally—and an adjunct professor with the Southern Cross University.

Robyn has written eight books on networking, self-promotion and building self-esteem. Her latest book is *How to master networking* (2nd edn, Sea Change Publishing, 2004).

To find out more about Robyn Henderson's work and recent publications, visit <www.networkingtowin.com.au> or <www.seachangepublishing.com.au>.

Robyn Henderson can be contacted at <robyn@networkingtowin.com.au>.

# Executive summary

This chapter provides an introduction to the power of networking and explores what can be learned about influence from 'master networkers'.

Master networkers are individuals who realise that networking is a life skill, not just something you do when you want something. Their networking includes connecting with different cultures, ages, special interests groups and networks. They are constantly making strong connections, following up, keeping in touch, identifying and making contact with spheres of influence, and forming win–win strategic alliances and mastermind groups.

Master networkers have much to teach leaders at any level about building influence. In fact, if you are not a master networker, it is highly unlikely that you will be an effective leader or have any substantial influence in your networks, communities or workplace.

However, influence gained through forming strong networks, and by becoming a sphere of influence, can be a two-edged sword. Master networkers understand that their ongoing success depends on treating their networks and the people within them with respect and integrity. This is one of the reasons why building networks takes time, effort and, most of all, sincerity.

The networking world is open to everyone, without exception, as long as your networking values are strong, ethical and transparent.

## Introduction

Great networkers make great leaders because they have unlocked the potential of networking in their busy lives. They have created simple systems that enable them to connect with others, stay connected and create valuable lifetime connections with key players, spheres of influence and other master networkers.

Great networkers are not born, they are created. And it need not be a complex process. The great news is that anyone can improve their networking and influencing skills. The networking world is open to everyone, without exception, as long as your networking values are strong, ethical and transparent. This chapter will show you how to create and maintain strategic alliances and mastermind groups and become a master networker who positively influences many connections within valuable networks.

Many people think that networking is something that you *do*, rather than a way that you *live*. In fact networking is a life skill, not something you do only when you want something.

The basic principles of networking discussed throughout this chapter are based on the following three universal laws:

1 *The law of abundance.* There are plenty of opportunities for everyone—plenty of ideas, clients, customers, jobs and so on. Just because your diary is empty does not mean that there are no opportunities around. Great networkers believe in an abundance of opportunities.

2 *The law of reciprocity.* What you give out comes back tenfold. If you give out help, you get back help; give out love, you get back love; give out information, you get back information. The challenge, of course, is that although for you the giving is instant and in the short term, the receiving may not happen for some time. Also, what is returned may not come from the person to whom it was given. However, great networkers believe firmly that what you give out comes back tenfold.

3 *The law of giving without expectation.* This occurs when you give without an expectation of receiving something in return. You do something for someone not to get something back, but because you want to help them achieve their goal. Great networkers do not keep a scorecard on their good deeds. They do something and then forget they have done it.

Great networkers also make heart-to-heart connections with people when they talk to them. They listen with their hearts as well as their ears—they are totally focused on the person in front them, regardless of whether they think that person could be a prospect, client, new friend or just someone to add to their network. They realise that every person they connect with forms part of their networking jigsaw, and every stranger has the potential to become an important connection within that network.

Today we live in a borderless society, where people can network nationally and internationally, as well as locally. Although networking is often business oriented, taking place in a business environment, there is also social networking, where the same principles are used less formally (at parties, sporting events, dinner parties, social groups, school events and so on). Wherever two strangers have the potential to connect there is a networking opportunity.

Anyone and everyone can network. There is no prerequisite, although having a business card or name card can create an opportunity for you to give the person you are meeting something to remember you by—a way to make contact with you in the future if they wish. Plus, when you receive their business card, you have a way of following up and also including them in your current network or database.

Great networkers network ethically, professionally and courteously—aware that every best friend was once a perfect stranger, and that you never know who that stranger in front of you actually has in their network. The basic philosophy of great networkers is to treat everyone the way they would like to be treated.

## The power of networking

The more people you know, the more people you can influence, either positively or negatively. People who work at developing strong clusters of networks across a broad cross-section of interests, age groups, demographics and cultures can often wield enormous positive or negative influence. These people are often referred to as *master networkers* and *spheres of influence*.

Master networkers have much to teach leaders at any level about building influence. In fact, if you are not a master networker, it is highly unlikely that you will be an effective leader or have any substantial influence in your networks, communities or workplace.

One of the challenges in our time-poor society is that many of us can't be bothered investing the time required to work at and create new networks. It is so much easier and a great time saver to stick to the networks that we know and feel comfortable with. Our comfort zone becomes very safe and non-threatening. However, it is also very limiting and the potential for influencing large numbers is almost nonexistent—unless our smaller networks are themselves filled with key spheres of influence who can network on our behalf.

One definition of people who are spheres of influence is 'someone who knows a little bit about a lot of things and a lot about one or two areas'. They often specialise in one area, while having a good general knowledge of many areas. They are very good at keeping in touch with their networks, they remember what is 'special' and unique about individuals, and they are generally extremely good communicators.

Smart networkers work at creating relationships with spheres of influence; they know that a positive word about them from one of these key players carries a lot of weight and influence. Bill Gates has spoken of a *trilogy of trust*—the trust that one person has in another, that is then passed on to the third party.[1] For example, Bob knows, likes and trusts Sue, who knows likes and trusts John. Based on this two-way trust, Bob will be open to discussions or possible connections with John, even though John has never previously had contact with Bob.

Master networkers don't switch on their networking skills at 9.00 am each work day and switch them off at 5.00 pm. They *live* networking and see it is a life skill, not something you do only when you want something. As Ivan Misner and Don Morgan say in their book, *Masters of networking*:

> Master networkers know that givers gain—that creating, maintaining, and serving a wide network leads to great business and personal rewards. Generating leads and referrals, building healthy relationships and delivering value over the long term, are at the heart of networking.[2]

You cannot buy a network, you must earn the right to ask a favour. You build your networks and influence people, one person at a time. However, once you have a strong connection with a master networker or sphere of influence, you in turn will be networked to many others, purely through their third party endorsement (the trilogy of trust).

The more you actively network, the more connections you make and the more influence you will ultimately have.

## Networking with integrity

The power to influence others is highly regarded and rarely abused by ethical networkers. This is one of the main reasons why building networks takes time, effort and, most of all, sincerity. Master networkers can smell insincerity from a mile away; they quickly identify people who want to use them, use their good name and benefit from associating with them.

It goes without saying that networking and influence are more effective when coupled with ethics and morals. Often when I am faced with a 'will I, won't I?' dilemma (for example, 'Is this a good career or business move or might it come back to bite me?'), I take what I call the *Sydney Morning Herald* test (substitute the name of your favourite daily newspaper): *If this incident or situation appeared on the front page of the* Sydney Morning Herald, *would I be embarrassed in any way, and would I need to do some serious explaining to my family and friends?*

If the answer is yes, I don't do it. Why? It takes years and years to build your reputation and good name, whether you are an employee or an employer—why risk your good name on anything that might, even remotely, be or be perceived to be unethical, illegal or lacking integrity. (Though, as an observation, our newspapers and magazines would have nothing to write about if everyone asked themselves the *Sydney Morning Herald* question before taking action!).

### Networks aren't for sale!

One of the quickest ways to damage your reputation is to treat your connections, or those of others, as a short-term, saleable item.

Many people try to take short cuts by buying their way into, or paying for access to, an established network, usually for sales purposes. 'Buying a network' is rarely successful, and can result in the people within the network resenting both the person paying for access and the person who 'sold' the network. I am sure that you, like me, have accepted an invitation from someone you know through your network to attend a social event or supposed business meeting, only to find that you are there to be 'sold to'—usually by an unknown third party. You may well be interested in the third party's product or service. The point is that you are there under false pretences.

What is important here is *transparency*. If the invitation openly states the involvement of a third party and their agenda, that is fine. You have a choice: attend or not. If you choose to attend, you expect to receive a sales pitch, but at the same time you will have the opportunity to gather information and meet with others who may have similar interests.

If third party involvement has not been declared, it is often because the organiser is getting a kickback for holding the event, or for the number of people who attend, or for who ultimately buys the product or service.

You can imagine how offended the guests at such an event would be when they realise what is happening. The organiser has insulted their guests and ensured that they will be put on the master networkers' blacklist (don't go to anything XYZ invites you to, ever). Bad news travels fast. By late afternoon of the next day, XYZ's name will be mud, and spheres of influence will close ranks to freeze that person out of their networks. Was it worth it? Certainly not in the long term.

However, there are ways to openly gain access to a specific target market or network. This traditionally comes in the form of sponsoring an event—business or charity—where the organiser has an opportunity to market their products or services to a specific group. Once again, transparency is crucial. People attend a business breakfast knowing that SSS is the sponsor for the event and, as such, will be given the opportunity to make a short presentation about what they have to offer to that target audience. Most people are absolutely fine about sponsorship; they just don't want to be lied to or marketed to without their specific permission.

Remember, *you cannot buy networks*. No one likes to be used, sold to or undervalued.

Please note that I am not saying you should never try to gain access to an existing network, whether for direct sales purposes or to create and build relationships with a target group. What is important is *how* you do so. The following are some guidelines to help you gain access to a network without jeopardising your reputation with potential clients.

### Tips for ethically accessing a target network

- Spend time researching where your buyers go to network and to build their businesses and careers.
- Attend at least two of these events prior to sponsoring an event yourself or forming an alliance with this network. You might find the network is already aligned with one of your competitors and ethically they would not become involved with you. Alternatively, you may find that the decision makers do not attend this network—they attend another.
- Be prepared to invest time, energy and effort to create a presence in this marketplace. In other words, you won't necessarily walk away with customers the first time you attend this network—you may need to become a regular before you build the trust of the master networkers in the group.
- Rather than your sole focus being 'who can I sell to', expand your thinking to include 'who can I connect the people I have just met with'. With the law of reciprocity, what you give out comes back tenfold; if you want referrals, start giving away referrals to those within these targeted networks. Eventually you will receive referrals from this network, but you must first invest time, effort and energy.
- Always be transparent in all your communications. 'I am having trouble meeting my targets this month. I am looking for companies who would use my product/service. If you were me, what would you do?' People automatically want to help others, but first they need to know what you want.

Finally, always remember that if you don't value your networks you won't have them for long.

## Lessons in influence from master networkers

If you are seeking to be more influential, there is much you can learn from the strategies of master networkers. This section will explore the following six strategies:

1 communicating and connecting
2 giving recognition
3 empowering others
4 role modelling
5 strategic alliances
6 mastermind groups.

## Communicating and connecting

One of the greatest opportunities for influence can arise when you build a strong connection with someone who trusts you.

If you build a connection of trust with another person, it is natural for them to speak highly of you within their own networks, thereby potentially allowing you to influence total strangers, based purely on the connection you built with the original person. Picture a house being built brick by brick. Imagine trust being built in the same way—conversation by conversation, contact by contact. The more contact we make, the stronger our connection becomes.

It is for this reason that master networkers are strong communicators—they constantly make heart-to-heart connections with the people they are speaking to. This means that they are totally present and 'in the moment' for the length of that conversation. They give the person in front of them total focus; they listen with their heart as well as their ears. The conversation may last for only seconds or minutes, but the recipient knows that they have been heard.

Here are some lessons to be learned from master networkers about communication.

- *Constantly work on improving your listening skills.* Strong networkers look beyond the words and observe the tone, inference and body language of everyone in the group.
- *Communication doesn't start and stop at the employment doorstep.* Good networkers weave networking and strong communication throughout their lives, embracing these skills 24/7. And they also see their listening, speaking and understanding-the-message skills as a work in progress or a journey.
- *Remember to use people's names.* 'Name calling' (using a person's first or full name) in conversations is a very powerful tool (more about this later).

- *The better you listen, the better you will remember.* An added bonus for having strong listening skills is that you will remember more about previous conversations you may have had with someone. Having the ability to recall some of those highlights at the appropriate time is invaluable in building more trust with that person. For example, you might recall the name of their child or partner, or the fact that they had been unwell, on holidays, studying, renovating a home—anything that shows that person that you actually listened to them.
- *Don't be afraid to ask questions or clarify details.* Master networkers are always ready to admit that they may not understand something. They do not see this admission as a weakness, but rather the opportunity to learn something new and to give the other person an opportunity to share their knowledge.
- *There is always more to know.* No matter how much you know, there is always more to learn and other people have the information that you need. All that is required is for you to find out where and how to make contact with these knowledge keepers. And if you don't know where to find them, someone you know will.
- *Remember that nobody is a nobody.* Master networkers know that everyone is connected to other people, and that everyone is a somebody, somewhere. So if you create a poor impression with someone, you will never know who that person knows, or with whom they might share their poor opinion of you.
- *Not everyone will like you . . . and that's OK.* Despite your best intentions and efforts, some people may not like you. Master networkers acknowledge this and accept it. That person's aversion to you may be well founded or not. You may have a very tenuous connection to them that you don't know about— you may have mistreated one of their friends; you may have offended them by talking about something they were very sensitive about (weight, money, politics, children, or whatever). It may have nothing to do with you. In time you may be able to forge a connection, but for now just accept that they don't like you—they are not a prospect and they may never be. If you approached this person in order to gain entry to a new network, I would start befriending others with lesser influence, but more openness to your friendship.

As already mentioned, master networkers understand the power of using a person's name to make and strengthen a connection. The easier you make it for people to remember and contact you, the more positive your impact and influence can be with that person.

An inexpensive strategy to increase connection between your staff and clients (and if you have a large organisation, between staff) is to issue staff nametags. For example:
- Staff often feel more accountable when they wear name badges and this can increase their work output and the quality of their customer service.
- Nametags make it *easier* to call people by name, thereby strengthening communication, increasing the chance of connection and increasing the opportunity for networking.
- Staff nametags (whether *first* or full names are used) make it easier for customers during transactions. It lets them know who they are dealing with, and alleviates embarrassment if they have forgotten a staff member's name.

*Influential leaders and master networkers are strong communicators*

## Giving recognition

Everyone likes to be valued, appreciated and recognised. This may take the form of using a person's name, acknowledging them with a 'please' or 'thank you' when asking for something, or even being given a name badge or business card in the workplace.

Master networkers realise that people are not their jobs—they are people who are currently working in a specific area, but may have a huge variety of skills, experiences and talents that may not be obvious. Master networkers usually have conversations about the whole person, not just the job they do. They make a heart-to-heart connection when they communicate with others; so, more often than not, they are remembered positively.

This genuine connection is not manipulated in any way. Master networkers are excellent communicators because they care about people. When you care about people, you naturally give them recognition. And there are limitless opportunities to do so.

Far too many people don't receive any form of recognition in the workplace. They work for organisations that take their staff for granted, treat them poorly, have no systems in place to recognise achievement or progress and are complacent—about both staff and customers. Often these are also the organisations with high staff turnover, low morale, erratic profits and a poor name in the marketplace.

Unfortunately, recognition giving is the exception rather than the norm within organisations. It is for this reason that master networkers and leaders who acknowledge the efforts of others can have such a positive impact and influence.

Master networkers know that one of the most powerful phrases in the English language is *thank you*—thank you for doing a great job, staying back to complete the project, covering for someone when they were delayed, doing that extra something that made a great difference. This phrase forms the foundation of recognition, which should be embedded in an organisation's culture.

So how can you use this strategy within your organisation to increase your influence? Here are some practical suggestions. First, it is important to understand that:

- Employee recognition is necessary in organisations of all sizes, from micro businesses (fewer than five employees) to large multinationals with 20 000-plus staff.
- The employee recognition process needs to be ongoing. Whatever recognition system is introduced must be continued for the life of the project or for a pre-agreed period. If you give recognition once and forget it the next time, morale often drops lower than it was to begin with.
- Acknowledgment must be given to the entire team—not just the obvious income generators. For example, often the business development team will be given sales incentives and rewards, while the role of the 'factory' or 'engine room' is ignored. The 'back end' staff make the sales person look good by completing the delivery on time every time—yet they are often forgotten when the bonuses are given out. A word of thanks and show of appreciation to the engine room can have a huge influence on future results.

Acknowledging the effort and contribution of your staff can happen on a daily, weekly or monthly basis, depending on the

logistics of your company. Smart organisations build systems to acknowledge the efforts of *all* workers when results are announced and targets exceeded. These may include simple things such as:
- movie passes for all staff
- lunch or dinner for the group at a local restaurant
- a paid afternoon early-mark to celebrate the results
- certificates of appreciation
- acknowledgment in company newsletters.

A very powerful way to show staff that you recognise the importance of their roles is to provide *all* of them (whether or not they have regular, personal contact with current customers) with business cards.

Apart from providing recognition, giving all your staff business cards has the potential to increase business. As master networkers know, every staff member has the potential to bring business to the organisation, through the people they meet during day-to-day business, and through their formal and informal networks. So, why not make the process easier by providing staff with business cards that they can hand out to potential customers? At the same time, educate staff on why they are getting cards, how to use them and ways that their use might benefit the organisation.

More than 50% of personal assistants, executive assistants, secretaries and support staff are never given permission to have a business card. Yet they come into contact with potential and current clients all day, every day. Many of them have the authority to sign off on thousands of dollars of work—yet they have never been issued with a business card. With such potential to network and influence, it should be automatic that they have a business card as part of their role.

If you doubt the figure quoted, just ask the next ten personal assistants you meet for their card. What a missed opportunity to give a very important cog in the business wheel some recognition, and a missed chance to generate business and to contribute to the overall influence your organisation has on the marketplace.

*Influential, strong leaders and master networkers make recognition-giving a regular part of their day—they always treat people the way they would like to be treated.*

## Empowering others

There is a great sense of satisfaction when you have the ability to influence someone by empowering them. A discussion of the means and mechanism of empowerment is beyond the scope of this chapter, but one of the easiest ways to empower someone else is to *give them information*. Information can equate to power—and the more information you have about a subject, the more powerful or influential you become.

Information is one of the major currencies of networking, and master networkers have much 'information power'. As a rule, they are extremely well informed. They work at gaining and constantly updating their information through sources such as newspapers, books and the Internet, but also through the information that circulates through their networks.

Master networkers also know that the greatest gift you can give someone is your sole focus. Whether it is for 10 seconds or 10 minutes, if your sole focus is on that person, you will have had a quality conversation with them. Simply giving sole focus to someone is sufficient to influence and empower them, as this action is so rarely experienced in our busy society.

Again, master networkers always use this form of influence with integrity—they live a set of ethical values and their behaviour is authentic and transparent. They can never be accused of 'Oh she was just being nice to me because she wanted something from me'. Master networkers are nice to you because they strive to be consistently nice to everyone in their networks.

Leaders and managers are always time poor, yet it takes such a short time to empower people once you set the empowerment wheel in motion. Imagine that the rim of the empowerment wheel has ten grooves. By spending time, and giving sole focus or information to a person on one day, the wheel may turn to groove number three. However, because the time you spent with that person was 'quality time', when you walk away the wheel does not fall back to zero, it stays there. When you next connect with that person, they recall the previous connection and turn the wheel further, to groove number five or six. And so it goes, until your connection with them is ultimately and regularly at groove ten. And all they have to do is see or connect with you and they are empowered again and again.

The following example illustrates how empowering staff can positively influence behaviour and performance within an organisation.

### Radio station: customer service empowerment

A successful commercial radio station in New Zealand introduced a 'fix it with the customer' system that empowers employees to solve customer problems.

Management taught the staff how to use a simple decision-making system that helps them to identify the real source of the customer's problem, to offer the customer alternatives and options, and to come up with a win–win outcome. At the same time, every staff member is empowered to fix customer problems using an 'allowance' system—up to a limit of $250. Here is an overview of the process:

1  State the problem from the customer's point of view.
2  State the facts.
3  State the real problem.
4  List the options for solving the problem, both outrageous and mainstream.
5  Based on the facts you have, choose the option with the best outcome for the customer and the company, within the $250 allowance.
6  Record the process on the client's record.

Armed with the decision-making process, knowing that the organisation trusts them to decide how a problem should be fixed and then take action to solve it, and having clear boundaries (the $250 limit), the staff have the confidence to independently handle customer complaints.

Since this system was introduced at the radio station, staff motivation is noticeably higher, absenteeism is at an all-time low and productivity is up. This simple empowerment strategy has influenced performance, but has also positively influenced the relationship that customers have with the company. (By the way, the $250 allowance has never been used—through the decision-making process, staff are able to come up with solutions that don't cost the company any money.)

---

*Influential, effective leaders and master networkers make people empowerment a daily habit and a life skill, enabling them to positively influence others.*

---

## Role modelling

Master networkers watch what other successful networkers do, and then do the same. That is how they become masters at what they do. Tradespeople, engineers, professionals, teachers and designers do much the same thing. They look to people they admire and want to be like—that is, *role models*—and then copy what they do, but without becoming their clones or stealing their ideas and concepts.

As a leader, you will know you have true influence when you become a role model for others. It is such a compliment to a leader when their team follows their habits and copies their positive behaviour.

This is not about creating an organisation of clones, rather an organisation of individuals who practise certain positive habits to achieve specific results. Modelling a leader's behaviour might be something as simple as returning calls between 4 pm and 5 pm, or reducing the number of coffees drunk in a day, or even the choice of time of day for working out or exercising.

In some ways it's a bit like reading a book: you read a book and gain information, hints and lessons that may have taken the author years of research and living to experience. When people read a book and then take action on the content, it usually becomes a very successful and well read book.

How do you become a role model for others? I don't think it is something you can force; it is something that happens as a result of what you do.

There is a well known phrase in the professional speaking industry: *walk your talk*. This means that what you speak about from the platform should reflect your traits and the habits that you live by. Employees are acutely aware of leaders who don't walk their talk. You will have the greatest influence when people can see that, as a result of certain habits and actions, you have achieved certain results.

As role models come in many forms, I will share the traits of my current role models.

- They are passionate about the work they do.
- They believe in themselves, even when others don't.
- Their mottos is: *The buck stops here* . . . let's fix it rather than find a scapegoat.
- They always stand by their staff, as long as they have the total truth told to them.

- They look for the good in others, even when it's hard to find.
- They make heart-to-heart connections when they speak to you.
- They are fun to be around.
- They laugh often.
- They don't overindulge.
- They don't hold grudges.

*Influential, great leaders and master networkers become a light for those who are living in darkness.*

## Strategic alliances

*To go fast—go alone; to go far—go together.*     African proverb

A leader can progress from zero to hero with the formation of a number of strategic alliances, both internal and external. In fact, it is very difficult to achieve hero status and major influence in an organisation without the support of a number of strategic alliances and collaborations.

The main reason why people form strategic alliances is to make it easier to achieve their desired results. Strategic alliances can be described as a coming together of two or more parties who agree to certain behaviours or procedures for the purpose of ultimately creating mutually beneficial results.

Leaders cannot perform effectively without a number of strategic alliances within divisions, organisations, teams and clusters in their workforce. Strong leaders also know that strong alliances will assist them to reach and influence many individuals that they may not physically be able to spend time with. The key, of course, is making sure that the selected allies have the respect and support of the leader's peers. Otherwise the alliance can do more harm than good.

The potential for influencing others via strategic alliances is huge. You will be connecting with so many different people to pull an alliance together, and each of these people will develop an opinion about your capabilities: how you manage things, how committed you are, how you interacted with other people, how you resolved conflict and so on.

Master networkers form *win–win* strategic alliances in order to expand their networks or influence for mutual gain. Unethical networkers will attempt to form *win–lose* alliances, which rarely work for any substantial length of time. Master networkers know that if there is not benefit to be gained for all allies, it is highly unlikely that sufficient effort will be made for the alliance to work.

The following points will assist you if you are contemplating forming a strategic alliance.

1. *Select your partners carefully.* Make sure you target like-minded people with similar values and ethics. You have spent considerable time and effort building your name in the marketplace—a poor choice of partner could result in your name being tarnished. Also compare your personal philosophies and core motivations; for example, an alliance between an environmental body and a paper mill might result in major ethical conflicts of interest.
2. *Decide how much you are prepared to lose or invest in terms of time and money.* In order to calculate a reasonable return on investment (ROI) for your time, you must first assess your costs. Here is an example:
   Number of meetings (twice a month over 6 months) = 12 meetings
   Time allocated per meeting (2 hours plus travel time) = 3 hours
   Total meetings over 6-month period = 36 hours of your time
   Your normal charge-out rate = $250 per hour
   Cost of the potential alliance in time and money = approx. 4 working days + $9000 (of course this is not billable time for you but you still need to place a value on your time)
3. *Make sure you have equal commitment from all parties.* People often get very excited about the possibilities of alliances and their potential earning power, and this can obscure the actual effort required to achieve even small results in the first instance. However, unless all parties are committed, there will be no substantial results. After all, you would not have gone to another party if you could have achieved the results you wanted by yourself. So ensure that each party is committed to XX amount of effort, time or money (whichever is the case).
4. *Be prepared to defer your project.* If your perfect potential partner is committed to forming an alliance, but unavailable within

your preferred time frame, be prepared to defer the project. However, only do this if you have their total commitment—a committed second choice is far better than an uncommitted first choice.

5  *Be clear about your desired outcomes.* The clearer you are on the results you are anticipating, the better you can communicate your requirements. 'Making money' is a very vague outcome. 'Making $550 000 by the end of the financial year' is very clear. Be as specific as possible.

6  *Never assume anything.* Clarify language, definitions, roles and responsibilities right at the beginning . . . or it could have a negative impact on your ROI. For example, never assume that 'urgent' or 'frequent' mean the same things to two people.

7  *Set specific timelines as well as short timeframes. Timelines* are necessary as every project needs a start and a finish. Many people have exciting meetings and lots of actions are discussed, but no timeline is ever mentioned and as a result the project flounders or never gets off the ground. Busy people need to have a clear idea of a specific timeline before they can make a firm commitment. At the same time, set short *timeframes* for achieving objectives. People's circumstances and commitment may vary from month to month, and something that seemed very possible in January may be impossible by June because of work pressure, health, finances and so on. For example, if you are collaborating on a writing project over the next 6 months, aim for 5000 words in the first month, rather than 30 000 at the end of 6 months. This will allow you to monitor your partner's commitment and your own. If you map out your project in short stages, you will be able to red-flag over-commitment or inability to complete.

8  *Document key points ASAP.* Many alliances fall over due to lack of action. Lots of great conversations and brainstorming happens, but no one actually says: 'This is my next task'. If you document key points during, or as soon as possible after, the first meeting, you give your partners an opportunity to clarify their involvement, action required, timelines, outcomes, and so on. This also provides an opportunity for sorting out misconceptions about who will do what, how and when.

9 *Be prepared to start small.* Large opportunities are often the result of getting it right with a smaller project. Starting small also gives new partners an opportunity to observe your management style, attention to detail, and ability to meet or beat deadlines and keep within a budget, plus your personal habits and attendance record. These are the things that will form the basis of your partners' opinion of you and add to the influence that you will have within the project group (not to mention the people that they may speak to about you).

10 *Brainstorm possible best and worst case scenarios.* Be up-front with best and worst possibilities. Transparency is critical with all alliances and collaborations. There is nothing worse than finding out that you have been misled when information was withheld or concealed. Ask your partners: 'What is the worst thing that can happen, and can we cope with it, individually and collectively?' If the answer to the second question is yes, then proceed. But if the answer is no, it might pay to brainstorm more options, or to scale back the project to a more manageable worst case scenario.

11 *Always aim to work win–win.* Over the long term, strategic alliances and collaborations based on win–lose will not work. Eventually the 'lose' partners will become resentful and stop pulling their weight in the project. Most alliances are not income generating in their start-up phase, and this can put added pressure on the alliance. If one side is generating income, while the other is contributing money and effort into the project with no return and no end in sight, why would they bother to continue with the project? (There may be exceptions, such as working on a charity committee or special event project—but strictly speaking, win–lose alliances are doomed to eventual failure).

12 *Remember to celebrate your successes.* It is important to record the milestones in your alliance; for example, as the stages of a project are completed, celebrate in some way. In today's busy, fast moving marketplace we are very good at dismissing our successes—'that was last month; what's on the board for this month'—regardless of how much effort went into the project. Acknowledge your progress and your successes, and

acknowledge your allies and the part they played in bringing the project together.

**13** *Provide an exit clause.* Often, alliances will be formed with people within your existing business and social networks and communities. Should the alliance come unstuck in unpleasant circumstances, this may cause difficulties for other members of your network. It may seem like a divorce, with network members feeling they have to take sides with one or other of the parties. Avoid this at all costs, as the repercussions will be costly for everyone. Instead, be prepared to provide an exit clause for an under-performing or under-committed partner; that is, an opportunity for your partner to exit 'without loss of face'. For example: 'John, you were obviously as busy as I was last month when our mutually agreed deadline passed. Let's put this project on hold until next year, when we have more idea of where the market is going.' This ensures a clean break and no discomfort for mutual allies.

**14** *If you are on the wrong road, walk away.* Many alliances start off with the best intentions, only to fall over because the idea or concept was not adjusted to meet changed circumstances or market variations and needs. This can often result in good money following bad money, again and again. Money does not fix a bad idea—if it is a bad idea whose time has passed in the market place, agree to walk away. If any part of the project is salvageable, then save that bit, but don't hang on for the sake of ego or pride.

**15** *Whatever the outcome of your alliance, always debrief and record any lessons learned.* Learn from every alliance how you can work smarter next time. Some strategic alliances work and some are doomed from the start. As the Dalai Lama says: 'Don't lose the lesson'. If things didn't go well, what would you do differently if you had your time over? What were the warning signs that all was not right and why were they ignored? Develop the discipline of debriefing and taking the time to record your findings. Then, when the next alliance opportunity comes along, you will be that much more prepared and will know the trouble signs to look for.

Strategic alliances are hard work. They are like many of the important relationships in your life; they take time to yield results.

However, they are a very interesting way to spread your influence to a much wider network. As Harvey Mackey says, it is not what you know, but who knows what you know.[3]

> *Influential, innovative leaders and master networkers know that without strategic alliances, it is difficult to move to the next stage of their evolution.*

## Mastermind groups

Another strategy master networkers use is to develop and participate in 'mastermind' groups.

Mastermind groups are informal or formal meetings where selected, highly regarded (by the group) people come together with a set agenda of sharing wisdom, creative ideas, solutions, possible outcomes and constructive feedback for each individual's problems, challenges or ideas. The information shared within mastermind groups is usually regarded as confidential, unless agreed otherwise. This enables individuals to speak freely about their challenges in an environment of mutual trust.

How can participating in a mastermind group increase your influence?

Mastermind groups can provide you with an opportunity to meet with peers from outside your organisations in an environment where you will not have to watch what you say, filter your conversations or be conscious of giving too much information to people who may not be privy to the bigger picture in your organisation. In other words, it can provide freedom of thought and connection that it might not be possible or appropriate for you, as the leader, to experience within the confines of your own organisation.

A leader may seek out or create a mastermind group to find solutions, tap into the power of collective thinking, increase visibility and strengthen bonds with select individuals from other organisations or networks. In return, the leader will gain influence with a key group of people who will learn to respect the leader's ideas and ability to share and contribute.

At the same time, creating mastermind groups *within*

organisations can be extremely helpful in tapping the organisation's potential, giving rising stars an opportunity to shine and hearing some great ideas from the workers. It is important to ensure that there is a formal facilitator who is not part of the group so that an in-house session does not bog down in day-to-day detail or become a complaint session about the company.

In summary, the long-term benefits of interacting with a group of open minded, supportive people include:
- a forum for brainstorming ideas and possibilities for careers or businesses
- access to honest feedback, support and encouragement for your new ideas
- encouragement to learn and move on from disappointments in your career and business
- a forum in which you can constantly stretch your mind out of its regular ways of thinking and comfort zone.

It is important to set up the mastermind group in a workable, participant friendly format to maximise your ROI. One of the most successful mastermind groups I have been involved with was one I started when I relocated my business to the far north coast of New South Wales in 2003. My motivation for forming the group was to ensure I remained 'in the loop' regarding what was happening in my profession in other cities, and about marketplace movements and trends. I was also concerned about maintaining my profile after moving my business to a new location.

At our first meeting, we discussed the viability of the group, how often we would meet, what outcomes we each expected, and what we were prepared to give to the group. We agreed to meet on a monthly basis and to allocate a day for each meeting (10 am–4 pm, plus travel time).

We agreed that we expected an ROI of $5000 per day (equivalent to lost income from potential presentation fees). Allowing for ten meetings a year (no meetings over the Christmas break), we were expecting an ROI of $50 000 per year—so we were looking for very big ideas from this mastermind group.

Energy follows thought. What we expected was what we got . . . big ideas and encouragement to make them happen. Individually and collectively we have created new CD series (joint and individual products), books (joint and individual), new business models and many referrals to new clients and prospects.

I found it invaluable to be able to ask for honest feedback about potential book covers, articles, proposals and so on. Criticism was always constructive and feedback was coated with kindness, even if they thought my idea or concept was dead in the water.

I know I have influenced decisions made by members of the group both positively and negatively, and vice versa. This is all part of the mastermind method.

Here is a checklist you may find useful if you are thinking of starting your own mastermind group.

1. Every mastermind group needs a driver—an organiser who keeps everyone on track, reminds people of meetings, outcomes expected and so on.
2. Always have an agenda and stick to it.
3. Be flexible with dates, taking into account people's varying circumstances.
4. Work out your personal ROI and detail exactly what you want to achieve with the group.
5. Always create an individual action plan at the end of each meeting.
6. Be prepared to reveal weaknesses as well as strengths—the mastermind members become mates as well.
7. Decide to go beyond 'talk fests' (all talk, no action).
8. Aim to arrive early and leave late—be committed.
9. Allow for exit clauses—if a member's circumstances or priorities change, that's fine, let them go.
10. Consider selecting members from outside your profession as well as within—variety brings lots of fresh ideas.
11. Make a list of potential mastermind group members today.

*Influential, smart leaders and master networkers understand the power of collective thinking—through mastermind groups they can influence as well as be influenced.*

# Conclusion

As technology drives our communication world further and further ahead, creating a time poor society—emails, mobile phone calls and information overload—networking has become more important than ever.

Wise networkers realise that their potential influence is directly related to the size of their network and base of connections. A network is a varying collection of people from all walks of life—some are CEOs and others are cleaners; some initially met by chance, through work or otherwise. In the jigsaw of life, you never know where that person might show up again or how much influence their opinion of you may carry . . . or the impact (for better or worse) of the influence you have had on them.

Master networkers influence others, both formally and informally, in matters small and large. So a smart manager or aspiring leader learns from them and works at developing strong, ethical networking skills. And remember, networking skills are a prerequisite for forming strategic alliances, which can enable you to move your organisation and your career to the next level.

If you are prepared to constantly hone your networking skills, value your current and expanding networks, consider forming strategic alliances and value the worth of such activities as mastermind groups, it is inevitable that you will have as much influence as you want to have.

Happy networking!

## How to become a networker of influence

1 *Understand that networking is a life skill, not something you do only when you want something from someone else.*

2 *Value your networks. Realise that every member forms part of the jigsaw of life and you never know where people will turn up later. The opinion they gain of you now can affect their future opinion of you (and the opinions of others).*

3 *Practise making heart-to-heart connections with people when you communicate with them. Aim to be totally present and 'in the moment' at all times.*

4 *Arm yourself with business cards and a nametag when you attend a networking event.*

5 *Befriend the gatekeepers—the people who assist or sometimes protect the people you are wanting to network with (secretaries, personal assistants and so on).*

6 *Walk your talk. Directly and indirectly you will become a role model to others.*

7 *Form strategic alliances based on quality not quantity. Make sure all parties are committed before you start taking your action steps.*

8 *Consider forming a small mastermind group, preferably with people not directly within your organisation, and open yourself to new ideas and constructive feedback.*

9 *The most powerful people are those who share information and don't hide it from others. Always be generous with information. Being able to give a person the specific piece of information they need (no matter how trivial it may seem to you) increases your influence enormously.*

10 *If you set out to build a strong network of people whom you admire, respect and value, the by-product will be that you will have great influence within this group. Yet if you set out to have influence without the firm foundation of a strong network of supporters you will fail and have no influence and a poor reputation.*

## For further exploration

- IR Misner & D Morgan, *Masters of networking*, Bard Press, USA, 2000.
  I enjoyed contributing a chapter to and reading this book. Ivan and Don have brought together many high profile identities (mainly US and Canadian), who share the common philosophy that 'you give without remembering and receive without forgetting'. It was fascinating to see this principle enacted in so many different forms, and told in such diverse stories.
- P Fritz, A Parker & S Stumm, *Beyond yes: negotiating and networking*, Harper-Collins, Sydney, 1998.
  This book provides a great insight into the links between networking and negotiating, and the potential overlaps when you expand your networks. The negotiating tips are uncomplicated and easy to follow.

## Notes

**1** W Gates, 'Be a referral giver', in IR Misner & D Morgan (eds), *Masters of networking*, Bard Press, USA, 2000.

**2** IR Misner & D Morgan, *Masters of networking*, Bard Press, USA, 2000.

**3** H Mackey, *Dig your well before you're thirsty: the only networking book you'll ever need*, Currency, USA, 1999.

# THE POWER OF KNOWLEDGE         6

Alastair Rylatt

Introduction

Knowledge as power

Knowledge contribution styles

The problem of ego

Discovering ground truth

Creating safe space

Permission and trust

Stimulating buy-in

Bringing campfires together

Coaching

Conclusion

For further exploration

Acknowledgments

Notes

# About the author

Alastair Rylatt, BBus, Grad Dip Employment Relations, FAITD

Alastair Rylatt is one of Australia's leading contemporary thinkers in modern business management. He is an inspiring presenter, expert facilitator and award winning author. His personal mission is to stimulate greater enlightenment and innovation in how work is undertaken in business.

Alastair's work has taken him to major conferences and clients throughout the world. He has a proven reputation as a consultant and coach who helps create high performing teams and smarter, better thinking. He does this by creating safe conversations on important issues.

He has written four books, the latest being *Winning the knowledge game* (McGraw-Hill, 2003). Alastair's earlier books include *Learning unlimited* (BPP, 1994) and *Navigating the frenzied world of work* (Woodslane, 1997) and, as co-author, *Creating training miracles* (John Wiley, 1997).

Alastair prides himself on making a difference in whatever he does. His great loves in life include hiking, yoga, film and bike riding. All these interests involve meeting and interacting with people from diverse backgrounds and cultures.

To find out more about Alastair Rylatt's work and to view selected articles, visit <www.alastairrylatt.com>.

Alastair Rylatt can be reached at <alastair@alastairrylatt.com>.

# Executive summary

If you wish to be influential in today's business environment, you must be able to lead thought and circulate knowledge, and do both well.

There are no short cuts to creating smarter, better businesses; managers need to foster a work environment full of knowledge contribution, passion and responsibility. Gone are the days when the 'brain' of the business could be the responsibility of a few. Modern business needs a culture of deeper thinking, exchange and critical review between the many.

The capacity of knowledge to transform comes not from control and overprotection but from stimulating flow and meaningful exchange. For too long, managers have failed in their efforts to uncover the hidden assumptions and barriers that inhibit such progress and contribution.

If we are serious about raising our performance levels, we need to grow a new code of learning DNA. One where the uncovering of our 'ground truth' is seen as a strength, and one where we are prepared to listen and build a better future together. For this to occur we need to put our egos aside and encourage improved connection and teamwork.

Increased influence can only come from exploring new boundaries, creating safe space and learning when to let go. This skill has been lost in a world where there is so much pressure to succeed, achieve quick wins and protect one's status within organisations.

## Introduction

Never in the history of management has the stimulation of knowledge flow been so important. No business can survive unless it has a strategy to ensure wisdom is circulated, shared and applied.

Managed properly, knowledge can be used to provide greater clarity, superior planning, world class processes and market responsiveness, while at the same time building the innate capability of individuals and organisations. When knowledge is managed poorly, there is leadership without wisdom, leading to endless cycles of disinformation and shallow thinking.

One of the great failings of management is that people often confuse positional power with influence. They get caught up with their identity, job title and role and forget that they need to create respect, trust and support to get work done. The success of any manager or leader is dependent not on their authority but on their ability to *generate the wisdom and capacity for people to act*. Such leadership and influence can exist at any level of the organisation.

This view is supported by the work of Jon Berry and Ed Keller, as described in their recent book, *The influentials*.[1] Berry and Keller found, based on 30 years of research, that the majority of successful, influential people:

- have a passionate desire to have strong relationships with family, partners, friends and broader networks
- live a life of integrity with a high commitment to honesty, authenticity and being true to oneself
- enjoy exploration, with an ongoing pursuit of knowledge, learning, open-mindedness and creativity.

Interestingly, the factors that build *least* influence are wealth, good looks, status and positional power.[2]

For me, the essence of influence is *intention*; it dictates what we do and how we behave. For example, when it comes to knowledge leadership, the type of influence you build will depend on whether your intention is to strictly control knowledge circulation or to encourage cross-fertilisation and freedom of expression.

As a leader and manager, you must be clear about the type of knowledge sharing that is vital for your organisation, its workforce and its customers. Without this sharp focus, your ability to influence can be adversely affected.

Personal and organisational assumptions, norms and systems will dramatically affect how the knowledge environment evolves. For example, a workplace full of strict controls and narrow job definitions will not encourage risk taking and innovative thinking. Alternatively, a more liberated learning culture will encourage new learning without fuelling unnecessary chaos or confusion. Although these work environments are markedly different, they each require a special breed of constructive leadership and positive influence.

If you think that your influence as a leader within your organisation will be greater if you adopt a strategy of knowledge sharing and stimulating knowledge flow, you should first examine your intentions. Answer this question honestly: do you really want people to learn and think for themselves? And if so, are you really prepared to change your behaviour in order for this to happen?

If you answered yes to both questions, this will be a good basis for improving levels of ingenuity and know-how in your organisation.[3] If you are not able to make this commitment, don't believe you can fool people otherwise. Your spirit will leave people in no doubt of your true motives and intentions, and will undermine the trust that is the foundation of knowledge contribution and sharing (more about trust later).

What makes the path of influence through knowledge so challenging is that the on/off switch for success is clear and self-evident. When we lose our positive intention or choose the wrong action we can cut off the flow of knowledge and motivation immediately. If, however, we build a track record for helping to make a difference in people we will be given more freedom and latitude even when mistakes are made.

Knowledge leadership is a complex science. It requires the ability to adapt to changing requirements while at the same time creating safe spaces for discovery and collaboration. It also requires a curious mind and a preparedness to question assumptions, ask insightful questions and change habits.

To use knowledge as an influence strategy, you must be prepared to constantly examine the factors that make what you do unique and hard to copy, and to explore how to sustain this advantage. Only then will you be able to influence events by acting upon the right knowledge, in the right context, with the right people and at the right time.

## Knowledge as power

There are many myths about how to be a successful leader or manager. One is that hoarding information and restricting the flow of knowledge will lead to job security or long-term career success for the hoarding individual.

Seeing knowledge as something that can be boxed in and manipulated is only helpful in a very insular and unchanging world. The fact is that most of us live in a world of constant change. In this world we must shift our role from protector and gatekeeper to one that encourages and facilitates new understanding and imagination, in the hope of increasing the awareness and know-how required to resolve the challenges we face.

Modern business, by its very nature, is full of networks, alliances and partnerships. It is a social and political place where excellence is often closely aligned with the quality of our relationships. *The power that comes from influence is built on how well we nurture trust and expansive thinking within these connections.*

When managers have a limited span of influence, they struggle to keep up to date and informed. They base their decisions and actions on what is often incomplete data. The result will be bad decisions and poor judgment (which is likely to decrease their span of influence even further).

Ask any senior executive what they would like most in a business and they will probably answer: 'A work culture that promotes teamwork, achievement and innovation'. Yet a host of competitive, defensive and selfish behaviours often lead to the exact opposite of what is hoped or desired. For example, a recent study by *Human Synergetics* found that nine out of ten Australian companies struggle with a culture of blame, indecision and conformity.[4] In many organisations office politics create an ugly game where individual protection and tribal warfare become more important than running a successful and knowledgeable business.

In this world, the benefit to the organisation of better knowledge and innovation may be the last thing in people's minds.

Influence through knowledge leadership is often hamstrung by a toxic blend of behaviours. The massive gap between intention and action is the major challenge to be faced when seeking to improve the quality of knowledge in an organisation.

The power of knowledge comes through the discipline of critical review, reflection and connection. In addition, if, as a leader and manager, you truly wish to stimulate the power of knowledge in your organisation, you need to reward and encourage some simple behaviours.

- Train managers to coach, rather than tell.
- Create ample opportunities for people to share their successes, expectations and frustrations.
- Throughout the organisation, value and treasure what makes it special. This means making the time and effort to celebrate insight and stories of experience.

## Knowledge contribution styles

Before we explore the ways that you can enhance and stimulate knowledge within your organisation, you must first understand the factors that determine an organisation's knowledge and learning culture, and the 'knowledge contribution' styles that exist within it. There are two primary issues to consider:

1 Who dictates the *agenda* for knowledge?
2 How much sharing or *flow* of knowledge is there within the business?

Let us look first at the *knowledge agenda*. There are two major parties that are involved in knowledge contribution and able to drive the knowledge agenda: the organisation and the individual.

If the organisation is dictating the agenda and holds the most power, it will prescribe a detailed plan of action for how knowledge is contributed and shared. Typically, there will be clear objectives, senior management support and strong accountability lines. People are expected to toe the line and work within organisational constraints. If the level of thinking is robust and expansive, this type of agenda will be driven by a solid and sustainable direction for the future that includes the needs of the customer and society. If it is not, the organisational agenda will be insular and ill-conceived.

By contrast, when individuals dictate the agenda, they have the freedom to pursue their own passions, desires and dreams. In some cases this may be due to the nature of work (for example, if the individual is working in a specialist area) or it may be because the business relies on volunteers, casual workers or community involvement, and direct lines of organisational control and command do not exist.

Individuals controlling the agenda may need clarification about how they fit into the organisation's wider knowledge agenda. For example, a scientist in a research laboratory may need to operate within a confidentiality agreement that details the rights and responsibilities for disclosure and protection of intellectual property. Such agreements help channel and clarify expectation. Of course, there are no guarantees that employees will choose to share all that they have learned. So special efforts must be taken to try to mobilise and codify what is being discovered as it occurs.

This leads us on to the other dimension of knowledge contribution; *knowledge flow*. Depending on the climate of the business, employees will either be restrictive or open regarding how and when they share knowledge. This could be determined by many factors, including how empowered the staff are, the nature of their work, the leadership style and the nature of the technical systems and operating procedures. Knowledge sharing behaviour will also be dictated by corporate folklore and the people involved (hence two corporations with identical business models may share knowledge and learning in quite different ways).

Figure 6.1 illustrates how agenda and flow result in four organisational cultures with distinctive knowledge contribution and learning styles. Each has advantages and disadvantages. In some workplaces several cultures may exist within different teams, departments and locations.

*Compliant learning (organisational agenda with restricted flow)*

In this culture, people feel obligated to follow firmly established rules and agendas regarding workplace learning. We often see this in bureaucracies and organisations where there are standardised

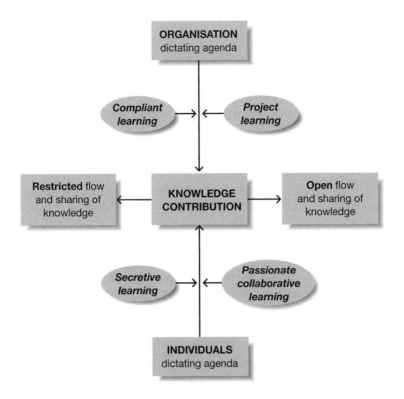

Figure 6.1 Knowledge contribution model

work functions. Learning is contained within a set range of expectations and capabilities. People are expected to follow the routine and procedures, and not rock the boat. Sharing of knowledge is restricted to finite areas, and will probably only occur when there is a compliance issue or an obligation to contribute.
- *It's an advantage* if you wish to build expertise in a highly specialised area of endeavour, such as technical systems or procedural matters; for example, occupational health and safety and risk management standards.
- *It's a disadvantage* if your business activity is starting to change its role or function. Staff in this culture will only seek to know enough to stay out of trouble or to obtain favouritism. They won't seek to contribute higher value knowledge to the organisation.

- *Making it work.* Every chance must be taken to help people to explore new ways to improve new systems and approaches. If managers and staff are paralysed by compliance and passive resistance, you may get some unwanted surprises. So regular communication is essential to build a shared commitment to required reform and renewal. In some cases this may mean bringing in outsiders and new blood to stimulate different thinking.

*Secretive learning (individual agenda with restricted flow)*

This is the secret world of specialists who are quietly working on their own learning. Sometimes they do not share what is unfolding—they are holding back for the right time and place. This is common in most organisations, but research and development and academia are classic examples. For example, 3M has actively encouraged and rewarded people to explore personal innovation and add ideas into the business brain. Post-It notes are one such successful innovation that came from this process.

- *It's an advantage* if you need to build specialised expertise. The emphasis is on individual activity and learning, and is devoid of some of the pitfalls that come from forced participation and 'group-think'.
- *It's a disadvantage* if people become too isolated and disconnected from organisational or business realities; for example, if a personal project is seen as more important than the broader interests of the organisation. This is common among knowledge workers who grow to love their area of discovery so much that they hide themselves away and do their own thing.
- *Making it work.* To stimulate a healthy relationship with this secret world, trust and recognition are everything. You cannot force people to share, particularly if trust is low! However, agreed performance targets, communication protocols and sound intellectual property agreements certainly help important insights and discoveries to surface.

*Project learning (organisational agenda with open flow)*

If the organisation drives the agenda, but there is open knowledge flow, there will be 'project-based' learning. People will collaborate on set areas for action. This could result in a variety of functional, cross-functional and virtual teams being established. The project learning process can be quite successful, but excellent scenario thinking, project management and team building skills are essential. Problems arise when the latest fad or political expediency drives the project process, rather than meaningful contribution. An example is when the needs of the customer or society are not considered.

- *It's an advantage* if you wish to focus on team learning or project learning as an organisational priority. Notably, where an organisational issue has never before been given collective importance. In the last decades various management approaches have used this method—Total Quality Management, Quality Circles and Six Sigma are cases in point where project learning was employed.
- *It's a disadvantage* if the project learning becomes a matter of compliance and expediency rather than a business necessity. Many organisational and business improvement programs have struggled because of a super-saturation of uncoordinated and unnecessary bouts of project learning. In such cases people have been unable to do what is necessary to really improve the organisation and are caught up in countless meaningless projects.
- *Making it work.* This requires a clear sense of purpose and excellent project management. Opportunities need to be created for people to influence the agenda and nature of projects to be undertaken. Extra up-front planning and thinking ahead can make a world of difference. A clear linkage to a broader organisational strategy or plan will also be very useful.

*Passionate collaborative learning (individual agenda with open flow)*

Here individuals drive the knowledge agenda, but there is a preference for teamwork and expansive sharing. This can lead to many forms of joint practice and networking. In industries such as education and training, health and community development, passionate collaborative learning has been very helpful. Shell, IBM, BP and the World Bank have well documented case studies of success through collaborative learning.

- *It's an advantage* if you wish to stimulate widespread sharing and learning on emerging issues. It is an excellent device to broaden commitment and cooperation across an organisation, business or marketplace. This style is often necessary for pioneering breakthrough thinking with a wide range of people. It can help people to 'think outside the square'.
- *It's a disadvantage* if the collaboration lacks context and meaning. Ground rules need to be established that encourage participation and deeper thinking. Where the activity fails to grab the imagination of the participants it is better to let it die rather than let it stumble along, pretending that it is worthwhile. For managers who crave command and control, passionate collaborative learning can be quite threatening. They want people to be reined in and the political dynamics to remain the same.
- *Making it work.* Studies indicate that an organisation benefits directly if there are clear feedback processes, or indirectly if knowledge contribution leads to raised personal resourcefulness, confidence and know-how. If this form of learning is to last, it requires energetic people who love to inspire, build momentum and celebrate success.

In summary, to influence knowledge contribution you need an acute understanding of the dynamics of knowledge circulation within an organisation. It is quite likely that a combination of all four styles discussed may be necessary. In that way the best of all worlds can be gained.

At a practical level, creating a plan of action for knowledge contribution, whatever style is best suited for your organisation, is vital. Take time to look at the business realities and the personalities involved to ensure a well formulated and coherent plan is developed.

## The problem of ego

Now that we have discussed the broader issues of influence through knowledge leadership, it is time to personalise the conversation. It is pointless creating new systems and approaches if you, as a leader and manager, are unable to set aside your own biases and entrenched learning habits. This can be a greater challenge than getting others to behave better or learn differently.

Your ego plays a major role in making you who you are and what you will become. It shapes your self-concept, identity and place in the world. This protector is like a trusted friend, always helping and directing you to preserve what it means to be you. Ego is like a sculptor constantly chiselling away in granite to perfect and finish a piece of art called 'I' . . . never completing, but always wanting to perfect and protect whenever possible.

When I conduct training, I often discuss the notion of ego and how it is both a 'friend' and a 'foe'. Most people can quickly list the benefits of an ego, but when it comes to listing the pitfalls they struggle. The pitfalls of ego can include:
- choosing to be hurt or not listen when someone disagrees or questions us
- becoming defensive and being vengeful
- avoiding important issues
- gloating, craving or being single-mindedly ambitious.

All quite unhelpful when it comes to long-term personal and professional growth.

I liken our relationship with our ego to turning on a car radio and switching to the same station all the time. This station is called EGO FM. We are magnetised by the frequency and message and rarely tune into the other stations. Why do we always stick to the same frequency or script in life? How about changing from EGO FM and trying a few other stations on the dial?

The fact is that ego can cage people's thinking in all walks of life. For example, when people undergo change, EGO FM blasts away giving all the directions and instructions and landing all the punches. We put labels on ourselves regarding what we can and cannot do, or we stick to a tired response to solve the situation. In many cases, making even minor changes is strongly resisted by the ego and leads to an unhealthy spiral of self-doubt, denial, panic and anxiety.[5] This is particularly the case when we are stressed. In such times our egos limit our ability to see alternatives and give us the freedom to let go of habits and make important changes.

Our ability to influence through knowledge starts and finishes with our ego. We have to remain open to *what is* and notice how our ego is driving our current feelings and choices. Only then are we in the right frame of mind to be open to our better insights and to be able to recognise and benefit from the knowledge and insights of others.

When it comes to personal and leadership growth, the reality is that we can only progress if we are prepared to be totally honest with ourselves, to move beyond ego, and to maintain a calm and alert state of mind. Whether it is in the field of sport or business, peak performance requires a passionate desire to be 'in the moment' and to improve.

## Discovering ground truth

In April 2004, I learned something very important about the value of accurate information.

> Towards the end of a speaking and study tour in England I met my friend Sharon and her boyfriend Alan, who introduced himself as a self-employed scaffolder. He talked with great pride about his job and his desire to deliver outstanding service. As the night went on we shared our deeper and more passionate views on a variety of topics from drug abuse to Alan and Sharon's dream to one day live in Australia. Alan was also in the Army Reserve and started talking about his role during peacekeeping duties in Bosnia in the 1990s. His primary role on the ground was what he called 'ground truth'. Alan explained ground truth as follows.
>
> Alan and another member of the British armed forces would live full-time in a village. They would walk around each day in the village and meet and greet the locals. Where possible they built trust by just sitting and listening. Alan and his fellow soldier were in uniform and were unarmed. Alan's brief was to discover the truth and learn the facts; nothing else. Each evening they would meet the senior commander over a cold beer and debrief, sharing their discoveries of the day with other Ground Truth teams. The commander found the process priceless. He was getting first-hand information that on many occasions was more accurate than classified intelligence.

As Alan told this story I could not help but realise its very strong relevance to the business world. How often do managers act on incorrect assumptions or poor information? What would happen if instead they found out the ground truth?

Unless we get accurate information on the ground, our

organisation will struggle and we will be unable to respond appropriately. In some cases our ground truth may involve market intelligence or updates on workload, or it could simply be about the current attitudes of staff. Whatever the case, our job becomes easier when we are acting on more truthful stories.

Of course there are limitations. People often know more than they say, so unless you build trust and confidence the process may be stifled. We also have to be aware that people may distort the truth based on unrealistic assumptions or analysis. In some cases this may be a deliberate distortion, but often it happens unconsciously—the mind just makes poor judgments based on incomplete data. So to help address these limitations, here are some guidelines to assist you to uncover ground truth.

- *Mine the hidden gems.* Go beyond written systems and procedures and look for deeper feelings and insights. Be prepared to listen to stories and spend more time creating the right social structures to get the work done. Help people to go past their entrenched habits and look for sources of inspiration. Spread your networks wide and nurture deeper thinking. Observe how habits in thinking can become a problem when people rely overly on what they learnt most recently or what they learnt first.
- *Discover how systems dictate know-how.* Whether you are operating a help desk or using an SMS system, how you behave with the technology depends in part on the system, but also on you. Knowledge is socio-technical in nature. Put two people in an identical car and see how they drive differently. So explore why people choose to behave the way they do and what decisions they make when they operate systems.
- *Clear wrong assumptions.* Each of us carries a long list of assumptions and mental models that should be questioned. A funny example of this occurred recently in my life when I decided to learn to swim again. I told my friend that I felt that I was a poor swimmer because I struggled to do as many laps of the pool as I felt I should. In my mind a lap was up and down once, which translates into a 100-metre journey in a 50-metre pool. In fact, as I recently learned, a lap is only one length of a pool (50 metres). So when I compared with other people the number of laps I had done, I would leave the conversation feeling bemused

or somewhat inferior. Not surprising, when most people seemed to be swimming twice the distance I was. It never once occurred to me to ask the obvious insightful question: 'How long is a lap?' The lesson for business: we have to have a healthy questioning of our assumptions and mental models.

- *Go past quick wins.* In any job it is very easy to give the impression you are resolving tough issues by being busy. I see this particularly in heavy workload areas where the primary goal is to complete the work at all costs. This leads to a culture of quick wins and 'getting runs on the board' rather than dealing with long-term issues of sustainability. Unless we deal with the fundamentals, our learning and capabilities will never be addressed. I would like a dollar for each time I have been to annual planning process meetings and the same tough issues were on the table as had been the previous year.
- *Explore stories and memories.* Encourage people to share their versions of the truth. This way you will uncover the powerful experiences that trigger motives, thoughts and decisions. You will also discover how perceptions can lead to generalisations, distortions and loss of knowledge. By identifying these insights we are much better placed to take better action in the future.

## Creating safe space

Organisations must be prepared to speak about the tough or unspeakable issues if they wish to move forward. Many people talk about the importance of teamwork, learning and smarter organisations, but for many, sadly, it is only rhetoric.

Think about the last time you truly felt safe to speak your mind, free from reprisals, not limited by fear, and able to have open and frank conversation. This memory is the best anchor you have when it comes to influencing people with knowledge. Hold on to this memory and never forget it. Build on the lessons learnt from this experience and apply them to your life and your work environment.

That is why creating what I call *safe space* is an essential skill for all managers, coaches and facilitators in businesses and organisations. Safe space is an environment where people feel comfortable to candidly and constructively discuss and explore issues without the fear of ridicule, retribution and bullying.

It is not always easy to create safe space. For example, people are often unwilling to let go of control and create space for new dynamics to occur. And it should be acknowledged that it takes courage to give the process a try. For some, creating safe space may seem too hard, particularly if they have had failed attempts in the past. However, experience has shown me that, when done properly, creating safe space is incredibly liberating and positive. Normally people are very thankful that hard-to-discuss issues have been aired and explored. My advice is to start small and build it up.

To make progress we must be prepared to take a risk and not let the fear of making things worse stop us. This is particularly the case if people are not comfortable with open and honest conversations, as the following example shows.

> Recently I was asked to put a proposal to a new client. They wanted a team-building day. I typically only do them if I can meet the team members in advance. This helps build rapport and enables me to custom design the exercise for the team. It also helps team members to articulate and share their expectations. When I met the team leader at her office she asked me to come in and close the door. She then told me what she wanted out of the process and that there had been a long history of conflict in the team.
>
> When I put my proposal in writing I suggested that I meet each team member separately before the team-building day. I would then submit an agenda based on input. She rejected my offer, advising me that she wanted to launch straight into the team day without meeting the team first. She said it would be too much for the team to share their feelings with me beforehand.
>
> It is obvious that this team leader was not ready for safe space. I sensed she was quite fearful and protective of her role and her ego was not willing to give it a try. The team leader chose another provider—my hope is that the other consultant had more success in helping the team get past square one. Without safe space I doubt the team would resolve its underlying issues.

A safe space will not happen by itself—you need some ground rules that will help to shape and flavour positive dynamics. Bob Dick and Tim Dalmau, in their book *Helping groups to be effective*,[6] have come up with the following guidelines, which I have found to be very helpful.

- Agree on and pursue common goals.
- Explore why people need each other.
- Show respect, and share time and decisions.
- Attend to each other and listen for understanding.
- Build on ideas and acknowledge feelings.
- Reveal assumptions before acting on them.
- All must take responsibility for the quality of conversation.

Having reached agreement on the basics, you can then try a few different group processes. Here are five of my favourites.

- Appoint someone to the role of process observer, to give feedback on how the ground rules are being demonstrated.
- Start meetings with each person completing statements such as these: 'What I feel like saying is . . .' and 'My major success or learning in the past week was . . .'
- Instead of having an agenda, frame each topic heading with a question. A burning, insightful question can clarify the issue much faster than a list of agenda items.
- Once a month, have a one-hour knowledge sharing meeting where someone brings work in progress to the table for which they would like opinions and insights.
- Change the location, seating, timing and venue of the meeting. Often our behaviour is wired and anchored into a routine.

## Permission and trust

Stimulating knowledge requires permission from all those involved. Without it people will not contribute with their full hearts and minds. As I heard Michael Grinder, master trainer in neuro-linguistic programming, say at a recent presentation in Sydney: 'You can only do as well as the permission you are given'.

So what do we mean by permission? Dr Alan Cattell, from Bradford University in England, once explained to me that here are four categories of permission. Depending on the nature of the tasks, all levels of permission will need to be discussed and clarified.

- *Level 1.* At the lowest level of permission, people wait to be *given permission* before they start. This may require a verbal or written assurance before they take an action.

- *Level 2.* People may feel they need to *ask for permission* before they proceed. This often occurs when boundaries are being negotiated and roles clarified.
- *Level 3.* Some individuals may believe that they must *earn permission*. This may mean people getting 'runs on the board' before permission is granted. We often see this in process delegation, when work is farmed out.
- *Level 4.* At the highest level, people *assume they have permission* or, even if they haven't, they go straight ahead and *give permission to themselves*.[7]

If you apply this permission category model, you will soon discover that it helps to raise the level of clarity and awareness. However, you will also discover it is not a miracle cure. Even when you feel you have agreed permission there will be some things that will remain unsaid. As Chris Argyris, Donald Schon and their many followers have said for over a quarter of century, there are always 'undiscussables'.[8] People prefer to self-censor, look fine, maintain the status quo and remain civil rather than share their assumptions, vulnerabilities and motives. Even when they are asked to tell the truth they may hesitate to do so, resulting in rather contrived and riddled conversations. Whenever possible, people would prefer to protect themselves and protect others rather than speaking their version of the truth.

This revelation is unsettling, particularly given our earlier discussions about ground truth and creating safe space. We must be resigned to the fact that even when we desire to be open, transparent and trusting, this may not be enough to encourage others to do the same. The only long-term remedy is gradually to create an environment where people are more prepared to share undiscussables.

Bob Dick and Tim Dalmau suggest asking each person to create a private list of their undiscussables.[9] For example, this list could include your inner concerns, biases and assumptions, and the behaviours of others that you like or that annoy you. It is also worth noting your judgments of other people's talents and expertise (though remember that this list may say more about you than the other people). Then identify which undiscussables you are most willing to share, either one-on-one or in a group setting. As trust builds and issues are aired, more challenging undiscussables may be disclosed. Trust your intuition—you will know when to stop. In many cases full disclosure of your list would be unhealthy and counterproductive. Finally, you need to realise that getting the whole truth out may be too ambitious.

In difficult situations you may need third party assistance in the form of a facilitator, coach or mentor. However, for most matters this will not be necessary. Over the last decade, I have seen many teams make massive inroads on undiscussables. I have also seen relationships or teams heal by simply taking the chance to be more honest with each other. Remember the goal here is not always about beautiful endings but about gaining better insight into what really matters.

## Stimulating buy-in

It may sound obvious, but unless people clearly understand why knowledge contribution is necessary, they will most likely resist and you will not get the 'buy-in' or the level of support required.

So how do we generate a buzz about knowledge? In my book, *Winning the knowledge game*,[10] I discussed research showing that people primarily want interesting and challenging work. They want to make a difference and to stamp their personal mark on how work is done. This is reinforced by the results of the 2004 Grey Worldwide *Eye on Australia* consumer research study,[11] in which Australian consumers were asked: 'What are the most important things in your life?' 'Freedom to be yourself' was rated number one across all demographics. Other priorities included being safe and secure; home; friends; and financial security (in that order). Interestingly, 71% of Australians wished they had more fun in their lives.

From this evidence it is clear that money is not everything. If we want to stimulate buy-in we need to identify and market more personal and emotional reasons for employees to contribute. Instead of detailing features of a system to improve knowledge use, we need to stimulate the emotions a little. For example, discuss how new or better knowledge will improve lives; increase mutual respect, reputation or identity; increase social approval; enhance personal freedom; increase self-esteem; and reduce stress. All of these emotional factors carry much more weight with people than benefits such as increased productivity and job efficiency.

When it comes to getting the buy-in of senior management for a proposal, reasons such as competitive advantage, profitability, customer loyalty or improved performance will gain immediate attention. If you wish to gain support and commitment at a deeper level, you need to find a personal or political trigger.

Motivating people to action must activate intrinsic needs, aspirations and desires, as in the following example.

> My fondest memory of stimulating buy-in and influencing knowledge occurred in Parramatta City Council in 2002. What started as a simple talent development program became a highly successful change program called MAD. MAD stood for 'making a difference'. It had its own logo, publicity and marketing campaign. With a little humour and loads of imagination, six cross-functional teams were established to study six business issues. The process included lots of ingredients, such as mentoring, training, teamwork and formal presentations on two 'recall' days. Using the MAD theme to stimulate more magic and excitement, the first recall day was called the MAD Café and the second gathering, three months later, carried a train metaphor—the MAD Express.
>
> At the completion of the program, over 75% of staff wanted to be involved in MAD 2, if it was to occur, while 100% of staff were aware of the MAD brand and what it was achieving. The MAD program was nominated and reached the final of the Local Government Management Association Management Awards in 2003.
>
> MAD succeeded because staff wanted to make a contribution and it had total senior management support. Most of all, staff passionately wanted to learn new skills, stamp their influence and make new friends and connections. There were also key staff who were motivated change agents and who kept a close eye on the buzz as it was generated. What surprised me the most was that even the most cynical were converted.

## Bringing campfires together

There is something magical about sitting in front of an open campfire. If you are lucky enough to be sharing it with friends the atmosphere can build a strong sense of community and friendship.

The campfire has been an important meeting ritual during the history of civilisation. For thousands of years people have sat in silence, pondered their thoughts or shared what is on their mind.[12]

There are also campfires in business and in organisations. They come in many forms—work teams, gatherings in tearooms, professional associations or just loose networks on the Web. Each group has its own purpose, bond or loyalty. No doubt our habits, loyalties and rituals are huge influencing factors in how these campfires are established and maintained.

In any organisation or area of expertise there are many campfires of knowledge—just as you will see separate fires in a busy camping ground on a chilly night, with each crowd doing its own thing. Unless someone takes the chance to meet with another group, the different groups may never connect. Of course if people feel comfortable and warm where they are, the desire to meet someone else may never arise.

How do we get the different campfires of knowledge to collaborate, network and share? Most industries and knowledge workers are working overtime to address this challenge. In recent years there have been numerous attempts to build connections between campfires of knowledge, whether through knowledge sharing events, cross-functional teams, directories on company portals, communities of practice or blogging. The Internet is certainly helping to open up new gateways of information and connection, but it can not be expected to solve the problem completely.

Just because someone creates a web presence or a video conference facility it does not mean they are creating the haven of knowledge or sources of inspiration we need. What is required is a *compelling and meaningful reason to collaborate*. Unless there is a strong igniting spark, campfires will never connect. Clear purpose is essential. Intention must be broad, challenging and over-arching. Without clear focus and motivation, efforts will fail. There must be practical ways for people to learn together. This may mean developing agreed protocols, procedures and common digital platforms. One such digital innovation is WIKI software. It enables diverse groups to build and edit a common website in no time at all.[13]

Finally, people must have a strong desire to contribute and take responsibility, supplemented with a little daring and fresh team processes. This is vitally important when people are struggling with multiple roles and very busy lives, and seeking instant gratification.

# Coaching

In all walks of life, coaching and mentoring play an active role. Whether it is in the community, in sport or in business, coaching helps to advance understanding and to build capability. We only have to consider how complex life can be to realise that a little help and guidance can go a long way.

When I wrote my first book, *Learning unlimited*,[14] in 1993 I made the observation that there was a corporate black hole when it came to widespread use and training of coaches and mentors. Little has changed in the past decade, except that there are now many consultants who are working as business coaches.

Coaching and mentoring can be two of the most effective ways a leader or manager can spread influence, yet often managers are too busy, or they are unmotivated or untrained for the tasks.[15] This observation is backed by a host of studies in career development throughout the world.[16]

I recently heard the Dalai Lama say at a public meeting in Darling Harbour, Sydney: *The greatest deficiency in education is not of intellect but of the heart.* No place is this truer than in the coaching role in business. If a manager is unwilling to show interest in and compassion for others, the coaching process will probably struggle. Such managers most likely become paralysed on task and structure and fail to discover important issues regarding motivations and feelings.

The relationship between a boss/coach and protégé is the most important factor in talent development. Good relationships and positive emotional energy lead to strong knowledge growth, openness and grace. Coaches must be champions for making work a positive experience. Freedom to express and discuss emotions and motivations is a vitally important part of this process. Not only will this help fast track learning but it will dramatically improve mental and physical health.

Gaining influence through coaching is about enabling people to know their strengths by helping them to gain meaning and to reach a higher purpose, and by exposing them to new challenges. It is not about getting people to do what you want; but it is about gaining commitment and inspiring contribution.

Individuals want a workplace where their ideas are respected. They want an environment in which their careers can develop and insight can blossom. This means a healthy connection between a good working relationship with your people and the task at hand. What makes the role of coaching so challenging is that many people are not trained or motivated to undertake it. However, with a little practical help, training and support you can make a solid start.

In closing, remember that coaching and influencing can be draining—particularly if you have other battles and challenges in your life. So be kind to yourself and others; be prepared to find a good mentor or role model to help guide *you* through the good and tough times. That way you will sustain the energy and drive to be a true champion of knowledge leadership and influence.

# Conclusion

The power of knowledge comes from creating networks, conversations and systems that build capability and awareness. You can influence the viability of an organisation by promoting a culture of cross-fertilisation and exchange. Certainly there will be times when specific matters may need to be kept confidential or protected. If general, however, knowledge is not something that can or should be boxed in or controlled.

Knowledge flow is a wonderful way to influence and to enable transformation and incremental change. When people feel confident that they can express what is on their minds without fear of retribution, there is more hope of creating intelligent and empathetic workplaces. To do this we must create a robust knowledge environment full of learning opportunities and exciting new frontiers.

Leaders and managers seeking to be of influence must remember that without knowledge there is no influence. Influence, at its core, requires a spark of insight and then the sharing of that wisdom so that people will act. It requires intention and then connection—some transfer, exchange or stimulation of knowledge is essential to the process.

With good and clear intentions, people can be mobilised and inspired into action. It is when we try to stifle flow and sharing that a business brain begins to shut down or become less effective.

As leaders, we need to put away some of the managerial jargon and buzzwords and just do what is required to be decent human beings. This means saying no to those organisational practices which reduce liberty, stomp on initiative and dehumanise workplaces.

For most us, what we want is a workplace and a society where we can genuinely make a difference and be treated well. It is nothing more complex than that. So let us not over-complicate the challenge. If we display simple reassurance, communication and trust in everything we do, we will make a positive difference.

### How to unleash knowledge flow

1. *Develop clear intention*
   Explore *why* you wish to improve knowledge levels and quality. Answering this question and then communicating the answer to stakeholders is central to stimulating interest and buy-in. Explore emotional and symbolic reasons why people may wish to be involved.

2. *Create safe space*
   Establish a common understanding of the ground rules for excellent listening and dialogue. Start with easy conversations then move to more sensitive and challenging ones.

3. *Stimulate contribution*
   Schedule events and opportunities where people can gain confidence and contribute. Make sure the projects have meaning. Mobilise joint effort on how learning can best be shared, reviewed and celebrated. Encourage people to share testimonials, stories and observations at every opportunity.

4. *Notice your ego*
   Constantly ask whether your ego is a friend or foe. Be prepared to go to new places and find out new answers to your questions. Become more curious and notice how ego shapes your own identity and capability and that of others.

5. *Let go of control*
   The more you impose, the less likely you will succeed. Forced participation is not only a killer of contribution, it also raises passive resistance that stifles the potential for quality answers, questions and solutions.

6. *Jazz up collaboration*
   Explore new ways to refresh and jazz up your collaboration, ranging from simple adjustments to meetings (such as having different people chair discussions), to high energy weekend retreats, to establishing easy-to-use websites and help desks.

7. *Build new campfires*
   Establish new networks, teams and projects where people are learning with new people about key areas of interest and enquiry. Connect people who have a desire to contribute and take responsibility. Use a blend of face-to-face and digital technology.

# For further exploration

- S Denning, *The springboard: how storytelling ignites action in knowledge-era organizations*, Butterworth Heinemann, Boston, 2001.
  This book is a practical case study about how story and narrative were used to influence change and stimulate knowledge flow within the World Bank. An excellent exploration of how momentum and opinion can be swayed by using such a timeless and simple tool as storytelling.
- R Dick & T Dalmau, *Values in action*, 2nd edn, Interchange, Chapel Hill, Australia, 1999.
  The work of Australians Bob Dick and Tim Dalmau has been an inspiration to me for over two decades. Their publications have been compulsory reading in preparation for many facilitation projects over the years.
- R Florida, *The rise of the creative class*, Pluto Press, North Melbourne, 2003.
  A compelling read about what is required to stimulate vibrant and creative communities. Although much of the book is focused on cities and broader communities, the discussion of building business capability and innovation is priceless. Values such as tolerance and diversity are proven key drivers for economic improvement and innovation.
- B Kaye & S Jordon-Evans, *Love 'em or Lose 'em*, Berrett-Koehler Publishers, San Francisco, 1999.
  Dr Beverly Kaye and her colleagues have for several decades been world pioneers in how to help managers guide and support the development, careers and learning of staff. This book provides a wide coverage of the topic of talent management and is an easy-to-read and practical book.
- N Kline, *Time to think*, Ward Lock, London, 1999.
  This poetic and beautifully written work explores how true listening can profoundly affect the quality of communication and decision making. I saw Nancy present in London in April 2004 and was profoundly moved by her depth of thinking and reflection. She gave the book out at the end of her lecture as a gift and it helped shape my thinking for this chapter.

- A Rylatt, *Winning the knowledge game: a smarter strategy for better business in Australia and New Zealand*, McGraw-Hill Australia, Sydney, 2003.
  My most recent book covers many aspects of knowledge management relevant to this chapter. Three themes of opening hearts and minds to smarter learning, growing competitive advantage and ensuring lasting success, enable managers to build on the wisdom of the book and create a more intelligent and wiser workplace.

## Acknowledgments

I wish to acknowledge the assistance of Cec Pedersen, from the University of Southern Queensland, for his practical support in reviewing my initial draft.

## Notes

**1** J Berry & E Keller, *The influentials*, Free Press, New York, 2003.
**2** N Simson, 'Why 10 per cent of people influence everyone else', *Marketing*, June 2004, p. 35.
**3** N Kline, *Time to think*, Ward Lock, London, 1999.
**4** S Nixon, 'Backstabbing in the workplace may not be as beneficial as the boss thinks', *Sydney Morning Herald*, 24 July 2003, p. 3.
**5** HeartMath Research Center, *Science of the heart*, Institute of HeartMath, California, 2001.
**6** B Dick & T Dalmau, *Helping groups to be effective*, Interchange, Chapel Hill, Australia, 1987.
**7** This model is from Alan Cattell. It will appear in his chapter in the forthcoming publication: JP Wilson (ed), *Human resource development: learning and training for individuals and organizations*, 2nd edn, Kogan Page, London, 2005.
**8** C Argyris & D Schon, *Theory in practice: increasing professional effectiveness*, Jossey-Bass, San Francisco, 1974; C Argyris, *Knowledge into action: a guide to overcoming barriers to organizational change*, Jossey-Bass, San Francisco, 1993; C Argyris, *Overcoming organizational defenses: facilitating organizational learning*, Allyn & Bacon, Boston, 1990.

**9** B Dick & T Dalmau, *Values in action*, 2nd edn, Interchange, Chapel Hill, Australia, 1999.

**10** A Rylatt, *Winning the knowledge game: a smarter strategy for better business in Australia and New Zealand*, McGraw-Hill Australia, Sydney, 2003.

**11** M Winter, 'Freedom is a powerful driver', *Marketing*, April 2004, pp. 40–1.

**12** A Rylatt, 'Campfires of knowledge', *Employment Review Australia*, November/December 2003, pp. 50–1.

**13** To see an example of WIKI visit the New South Wales Knowledge Management Forum at <http://www.nsw-km-forum.org.au/>.

**14** A Rylatt, *Learning unlimited: practical strategies for transforming learning in the workplace of the 21st century*, 2nd edn, Business+Publishing, Sydney, 2000.

**15** T Gutteridge, Z Leibowitz & J Shore, *Organizational career development*, Jossey-Bass, San Francisco, 1993.

**16** A Rylatt, 2000 (see note 14); B Kaye & S Jordon-Evans, *Love 'em or lose 'em*, Berrett-Koehler Publishers, San Francisco, 1999.

# INFLUENCING BEHAVIOUR IN ORGANISATIONS

## 7

John Eales and Liza Spence

Introduction
Leading behavioural change
   Change the message
The change journey
   Stage 1: the game plan
   Stage 2: developing and leading
   Stage 3: maintaining momentum
Conclusion
For further exploration
Acknowledgments
Notes

# About the authors

John Eales, BA (Psych) (UQ)

John Eales captained the Australian rugby team to their 1999 World Cup win, and has built a reputation for outstanding leadership based on strong values. He is the most capped Wallaby captain, and the medal presented to the best and fairest rugby player in Australia is named after him—the John Eales Medal.

Since he retired from rugby, John and his business partners have been building a series of leadership and team development tools designed for corporations and sporting organisations. This material assesses and develops an individual, in line with the desired values of their organisation. Many corporations seeking to provide their leaders with an edge have used John's insight into leadership and teams.

John is a Director of the Australian Sports Commission and QM Technologies and also consults to BT Financial Group, particularly in the area of financial planning. In 2001 he founded JohnEales5, a company that was a leading sales agent for corporate hospitality during the Rugby World Cup 2003 and has now expanded to incorporate sports marketing, sponsorship and hospitality.

John presents rugby with the Seven Network in Australia and is a columnist with the *Australian Financial Review*. He was chosen as an Athlete Liaison Officer for the Australian Olympic team in Athens 2004.

John Eales can be reached at <editor@aim.com.au>.

## Liza Spence, MA (Psych)

Liza Spence is the Managing Partner of Mettle Group, with responsibility for shaping leadership and business solutions. She is an experienced and visionary consultant, with an exceptional track record as a 'thought partner' for some of Australia's top business executives.

Liza has been described as an architect of personal and organisational transformation. She focuses on providing integrated performance improvements that address the key areas of strategic context, business imperatives and organisational culture; and the implications for team and individual behaviour.

She has developed a passion for applying her understanding of human psychology to enable leaders to shape their organisations. She has brought transformation to the senior executives and top level teams of some of Australia's premier companies.

Liza has extensive experience in a broad range of industries, including retail, banking and finance, IT, hospitality, health, insurance, manufacturing, telecommunications, mining and professional services. Her clients have included Astra Zenica, CSC, Commonwealth Bank of Australia, David Jones, DOCS, Esso, Lion Nathan, National Australia Bank, Oracle, Qantas, QBE, Telstra, and Woodside.

To find out more about Liza Spence's work, visit <www.mettle.biz>.

Liza Spence can be reached at <lspence@mettle.biz>.

# Executive summary

Influencing change is at the heart of effective management. The world we live in is a moving feast and to remain relevant within it we must constantly evolve. This is especially so for managers and team leaders.

For a team to remain relevant, individual team members must constantly adapt their behaviours to conform both to the team's new way of operating and to the new environment it operates within. So one of the critical roles of a team leader is to influence the behaviour of the people in their team and thereby bring about change.

There are two ways to influence behavioural change. You can either drive it by changing the environment people operate within or you can expose individuals to new information so that they decide to change themselves.

This chapter will show you how, through effective change leadership, you can influence both the way things are done within your organisation and the individuals within it.

Change is driven by working simultaneously on the behaviours, symbols and systems of your people and your organisation. The results of any change program are not immediately evident, so change must be approached as a staged process.

# Introduction

Not so long ago, John was negotiating his way around the streets of Dublin, unsure of how to get to his next appointment. His skill with the street map (or lack thereof!) led him to seek the help of a local. The reply that was proffered was typically Irish: 'If that is where you want to be going then you don't want to be starting from here'.

Thanks for that!

Though the Irishman's advice wasn't particularly useful at the time, when it comes to change, it really resonates. Most of the time you won't feel like starting anywhere! People's initial reaction to change is often to automatically and instinctively oppose it, but the ability to recognise, adapt to and cope with change is now a fundamental survival skill of modern society. Everything is subject to change—our personal lives, the communities and societies we live in, and the organisations we work for. Some changes are gradual, others traumatic. Some we create, many are beyond our control—but ultimately they all need to be managed.

Transforming yourself or your environment can be an incredibly challenging and stressful experience. Think about the stress involved in changing jobs, being made redundant, moving house, divorce and so on. If these types of changes cause anxiety levels to rise, imagine how they would soar if you try to change aspects of the very core of your identity, such as reinforced habits and ingrained behaviours.

Change takes people out of their comfort zone. It challenges accepted norms, questioning whether they continue to be relevant. If understood and supported, these change events can be turning points and opportunities. If not, they can lead to serious errors of judgement, depression, breakdown, broken relationships and/or careers.[1]

From an organisational perspective, anything that is as confronting as change will incite an intense reaction from stakeholders. Those who bat for change will espouse the maxim: 'The only constant is change', or live by the motto of US Army Chief of Staff Eric Shinseki: 'If you don't like change you're going to like irrelevance even less'.[2] The naysayers will adhere to the age-old: 'If it ain't broke, don't fix it'. The reality, like most things in life, is neither black nor white—it is genuinely somewhere in between. The change experience itself will undoubtedly be an adventurous one. If managed correctly, it also has the potential to be very rewarding, both personally and professionally. For this to occur, though, your ability to influence stakeholders and engage and co-opt them will be the key.

Influence is the effect that all of our actions, both conscious and unconscious, have on our surroundings. Whether we like it or not, our actions are always influencing something. Part of any leadership journey is to become very conscious of the outcomes of our intended or unintended actions. This is particularly applicable when leading the change process.

## Leading behavioural change

Familiarity breeds comfort. You will find that many people are comfortable behaving as they do, regardless of whether or not others find their behaviour acceptable. Therefore, a significant and obvious stimulus of some sort must be provided to cause people to change. *Leadership is the perfect stimulus.*

As a leader, you can effect change by focusing on and encouraging the behaviours that will facilitate your desired outcomes, and discouraging those that won't. However, to understand how to change behaviour, you must first understand what it is, and what drives it.

'Behaviour' can be broken into three broad categories:
- the decisions people make
- the way they spend their time
- their interactions with others.

At its simplest, behaviour is a product of both the individual and the environment within which they operate. There are two levers a leader can use to drive behavioural change:
1. *Introducing environmental factors that will cause people to change their behaviour.* When you change the environment in which people operate they are forced to choose either to adapt or not. For example, if your aim was to increase communication and collaboration you might change the physical environment to an open office plan. Changing the *environment* is a powerful stimulus for change.

2. *Getting people to choose to change their behaviour*. People will choose to change when they understand that the new information they are processing has become more important than the old information to which they once subscribed. The *messages people receive* will determine whether people decide that there is a better way of doing things.

A leader can influence people and their behaviour by working both these levers simultaneously. As the second lever is the one that many leaders have difficulty understanding, the next section will concentrate on how to get people to choose to change their behaviour by working on the messages they receive.

## Change the message

We believe that the fundamentals for creating a healthy and sustainable change of any sort are established by focusing on *aligning the messages people receive* about what is important.

Messages come through three distinct channels (outlined in Table 7.1):

**1** *Behaviour*: the actions of individuals; what is said and what is done.
**2** *Symbols*: observable events, artifacts and decisions to which people attribute meaning.
**3** *Systems*: mechanisms for managing people and tasks.[3]

Table 7.1 How people receive messages

| Channel | How the message is sent |
|---|---|
| Behaviour | • one-on-one, in teams, in larger forums<br>• senior managers (especially) and key influencers<br>• peers, internal customers and suppliers<br>• what is said and what is done |
| Symbols | • where time is spent<br>• where resources are invested<br>• physical environment<br>• what and who is rewarded<br>• who is involved in what<br>• use of values statements<br>• rituals *(continued)* |

| Systems | • goal setting and budgeting
• reporting and measurement
• reward
• performance management process
• communication
• career development
• feedback
• structure |
|---|---|

In order for individual, team or organisational transformation to have a real and lasting effect, it is essential to simultaneously align the messages that stakeholders receive through all three of these channels.

*Messages sent through behaviour*

An individual's *behaviour* is their most defining characteristic. It doesn't matter what they preach, it is all about what they practise. We're sure you know of some people who put great emphasis on what they say and little on what they do. Think of the lack of impact this has. Ralph Waldo Emerson articulates this as: 'I can't hear what you say, who you are is too loud.'[4]

If leaders wish to ensure that behavioural messages are aligned, then the most effective thing they can do is to model the desired behaviour. Although this is easy to say, it is sometimes harder to achieve. Leaders and change agents need to *be* the change they want to create, and demonstrate this in their behaviour (because behaviours are so visible).

*Messages sent through symbols*

Symbols are events or decisions to which people attribute a meaning. They are created when one event is seen to be indicative of a larger pattern, and thus symbolic of that pattern.[5]

For example, while John was on a corporate visit in Sydney with one of his business partners, Ian Basser, they entered an organisation that had the senior management's offices located in the central floorspace of the building while all 'the workers' enjoyed the window desks with harbour views. Ian immediately commented on what a powerful symbol this was; it embodied the 'leader as servant' philosophy of the executive team of this organisation. The message was loud and clear: 'We value our employees'.

Symbols have the potential to be powerful both in a positive and a negative way. When a German institution bought out one of Mettle Group's clients in the late 1990s, there was a lot of concern within the organisation about how things would change. The employees were in a state of flux—none had ever worked for a German company before and they were aware that there was potential for cultural clashes. The most prevalent fear (as is the case in any merger or acquisition) centred on job security. Employees wondered if they would still be employed under the new regime.

Their fears were soon strengthened when a global video link took place. Although the conference was set up to allay the fears that naturally arise in the face of a merger, the opposite occurred. At one point someone asked a question of the German president: 'Will there be any job losses?' To which he replied: 'There will be job losses, but there will be none in the homeland.'

The screen in Australia, watched largely by aggressive investment bankers, was soon sprayed with pens, staplers, drinks, food and almost everything else that was within arm's reach in the office.

The president's dismissive tones were taken as a symbol of what the future held for the organisation and the people within it. Within 12 months, people's fears were realised. The parent company had broken up its acquisition and on-sold it to two other companies.

Symbols are often unique to a particular organisation or team, and can sometimes be confusing for an outsider to interpret. A good example of this is the symbolic 'ringing of the bell'. In many sales organisations, a bell is rung to indicate that a significant sale has been made, whereas in the head office of the insurance group Lloyds of London, the long-held tradition is to ring a bell whenever one of their insured vessels sinks. Though the action is the same, both powerful symbols send very different messages.

## Messages sent through systems

Systems are the management mechanisms that control, plan, measure and reward an organisation and its people. They are the result of historical decisions that have been made within the organisation around such disciplines as human resources, finance, budgeting, performance management and communications.

Systems can be a very powerful way of reinforcing behaviour and gaining alignment between individual actions and organisational needs.[6]

### The game changes for the Wallabies

*A good example of changing behaviours, symbols and systems can be found in the way the Wallabies adapted when rugby union became professional in 1998. It was John's third season of international rugby and the traditional way of doing things just wasn't working.*

*Before each test match the team would assemble in the town in which the match was to be played. With at least ten test matches per season, this meant creating a new training environment up to eight times each year. To solve the problem, the Wallabies set up a base camp in Caloundra, one hour north of Brisbane, for all pre-test training. At the same time, the camp was opened up so that the families of players could live in as well. Basically, the Wallabies transformed their system—the way they prepared as a team.*

*Not only did the Wallabies now have a consistent training environment, but a powerful symbolic message was given to individual players, the team and the country through the invitation for partners and family to join the team environment. This was a significant change that shifted and softened the dynamics that had existed for the previous 100 years.*

*The onus was then on the players to consider the obvious behavioural expectations and make some choices. Do these changes fit with my values? Is this where I want to go? Will I accept these decisions? Does the new culture of the partner/family dynamic and the 'physical place of base camp' align with the developmental goals of the team? Will the changes prove distracting?*

*Essentially the team adapted extremely well to the change. The Wallabies of the next few seasons were recognised as being the most successful in history. By July 2001, they had won every trophy that they contested. The change was a success!*

Throughout any change journey, people will 'self-select' in or out of the team based on the new input they receive and the new environment they experience. If it is not the way they want to go then they will either move on or, alternatively, the team will move them on. If individuals self-select in, they will choose to belong, adapt or embrace the change and therefore the future.

Transformational, ongoing change is created through the effective manipulation of cultural levers. It is the leader's responsibility to first identify and then frequently readjust levers throughout the change journey. Using levers correctly creates powerful messages that, when consistently reinforced, result in change.

It is fundamental to the change process that leaders consciously use their own behaviours and the behaviours of other senior leaders to identify the key organisational symbols—to let people know what is acceptable and what is unacceptable. It is also vital that they ensure the organisation's systems reinforce the desired behavioural norm. For example, it is symbolic to promote or recognise individuals who are demonstrating the behaviours a leader wants within the organisation.

## The change journey

So far we have covered *what* you need to do to influence change—simultaneously using the two levers of changing the environment and getting people to choose change (by working on the three message channels of behaviours, symbols and systems). The remainder of this chapter will take you on the journey of *how*, through effective change leadership, you can influence both the individuals within your organisation and the way things are done within it.

The journey we are about to map out has been designed to stimulate change in an individual, a team or an organisation. For the purpose of this chapter, however, we will focus on its application within a *team environment*.

There are three distinct stages to travel through when changing a team's behaviour:
**1** establishing the game plan
**2** developing and leading
**3** maintaining momentum.

These stages are illustrated in Figure 7.1 and are then described in detail.

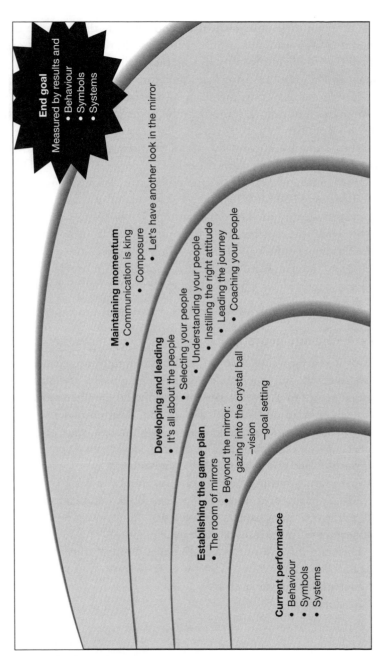

Figure 7.1 The change journey

The nature of behaviour is dynamic and multi-dimensional and so are the methods used to change it. You must therefore systematically work the two levers and manage the three message channels through each of the stages illustrated in Figure 7.1.

## Stage 1: establishing the game plan

You must begin this first stage by understanding where you and your team are now, and then deciding where you want to be in the future. Then you can formulate a 'game plan' for change.

### The room of mirrors

To appreciate where you want to go, you must first understand where you are—your current state of being. Imagine how useless a roadmap would be in trying to find your destination if you didn't know your current location. Maybe that Irishman in Dublin was on to something!

Sun Tzu, in *The art of war*, espouses the virtue of awareness. Although he discusses it in the context of war, its application remains pertinent for everyday modern life.

> *If you know the enemy and know yourself, you need not fear the result of a hundred battles. If you know yourself but not the enemy, for every victory gained you will also suffer a defeat. If you know neither the enemy nor yourself, you will succumb in every battle.*[7]

People love stories and quotes and tend to cling to them in times of transition and competition. Sun Tsu is a favourite of many, including former Wallaby coach Rod Macqueen. He would often refer to *The art of war* and, although the words he quoted were sacrosanct, he constantly mistook the author! He was renowned for getting so caught up in the passion of the moment that he would say, 'as Kostya Tzu [Australian world champion boxer] says . . .' His point was noted nonetheless.

To understand the current state of your team, you must enter a metaphoric *room of mirrors* to conduct a really frank assessment. In this room there are no illusions, only reality. Here, you and your team look at yourselves without fear or favour—nothing is hidden, exposure is total and reality reigns supreme. In order to be clear about what you see in the room of mirrors, you can use formal quantitative or qualitative measures to establish where you are, or you can simply rigorously discuss, debate and then agree on your current state. However, if you take the informal route, it can be more difficult to achieve a frank and open review. So it is advisable to complement informal conversation with a thorough, qualified and objective diagnostic process.

After emerging from the room of mirrors you should begin to get a sense of:
- who the members of your team really are
- how your team behaves at present
- whether you are on track to reach your current goals
- which behaviours and mindsets are typical
- which behaviours and mindsets need to be either further embedded or changed
- what needs urgent attention.

Learn from the past, but don't live in it. As the saying goes: 'Love what you do, not what you did!'

### Beyond the mirror: gazing into the crystal ball

Once you know and understand the current state of play, the next step is to decide where you want to be; that is, your end state. This step involves looking into a 'crystal ball' and visualising the end state you would like to create. When the visualisation is complete, it will become clear what you need to do to make the transition. Questions to consider include:
- Who do we want to be?
- What do we want to represent?
- Where do we want to be?
- What do we need to do to get there?
- What is mission-critical?

The team and the individuals in it must be clear about their roles and responsibilities within the organisation, and ensure that the direction in which they are heading is aligned with that of the organisation. Everyone needs to be 'singing from the same song sheet'. So when defining your end state, ensure that you express it in terms of behaviours, symbols and systems.

There are two important tools that are invaluable for this stage of the process, both of which generally receive more lip service than anything else in Australian business. First, you need to have a *vision*. Second, you need to work out how to achieve that vision through the process of *goal setting*.

A *vision* is an understanding from within yourself and within your organisation of exactly what success looks like. It entails much more than how much money you make, or how many games you win. It is about the type and quality of team you want to create and the values and principles you intend to represent.

Creating a vision for a group of people is important because it gives them an understanding of what they are working for and of where they are going. Some of the most successful people in the world have developed corporations and initiatives simply based on the fact that they had a vision they were able to communicate.

A vision is an open and honest way to get everybody 'on the same page'. Such a public statement of intent allows individuals to make personal choices about aligning themselves and their behaviour with strategic objectives. It allows members to assess whether they want to, and indeed can, change any necessary behaviours in order to assimilate. That is why it is most useful to have as many team members as possible actually discussing, deciding about and engaging emotionally with the organisation's vision for the future.

A good example of a visionary is Lang Walker, one of Australia's most successful property developers. His empire has grown from a one-man band to an organisation employing more than 300 people. John once asked Lang how he got his start in property development. The story Lang told not only illustrates the value of having a vision but also the importance of being able to articulate and sell that vision to other people.

## Building a vision

> Lang Walker used to ride his bicycle past a new housing development on his way to college every day in the outer suburbs of Sydney. Eventually, the development caught his attention and he entered the sales office to take a closer look. Upon investigation, he realised that the 100 or so blocks in the development were scaled in price from the most expensive on top of the hill down to the least expensive at the bottom of the hill and near a main road. He also noticed that, although there was an obvious difference in the price of the blocks, the difference in their apparent value was less clear. Though the blocks were staked out, there was no obvious differentiation.

Then and there, Lang had a vision and identified an opportunity. Rather than hope that the purchasers saw his vision he decided to illustrate it for them—to make it a reality, something they could experience themselves. Armed with this confidence, he purchased the cheapest block in the development on a delayed settlement and hired a bobcat to do a bit of digging. He took the bobcat to the bare lot and began to inscribe his vision into the block. First he cut out a driveway, then an area for the house and, finally, a hole for a pool. He certainly got a reaction. 'I didn't realise a house that size would fit in there.' 'A pool works well there, doesn't it?' The prospective customers were talking.

Before he even had to pay his settlement on the block he had on-sold it for the same price as the most expensive block in the development. Essentially, he sold his vision. He achieved success with just 2 hours worth of work. Soon he was doing the same thing with five or six blocks at once. The vision just kept selling.

Before the year was out the original developer had gone broke and Lang bought him out with the proceeds of all the sales he had made through the application of his vision. He was on his way.

Next comes *goal setting*. Knowing your end goal is often easy. If you are an international rugby player, then you want to win the Rugby World Cup. If you are a 100-metre sprint star, then you aspire to win Olympic gold. If you are a top salesman, you want to exceed your annual targets and hit bonus. If you are a consultant, you want to finish a project on budget and on time. The end goal is normally the easy part.

What is difficult is establishing the milestones you need to reach along the way, and understanding which steps you need to take to get you to your end result. You might establish these steps by asking yourself, for example: Where should I be in one year's time? How fast do I need to be running? What do I have to do to avoid re-injuring my hamstring? Who is going to be doing these specific jobs for me along the journey? And so on.

Goal setting is a very effective process, particularly in relation to motivating employees. Research support is more consistently favourable for goal setting theory than any other single approach to employee motivation.

Goal setting should be a pragmatic rather than magical process. It should take place on a regular basis and should be a collaborative effort between the leader and each team member.

Rewards should be directly tied to the achievement of negotiated goals.

There is a very simple but effective checklist for goal setting—the often-quoted SMART. Goals should be:

- *Specific.* Vague goals lead to vague, halfhearted attempts to achieve them.
- *Measurable.* It is hard for people to stay motivated in the absence of milestones to indicate progress.
- *Attainable.* Goals should give people something to stretch for, but must not be out of reach.
- *Relevant.* The goal must have an impact on performance.
- *Time-bound.* People are better able to focus when they are committed to deadlines.[8]

Regular goal setting also paves the way for consistent activity—the establishment of routine. It is through the sanctuary of routine that many high performers shut out distractions. Olympic swimmers are a great example of using the power of routine to remain focused. Their punishing schedules involve 5.00 am starts, six mornings per week, which means that early nights are a must and distractions are largely avoided. In the corporate world, the need to achieve performance 'deliverables' and to make check-ins on a regular basis can have the same effect of reducing distractions.

Goals should be regularly reviewed and aligned and should exist simultaneously for the organisation, the team and the individual.

## Stage 2: developing and leading

By now, you should know the basics of your game plan. You will know where you are, where you want to be and how you think you should get there. The people around you should be aligned to that direction and aware of your vision and their goals, all of which will bolster the game and improve the performance of all involved. Now it's time to start applying your knowledge and leading the change.

### *It's all about the people*

The next phase is about leveraging your most important resource—your people. By ensuring you have the right people, by making an effort to understand them, and by identifying, instilling and reinforcing the right attitudes, you will be one step closer to success.

## Selecting your people

During a change process, selection can occur in either direction. Some people will consciously choose to assimilate and engage in the new way of doing things. These people choose the organisation—they select you. Others will choose not to assimilate; the change will create an environment that is too different, or it may be misaligned with their values and goals. Eventually these people will either self-select out, or the team or organisation will reject them.

It is often advantageous when you are planning for the change journey to estimate the number of people you expect to self-select out. For example, a recent client—a telecommunications company—had a 25% resignation rate following a cultural and change program rollout. Some felt they could no longer align themselves with the direction of the company, either because they didn't want to, they couldn't (due to a values conflict), they didn't believe in the new direction or they 'wanted to do something different with their life'.

Having the right resources to support the change you are trying to create is essential. However, it is worth thinking through the short-term implications of potentially losing people.

Selection of any new staff should be about finding the best player *for* the team, as opposed to the best player on the team. This is an important distinction. Jim Collins is a great advocate of this principle and in his books, *Built to last*[9] and *Good to great*,[10] he emphasises this point by talking about who is on and who is off the bus. Once you are sure you have the right people on the bus, then you can work out where you want them to sit.

Jack Welch has also taken a practical approach to identifying high potential individuals. He has educated a whole generation of leaders by providing a good dose of common sense. In his book, *Jack Welch and the GE way*,[11] Jack notes that high performers without values can be like cancerous cells, in that they will undermine everything you do. These people have a high profile and are visible yet without values alignment—they send the wrong messages and are damaging. Supporting these people undoes all the hard work you have accomplished and only confuses the rest of the team and organisation.

A charismatic CEO shared his philosophy with us about high performers who were void of values: 'Hunt them down and shoot them!' Though it was said with tongue in cheek, and is clearly extreme, it highlights the importance of a balance between values and performance.

When seeking to identify high performance individuals, measures of individual success should be holistic and need to include alignment with the stated and aspirational objectives and values of the organisation. Table 7.2 identifies a strategy that can be used when considering individual cases.

Table 7.2 Identifying high performance individuals: values versus performance

| Values | Performance | Management strategy for employee |
| --- | --- | --- |
| ✓ | ✓ | Keep, promote, turn into a role model |
| ✓ | ✗ | Train, develop |
| ✗ | ✗ | Out |
| ✗ | ✓ | Out |

## Understanding your people

To get the best out of your people you must know them as more than a group of job descriptions. Sporting teams often develop strong team-based cultures because they know each other so well. In spending so much time together training, playing and travelling, they are forced to understand each other as people as well as positions.

Understanding your people is essential to building trust, and trust is essential when asking people to deal effectively with change. It is vital that you:
- know their strengths and weaknesses
- understand what makes them tick (for example, is family important?)
- know when they are under stress.

One way to get to know each other is to spend time together doing things other than those you would normally do in the course of business. This can be one of the roles of off-site meetings and workshops.

An alternative perspective is offered in the contemporary management book, *The managed heart*.[12] The author argues compellingly against getting too personal, and suggests corporations and employers have no right to claim any mindshare or emotional attachment. The valuable point that this book makes is to be cautious. Entering the hearts and minds of people carries with it a certain responsibility. You must be careful to distinguish between building relationships and leveraging them to productive effect, and manipulatively trading in people's hopes and dreams.

A quote by Natalie Banks in *The golden thread* sums it up nicely:

> *Leadership is being non-possessive in human relationships. Having the capacity to be warm, open and inclusive as well as impersonal and unsentimental when approaching the reality of a situation. Yet, while not being drawn to sentimentality, still being humane and truly compassionate. Possessing an active and creative mind capable of understanding the needs of all while still being able to work for the larger whole. To achieve this may mean sacrificing individual feelings the leaders own and sometimes those of others.*[13]

## Instilling the right attitude

Once you have got 'the right people on the bus' and have begun to understand how your people operate and why, then you can start the process of building the environment you wish to create.

People are defined by their attitude. How many times have you heard a person categorised as one for whom the glass is either half full or half empty? An individual's attitude can make a huge difference to the state of the team. People can disguise an unhealthy attitude for a short period of time, but while the short term is a great concealer, time is the great revealer.

Can you create new attitudes? Absolutely! Investing the time in teaching people to manage their own attitudes is like gold dust on the change journey. Furthermore, it works the levers of individual choice and environmental focus.

One key skill that most successful business leaders and good sportspeople have is the ability to keep focused on, and take responsibility for, achieving their personal best and *facilitating it in others*. As Steve Waugh is reputed to have said: 'Attitudes are contagious—is yours worth catching?'

Bad attitudes can spread quickly. For example, how uncomfortable and tedious is it to be around people who see the world as having done something to them; who wallow in a victim mentality? In order to raise awarness of this type of negative attitude and to encourage employees to move to a more positive one, several clients of ours use the 'V for victory' hand signal to indicate (in a light-hearted way) to a team member that they are acting in a victim-oriented manner, and should amend their behaviour. This is an example of a behavioural and attitudinal expectation being translated into a habit through reinforcement. Once you have established that a victim mentality is unacceptable in individuals, shifting away from this attitude will soon become a team norm, and with consistent reinforcement and leadership role modelling, it will become a team habit.

The key to having the right attitude is to take personal responsibility for, or ownership of, your circumstances. In the 1968 Olympics an injured Tanzanian marathon runner, John Akwari, struggled throughout his race, but remained determined to finish. Over one hour after the medal presentation, with the grandstands largely empty and the stadium clothed in darkness, Akwari staggered home. He was injured and sore, and did his final lap in front of no more than a few hundred supporters, most of whom were journalists. After he crossed the finish line, a reporter went up to him and said: 'John, why did you bother to finish the race?' John's reply was one of ownership: 'My country did not send me 5000 miles to start the race, they sent me 5000 miles to finish the race.'

Most people will start the race; their attitude will determine how they finish.

## Leading the journey

Leadership is about enrolling others in a cause and then setting clear rules and consequences to guide the outcome and the expected behaviour. Once again, personal choice and the environment determine and reinforce this process.

In talking about leadership, we would like to blow two common misconceptions straight out of the water:
- You don't need to be born a leader to be a great leader (how depressing would that be!).
- Leadership is not something that is the sole responsibility of the figurehead or obviously nominated leader (CEO, captain, coach and so on). It is important that there is accountability at all levels of an organisation. Whether it is leading a one-off meeting, running an event or organising a conference, at some point everyone will be expected to take the lead on something and, in doing so, embody the values of the organisation.

Although there are many misconceptions about leadership, there are also many truisms.
- *Leaders must fit well in their own skin.* You must be comfortable with yourself, portray yourself consistently and watch your attitude.
- *Leaders will be watched*. It will be how you behave rather than what you say that will be seen by your people. Know that at all times you will be observed for your behaviour.
- *Leaders must maintain the standards of the team.* Just as a sheepdog snaps at the heels of the sheep, so will a leader shape the behaviour of his or her team.
- *Leaders must make decisions.* You can't sit on the fence as a leader. By all means, weigh up the risks and rewards, but don't procrastinate. When making a decision you will rarely be 100% correct, so don't worry abut it. Your philosophy should be: 'make a decision and then go about making it the *right* decision'. Your people will quickly develop a thirst for improvement and ultimately action.

## Coaching your people

Coaching is truly one of the areas where business has a lot to learn from sport. Sports teams are only 'on field' about once a week and the rest of the time they are developing and honing their skills. In a sports environment the coach takes full responsibility for the performance of the team and is therefore generous with his or her investment of energy and effort.

Constraints of time and complexity don't allow for the same

focus in business. However, coaching is an important tool in monitoring individual journeys and taking responsibility for extracting the very best out of your people. It is also a great way to stay informed and to build relationships with your most valuable resources.

Although we don't have the scope in this chapter to explore leadership and coaching in significant detail, the 'For further exploration' section at the end of this chapter lists some breakthrough titles and theories.

## Stage 3: maintaining momentum

Now that you have the right people, who understand the way they are expected to behave and who see that behaviour consistently reinforced, it is time to consider how you will maintain momentum following the initial 'jolt' of change.

### *Communication is king*

Communication is such an obvious component of change. A program can thrive or die on the communication with and between its participants. Mark Twain summarised it beautifully when he espoused the simple philosophy: 'Tell them what you are going to tell them. Tell them. Tell them what you told them.'

When considering the content, process and intensity of your communication you should use as your basis the three-stage rule: Know your story, tell it well and tell it often. This works just as effectively for verbal as for written work.

Communication up and down and across the organisation is essential. Used effectively, it will assist you to: engage your people; manage change; set the organisation's priorities; and demonstrate progress and achievements. It will afford you the opportunity to galvanise the organisation's commitment to the future; acknowledge and celebrate achievements; and diffuse any negative talk.

What is crucial is that you know what you are trying to communicate and you are able to communicate it effectively and consistently. Get this right and your message will have traction.

In the 'For further exploration' section at the end of this chapter you will find a selection of quality material on the power of communication and its virtues during times of change.

## Composure

Rosabeth Moss Kanter, Professor of Business at Harvard, says: 'All change looks like failure in the middle.'[14]

Although well-laid plans minimise mistakes and stress, they will never eliminate them. So composure is particularly important throughout a process that is, by its very nature, stressful and resisted. Composure manifests itself as *calmness under pressure*. It may enable you to make a critical business decision under difficult conditions or to kick a penalty on the full-time siren. It is the result of having faith in yourself, faith in your teammates and faith in the systems that you operate within.

Bruce McAveney, doyen of Australian sports reporting, alerted us to the following story about Carl Lewis that highlights the value of composure. When Carl Lewis lined up for the 100-metre final of the 1991 World Championship Athletics in Tokyo, he was the favourite for the race. At the halfway mark he was coming last. At the finish line he was the winner of the fastest race that had ever been run up to then—it was a world record time and six men ran under 10 seconds.

A reporter approached Lewis immediately after the race and asked him what he did at the halfway mark that made the difference that resulted in his win. Carl Lewis replied: 'I didn't try to run any faster.'

This is a seemingly simple statement, but very hard to put into action when things aren't going well. It wouldn't have been in Carl's game plan to be coming last at the halfway mark and it would have been easy for him to panic. But he had faith. He had faith in himself and his ability. He had faith in how his team of trainers had prepared him for this race. He had faith in the system that he was operating within. This faith enabled him to trust himself, not panic and not try to run faster. Consequently, he won the race and broke the record.

## Let's have another look in the mirror

Regular testing and re-testing will determine how much traction you have gained, what performance improvements have resulted, and where you need to continue to focus.

This is where you formally and informally monitor and record

the individuals', team's and organisation's behaviour, symbols and systems so that you can make the necessary adjustments to the pressure on different levers in order to maintain your momentum.
There are two components to re-testing:
- correction
- keeping score.

*Correction* is vital in everything we do, as it keeps us focused on our goal and improves our potential for resounding success. A great example of the use of correction is in a rocket's trajectory on its mission to the moon. How long do you think a rocket that aims to land on the moon is specifically on target for its destination? If you answered less than 3% of the time you would be right. The astronauts spend the rest of the time assessing and correcting their flight path, ensuring eventual alignment. Their quest for constant correction, along with superior feedback, communication and measurement systems, ensures their success. So correction is an important element of any journey.

The other part of the re-testing process is *keeping score*. This is about bedding down physical data that document your journey, and establishing benchmarks and measures of success.

Measurement is an important part of any change program. Interpreting behaviour can often be subjective and open to debate, so it is important to have agreement about new behavioural standards, and ways of measuring whether they have been met. This includes defining values, expectations and indicators of success, and ensuring that progress is measured and documented over time, and that individuals and teams are accountable for their role in the process. All those involved in the change program need to know what is in and what is out; what is acceptable and what is not. Keeping score helps to remove the 'grey areas' and therefore set smaller and tighter parameters for performance.

## Conclusion

All of us, in some capacity, are trying to influence people—to get them to do things, to change. Whether it is for ourselves or for other people, we each try to elicit certain behaviours in order to achieve an outcome. This applies in our jobs, our families and our communities.

It is for this reason that this chapter has addressed the complex and dynamic field of change, specifically around behavioural expectations and cultural and values alignment.

Organisational change is possible through the management of messages, specifically through behaviour, symbols and systems. Behaviour can be broken down into the categories of the decisions people make, the way they spend their time and their interactions with others.

Change is then created through managing various levers and messages and through the following three stages:

**1** establishing a game plan
**2** developing and leading
**3** maintaining momentum.

The *game plan* involves understanding where you are today, where you would like to be in the future, and how you should get there. This includes building self-awareness; creating and articulating a vision; and goal setting.

The second phase, *developing and leading*, is all about the people. It investigates how to select the right people or, better yet, have them select you; the benefits of investing the time to really understand them; and the importance of effective leadership and coaching.

The final phase of the journey, *maintaining momentum*, is achieved through communication, composure, regular testing and correction.

We think that the best way to influence others and achieve change is through the process detailed in this chapter; that is, through giving people the freedom to choose, while at the same time tightly controlling the environment that surrounds them in order to support the required outcome.

There is now an enormous base of research that shows that the happiest people in the workplace are those who can attribute a sense of meaning and purpose to the work that they do. This 'importance of endeavour' creates a context whereby not only can we be happy, we can also inspire others.

If you are a leader, no matter at whatever level of the

organisation, we urge you to clearly identify what is meaningful and purposeful in the work that you and your teams undertake and to identify what legacy they can leave behind. This in itself will provide a huge sense of satisfaction for all concerned.

As leaders, we have a responsibility to ourselves, our families and our collegues to provide a positive environment for people to work in and to achieve the best performance for the organisation's stakeholders. These are not mutually exclusive goals.

We suggest that if you do nothing else but identify and share the purposefulness of your work, and that of those you lead, your influence will be both strong and positive.

### Points to consider when seeking to influence change and behaviour

1. Change is stressful but managing it is a skill fundamental to survival and evolution.

2. Changing behaviours and ingrained habits can be even more stressful as you are changing aspects of the very core of people's identity—changing the lens through which they view the world.

3. Behaviours fall into three distinct categories: the decisions people make, the way they spend their time, and their interactions with others.

4. Leadership is a powerful stimulus and lever for changing behaviour. Your role as a leader is to reinforce, role model and be the change you want to create.

5. As a leader, you can influence the change process by having people choose to change and/or by controlling their environment.

6. Managing the messages people receive creates sustainable change. Messages come from three distinct areas: behaviours, symbols and systems.

7. A change journey can be broken into three phases: establishing the game plan (that is, planning what you are going to do); developing and leading (that is, learning how to do it best for your team); and maintaining momentum (that is, doing it better and better).

8. Self-awareness, vision, leadership, coaching, communication and composure—you will use all of these skills in the process of influencing change!

# For further exploration

## Leadership

- MJ Wheatley, *Leadership and the new science*, Berrett Koehler Publishers, San Francisco, 1999.
  A great text and easy read if you wish to know more about the application of quantum physics and organisational dynamics.
- D Ryback, *Putting emotional intelligence to work*, Butterworth Heinemann, London, 1998.
  This book will give you great practical ways to develop and practise emotional intelligence at work.
- RA Heifetz & M Linsky, *Leadership on the line*, Harvard Business Press, Boston, 2002.
  This one provides challenging but useful concepts on leadership and raising our expectations of ourselves.
- P Jackson & H Delehanty, *Sacred hoops*, Hyperion, New York, 1995.
  For the sports-minded, this book has some great examples of real team interventions.

## Coaching and empowerment

- P Block, *The empowered manager*, Jossey-Bass, San Francisco, 1987.
  A great 'how to' book.
- R Kegan, *In over our heads*, Harvard University Press, Boston, 1994.
  The author's deep reflection on the natural state of complexity that we all live in and his thoeries on cognitive complexity.
- WC Byham, *Zapp! The power of enlightenment*, Ballantine Publishing Group, New York, 1998.
  A short though great story of empowerment.
- AR Hochschild, *The managed heart*, University of California Press, California, 1983.
  An analysis of the ethical and moral implication of businesses saying they have the right to the hearts and minds of their employees.

## Communication

- H Cornelius, *The gentle revolution*, Simon & Schuster, Sydney, 1998.

A fabulous book on communication between the genders.
- GR Sullivan & MV Harper, *Hope is not a method*, Times Books, USA, 1996.
A practical book on how to build hope and pride, this refers to a command control culture (should you find that important to your situation)
- J Hawley, *Reawakening the spirit in work*, Berrett Koehler Publishers, San Francisco, 1993.
A solid semi-spiritual approach to providing more spirit and meaning at work.

*Teamwork*
- JR Katzenbach & DK Smith, *The wisdom of teams*, Harvard Business School Press, Boston, 1993.
A solid reference guide that describes different types of teams and the various developmental stages they go through.

# Notes

1 D Williams, 'Human responses to change', *Futures*, vol. 31, no. 6, August 1999, pp. 601–16.
2 E Shinseki, as quoted in T Peters, *Re-imagine! Business excellence in a disruptive age*, Dorling Kindersley, London, 2003.
3 C Taylor, *Walking the talk*, Random House, London, 2005.
4 RW Emerson, *Letters and social aims*, University Press of the Pacific, USA, 2001.
5 C Taylor, 2005 (see note 3).
6 C Taylor, 2005 (see note 3).
7 Sun Tzu, *The art of war*, Oxford University Press, Oxford, 1963.
8 RD Duncan & EJ Pinegar, *Leadership for saints*, Covenant Communications, Utah, 2002.
9 J Collins & I Porras, *Built to last: successful habits of visionary companies*, Random House Business Books, London, 2000.
10 J Collins, *Good to great: why some companies make the leap and others don't*, Random House Business Books, London, 2001.
11 R Slater, & J Welch, *Jack Welch and the GE way: management insights and leadership secrets of the legendary CEO*, McGraw-Hill, 1999.

**12** AR Hochschild, *The managed heart*, University of California Press, California, 1983.
**13** N Banks, *The golden thread*, Lucis Press, London, 1967.
**14** RM Kanter, *Change masters*, Simon & Schuster, New York, 1983.

# INFLUENCING FUNDAMENTAL CHANGE     8

Phil Harker

Introduction

Influence: learning to see things differently

The deep structure of human behaviour

   'You need to change the way you behave (or else!)'

   'You need a change of attitude'

   'We need to agree on our values'

   'We all need to see and understand our assumptions more clearly'

   'Maybe we need to take a closer look at what drives us'

On influencing the paradigm shift from fear to love

The role of the leader in influencing change

Conclusion

For further exploration

Acknowledgments

Notes

# About the author

Phil Harker, MA, PhD, FAIM

Phil Harker has spent the last 30 years lecturing and practising in the twin fields of organisational and clinical psychology. He has worked as an academic at the University of Queensland, the Queensland University of Technology and Griffith University, and as a consultant to a wide range of government departments and private enterprises in Australia and New Zealand. Clients have included the Australian Institute of Management, Telstra, Comalco, Royal Brisbane Hospital, Criminal Justice Commission, Queensland Fire and Rescue Service, Queensland Ambulance Service, and the electricity generation industry in Queensland and New South Wales. At the same time, he has also conducted a practice in clinical psychology and a personal counselling service, with over two thousand clients from business, educational and family settings.

Phil is a co-author, with Ted Scott, of the popular books *Humanity at work* (Phil Harker & Associates, 1997) and *The myth of nine to five: work, workplaces and workplace relationships* (Universal, 2002). *AFR Boss* magazine included this latter book in its list of the top ten management texts reviewed during 2002.

Phil Harker can be contacted at <philharker@yahoo.com.au>.

# Executive summary

Organisational change programs put great pressure on employees to 'translate' new ideas into their daily routine. When individual employees espouse the new ideas, they gain approval and favourable attention from the leadership team. However, as many writers have pointed out, all too often there is no long-term or fundamental change in that person's core behaviour. Fervent espousal of the new way of working does not necessarily reflect any real change in the deep structure of the employee's thinking.

If a program of organisational learning and change is to be successful, leaders must ensure that their espoused values are fully consistent with their more deeply held assumptions regarding human nature. The best way for leaders to do this is to themselves become *deep-structure learner*s. That is, as unsettling as it may first appear to be, they need to investigate their implicit assumptions, even down to the core motive that drives their unconscious decision making—fear (individualistic self-preservation) versus love (collective wellbeing).

By becoming deep-structure learners, leaders will have little need to force-feed employees by constantly preaching about the new values. They will naturally demonstrate or model the values, both consciously and unconsciously, during the normal stresses and strains of day-to-day business operations and interpersonal relationships. In other words, effective leaders become living examples of the new culture and in so doing 'set the tone' for a more natural learning process.

## Introduction

Bring to mind some event or occurrence in your present situation or in your past, and think about *the meaning it has*. Just take a few moments to ponder on that.

You probably found that fairly easy to do—yes? Well, if you did, you really didn't understand the task that I gave you. You see, my words were very precise. I asked you to ponder on the meaning it *has*, not the meaning you *gave* it. There is a big difference between the two.

The meaning that we each *give* to the world is based on our individually learned assumptions and beliefs. That meaning becomes our personal 'interpretive filter', and ultimately determines how each of us reacts and interacts with our world—materially, socially, psychologically and spiritually.

This chapter addresses how a leader—at any level and in any setting—can influence, for better or worse, the interpretive filters of followers and thereby work towards changing followers' deeper core motives, implicit beliefs and assumptions.

Leaders must also be aware of the implicit assumptions that may be deeply embedded in *their own thinking*. These assumptions can and will have a pervasive influence—for good or ill—first, on how they interpret their world, and second, on the 'tone' they set for their organisation's culture. These implicit assumptions can help or hinder leaders in their efforts to facilitate fundamental, deep-level change.

## Influence: learning to see things differently

What is influence? Some have defined it as 'the ability to create or change the behaviour, attitudes and beliefs of others'. My approach to influence and, in particular, influence in a leadership setting, is somewhat different. Instead of focusing on getting others to *do things differently*, my approach is about all parties *seeing things differently*. First, the leader learns to see things differently; then, through example and dialogue, the leader fosters an environment where others are enabled and encouraged to also see things differently.

It seems to me that, when leaders have difficulty managing others or influencing them to learn new ways, it is because their attempts to do so are based on the motives and assumptions they learned in childhood, which may not reflect how things actually are. The organisational learning process, as I understand it, is not a top-down one, proceeding from superior to inferior. It is a joint growth process in which all parties participate in a collective journey to discover how things really are, as opposed to how leaders wish people and things to be in order to fit in with their own misunderstandings and assumptions.

The most effective and long-lasting influence that leaders can have will arise from changes that occur at both the conscious and subconscious levels for both leaders and followers, as together they grow and develop on a personal level. This form of deep influence is an *educational* process, helping all involved to learn and change by seeing things collectively and in a new way.

Educational influence can be either positive or negative, and can contribute to the betterment or detriment of both individual and organisational life. An organisation's educational curriculum goes far beyond the explicit curriculum of the staff training program. It includes the 'hidden' implicit beliefs and assumptions that exist within the organisation. Of the two, the hidden curriculum will have the greatest influence on the long-term effectiveness of change initiatives and the inculcation of new beliefs and assumptions into the minds of employees.

Leaders who fail to understand the subtleties of the levels in the education process (explicit and implicit; deliberate and involuntary) are likely to end up with serious contradictions between the messages they wish to convey and those that employees actually receive. When 'espoused theory' is not consistent with 'theories in use', to use the well-known terms of Chris Argyris,[1] the contradictions lead to credibility gaps that contribute to employee cynicism, defeat the education process and diminish leadership influence.

## The deep structure of human behaviour

In order to describe the interlinked levels of the change process, I will relate the story of how my understanding of the process of behavioural change evolved. This story reveals how my thinking has changed over the past 40-plus years and the title of each section—a simple statement—is a simplified reflection of my own beliefs at the time. I believe that my progress also reflects the evolution of management's attempts to change organisational culture and employee beliefs, motivations and behaviour.

Figure 8.1 provides a model of the underpinnings or deep structure of human behaviour, and also offers a diagrammatic summary of the successive steps in my story. Note that the 'arrow of influence' in the model goes from depth to surface (that is, each successive level in the model is highly influenced by what lies beneath it). However, with respect to the steps in my own journey, the path of understanding has been in the reverse direction (working down from manifest behaviour).

Another characteristic of the model, in terms of its implications for the change process, is that as you go down successive steps in the model two things become very apparent:
- The deeper you go into the deep structure of human behaviour, the more difficult it is to 'see' and understand what

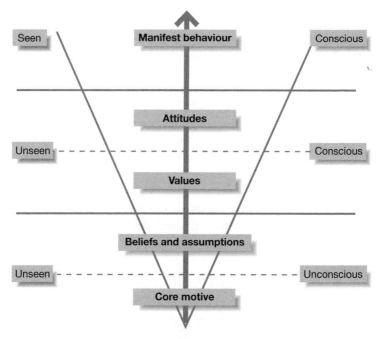

Figure 8.1 The underpinnings of human behaviour[2]

is really going on at that level and the more difficult, and perhaps even more psychologically 'painful', will be the process of adjustment and change.
- On the other hand—and this should encourage leaders to persevere with the process even if it be a little unsettling—the deeper in the structure that change occurs, the more comprehensive will be the coverage of the newly clarified perception and the more effective, satisfying and long-lasting will be the benefits of the natural change that occurs as a result of such a change in perception and interpretation.

## 'You need to change the way you behave (or else!)'

My journey begins in my pre-university days. At that time I unquestioningly believed that the voluntary behaviour of each human being was directly governed by his or her own separate and autonomous mind. I believed that, if controlling environmental factors were not evident, then it was only reasonable that people should be held directly and culpably responsible for their behaviour. Furthermore, I held this belief despite the rather obvious fact that neither I nor anyone else chooses the conditions of his or her birth or circumstances.

My attribution of deliberate, conscious intent to human behaviour led to feelings of pride, guilt, adulation or blame, depending upon whether my behaviour or that of others was evaluated to be worthy or unworthy of merit.

I believed that an individual's behaviour was under their conscious control. So my responses in social settings were based on the view that 'if you want to get along with others or get ahead in life you should just change your behaviour'. Or perhaps more accurately: 'If you change your behaviour *appropriately* you will be rewarded with approval and all that goes along with such approval, but if you don't change your behaviour appropriately, then you will be punished with disapproval and all that goes along with such disapproval. So if you don't change, you must be either stubborn, bad or just plain stupid!'

Of course, there was little question regarding whose definitions of *appropriate* behaviours were correct—mine and those of the social groups to which I belonged or identified with.

Consequently, I viewed with a certain amount of scorn or pity anyone who was outside the circle of acceptance.

Within the social groupings to which I belonged, there were two persuasive, socialising forces:
- *comparative*: 'I want to be like them'
- *normative*: 'I fear their disapproval'.

These two forces effectively produced a strong degree of conformity of behaviour amongst group members.

For most of us, group membership is largely voluntary prior to undertaking paid employment, and the benefits of such membership are mostly related to the intrinsic satisfaction and joy of the social involvement itself. Within such voluntary groups, the comparative socialising force ('I want to be like them') is the strongest, and so there is a high degree of group cohesion.

Between high school and university, I spent a couple of years as a farm and factory labourer. My understanding of human behaviour didn't change, but what did become obvious was that the balance of persuasive social forces had shifted towards the normative ('I fear their disapproval'). This was fostered by the management team, who held considerable power through potential administration of rewards (money, interesting work and career advancement) and punishments (less money, dull work and a more stagnant future). However, the social forces within employee subgroups were often the direct opposite. This was the situation:
- Management team—strong normative forces but weak comparative forces.
- Employee subgroups—strong comparative forces and less obvious normative forces.

In this 'us and them' situation, they (management) invented cunning little control games, so we (the employees) invented cunning little avoidance games. Of course, management's crude indoctrination efforts were only effective if we wanted to move up the organisational ladder. In this case, we allowed ourselves to be more persuaded by the comparative socialising forces of the employer's management team, while still convincing ourselves that we were doing so of our own free will!

Up to this stage, my notion of individual free will and self-determination was unquestioned. Hence, when I was persuaded by the group it was obvious to me that 'I chose to be persuaded', and when I was not persuaded by the group then it was equally obvious that 'I chose not to be persuaded'. *I was running my life.* Within the more obvious constraints imposed by my environment I, like anyone else, was in direct control of my thoughts, decisions, and behaviours as I responded to the varying circumstances of my world. *I was king*—or so I thought!

## 'You need a change of attitude'

In 1967, I commenced studies at the University of New South Wales and soon discovered that my illusions of personal autonomy and self-control were apparently totally false. In philosophy I learned about *determinism* (that is, that all events, including human action, are caused by events external to the will). In psychology, I learned about *behaviourism* (that is, that human behaviour is determined by conditioning, rather than thoughts and feelings). I studied the work of BF Skinner, the father of modern behaviourism. His deterministic process seemed to explain how behaviour occurred, but completely wiped out any notion of human freedom or responsibility in an individual's thinking.

I revolted against what I saw as the pointlessness of scientific determinism and came up with a comfortable rebuttal to the determinist's position. If determinism is a *true* model of reality, then either my belief or my disbelief in determinism would be equally determined (so I wouldn't have a choice in the matter anyway). If determinism is *not true* and I believe it to be a true model of reality then I am an idiot! Ergo, the only sensible position to take was that determinism was *not true*, even if such a position could not as yet be fully explained.

Armed with this smug little argument against determinism I retreated into the comfortable shelter of *rationalist humanism*. I found solace in its naïve assumption that an individual's conscious mind somehow possesses the direct ability to organise its own cognitive content, independent of its developmental history. In other words, that my thinking was my own personal creation and was not simply controlled by the impersonal forces that produced me (more of this later).

Temporarily back on track again, I discovered in the social psychology domain the wonderful role that *attitudes* play in reducing the infinite diversity and complexity of day-to-day life to cognitively digestible bite-sized chunks. I also discovered that changing behaviour is as easy as ABC!

Most social psychologists accept that any attitude has three essential components:
- *affective*: emotional ('I feel so strongly about . . .')
- *cognitive*: thoughts and ideas ('this company's disregard of fundamental safety issues . . .')
- *behavioural*: actions ('that I am seeking employment elsewhere.').

It appears that almost all our voluntary behavioural responses to the many stimuli that we experience in daily life actually came from: a *tendency to act* (behavioural component) in accordance with a *cluster of thoughts and ideas* (cognitive component)—whether they are objectively right or wrong—held in place by a *set of emotional attachments* (affective component). I also found that the less verifiable the cognitive component, the stronger the emotional component and vice versa. In other words, it seems that we are most emotionally attached to the ideas that we can least sustain!

Was the mind not rational after all?

Enter the 'power of persuasion' and the reams of material to be found in every textbook in the field of social or organisational psychology that deals with attitude development and attitude change. I had discovered the way to change the world.
- Feed people accurate and timely information.
- Make sure that there is enough fire in the proposition to stimulate their emotional attachment to the new ideas.
- Get them to participate in a simple activity that demonstrates the new ideas in practice in order to lock in the emotional attachment through self-confirmation.

It was that easy—or so it seemed! But if that was the case, why were people so resistant to having their attitudes 'readjusted'?

For example, in almost every organisation I have consulted with, at some point a member of staff will state, with nods of agreement from others, that 'there is poor communication around here' or that 'people don't work as an effective team'. And yet, these same organisations have inevitably (often repeatedly) invested money, time, effort and training to try and rectify these problems. But the situation does not improve.

I began to suspect that there was more to the story than I had found so far.

### 'We need to agree on our values'

The 1970s turn into the 1980s. That was the time of the rise in emphasis on social and organisational ethics. I discovered that people didn't want to have their attitudes changed by those whose values they perceived to be out of alignment with their own.

Enter the era of 'values clarification' workshops and 'values driven' leadership. This was a real plus in the organisational education process. It moved the focus of attention one level deeper into the structural underpinnings of human behaviour— from 'you (employees) have bad attitudes and we (management) need to work on changing your attitudes' to 'maybe we can find some common values that underpin our attitudes'. This was the very beginning of the concept that everyone is both a teacher and a learner at the same time (more of this later).

During this period, I was working as an academic, organisational consultant and clinician. I discovered that it was not very difficult to move people to a position where they could agree on values. Why? Because they were agreeing on how they wished to be treated and how they wished their world to operate. They wished, of course, to be treated with respect, dignity and trust; to have honest communication; and to work in a safe and secure environment where people valued their intellectual and material contributions, and where there was respect for the customers and all the other stakeholders.

I found that there was a good deal of support for, and justification of, agreed values. However, there was very little clarification of *why* these values were agreed upon, and what dynamic processes would magically transform 'espoused values' (what you *say* you value) into 'values-in-use' (what your actions *demonstrate* your real values to be).

In many organisations, there seemed to be an assumption that if values had been agreed upon, then it was only natural that people would live by those values. After all, aren't human beings rational creatures that, having honestly and sincerely agreed upon a set of values, would then naturally put them into operation?

Unfortunately, this wasn't the case and the *credibility gap* between espoused values and values-in-use created a degree of scepticism and cynicism regarding people's sincerity. This made management's job even more difficult.

To help with the process of interpretation and implementation, some organisations took the extra step of having the employee–management teams spell out, in behavioural terms, what they would expect to see happening or not happening if the agreed values were actually in use. This, of course, only tended to increase the normative pressure for behavioural conformity and had little long-term effect on the intrinsic motivation towards real change.

In many instances, including the following case study, the credibility gap problem had less to do with a lack of sincerity and more to do with a lack of understanding of the necessary underpinnings of the values themselves.

> In the early 1980s I was working as a consultant with a management team in a large national telecommunications company, and was asked by one of the senior managers to undertake some team development work with the staff who reported immediately to him. On first meeting with him, I asked him to give me something to read that spelled out his management philosophy. He looked a little confused, but left the room and returned with the team's mission statement. I explained that this was a statement of the intended focus for the team in terms of its targets and goals for the next year or so. Instead, what I needed was a statement regarding how he intended to manage the human side of that process, and the underlying philosophy that supported the process.
>
> The manager thought for a moment, and then turned several pages into the document and pointed to a heading that read 'Values statement'. Under this heading was the phrase, 'We believe in people', followed by a list of the usual corollaries—trust, openness, honesty and so on.
>
> I found this interesting, because I had heard the current joke doing the rounds in the organisation: 'Question: What's the definition of optimism? Answer: A

manager who brings his lunch to work!' Why was this the current joke? Because there had been a spate of occurrences where a manager had arrived in the morning and, without warning, been met at the front door of the building by security staff, barred from entering the building, and given a walking ticket along with a box of any personal contents from his or her desk (after someone else had sorted through them).

Consequently, this was a fear driven organisation, and yet the senior managers were attempting to establish the type of team-based working culture that could only operate effectively in an environment where fear was not the prime motivating force.

The senior manager also said that he hoped that, through my work with his team, I would be able to 'fix up a few of the troublemakers' who didn't agree with the way he managed the team (and here was one manifestation of his real values-in-use).

The manager and his team had espoused agreement on their joint values, and this agreement seemed quite genuine and sincere, at least at the level of their conscious awareness, but for some reason these values were not acting as the key drivers of team behaviour.

The problem with this team, and many others like it, did not seem to reside at the conscious level. The question formulating in my mind at the time was: If you do not doubt the sincerity of people's belief in their expressed values, and if you assume that sincere people don't operate according to malicious intent or duplicity at the level of their conscious awareness, then could it be that something was going on at the subconscious level that gave rise to the gap between espoused values and values-in-use?

### 'We all need to see and understand our assumptions more clearly'

The senior manager in my previous case study didn't understand that his own *implicit assumptions and beliefs* regarding human nature and human motivation (as revealed by his comments about 'troublemakers') contradicted and undermined his *explicitly espoused values* ('we believe in our people' and so on). Why was this so?

In the early 1980s I happened to read the second edition of Thomas S Kuhn's *The structure of scientific revolutions*[3] and it set off a revolution in my own thinking. It completely changed the way I regarded the nature of education and learning in organisations and in general.

According to Kuhn, the basic beliefs and assumptions inherent in a researcher's world view or *paradigm* made strict objectivity in the observation and interpretation of data nearly impossible (and this included not only the hard data of objective science but also the soft data of our everyday experience of physical and social life). Furthermore, Kuhn asserted that the crucial points in the development of new scientific knowledge came when an investigator looked at familiar data through an *entirely new set of paradigm glasses.*

This is illustrated in a story related by the Australian cosmologist, Paul Davies.[4] While he was a student of theoretical physics, he had the opportunity to ask a question of the famous physicist, David Bohm, regarding the origin of the random-phase assumption. Davies said: 'To my astonishment and dismay, Bohm merely shrugged, and muttered: "Who knows?"' To which Davies protested: 'But you can't make much progress in physics without making that assumption.' Bohm replied: 'In my opinion, progress in science is usually made by *dropping* assumptions!'

Kuhn argued that *paradigm leaps* came about only when the investigator dropped an existing set of assumptions as a result of deeper subjective and intuitive processes. The internal pressure out of which a new paradigm is born—or adopted—comes when the old world view no longer provides adequate explanations of experience, or is no longer able to answer the questions that arise from an exploration of the domain of experience that the old paradigm addressed. In other words, a new paradigm is born out of frustration.

A paradigm is meant to allow an answer to the question: 'Why?'—'Why is this not working?' or 'Why does this happen or not happen?' When the old paradigm cannot be used to answer such questions, then it may be time to look for a more adequate set of explanatory assumptions. What once was 'assumed' to be true about the nature of reality needs to be readdressed at the first-principles level. Time for a new way of 'seeing'.

Kuhn's thesis was a wake-up call for me. If this was true of the physical sciences, where there was reasonable agreement amongst scientists regarding the fundamental assumptions about the nature of physical reality through which they interpreted their data, it was far more true of the social sciences, where there had never been agreement about even the most basic assumptions regarding human freedom and responsibility—assumptions that lay at the very core of any interpretation of personal and interpersonal behaviour.

In the early 1960s, organisational theorists in Australia had extolled the virtues of participative work designs (that is, greater employee participation in both the short- and long-term decisions that determined their life on the job). But, despite the wealth of literature and the quality of discussion, very few organisations seemed to be willing to make more than token changes to their thinking. This was because the successful implementation of such a program depended upon the presence in the organisation of key individuals in senior management positions who understood the underlying theoretical foundations of this type of program. Such individuals had, in Kuhn's terms, made a paradigm shift and 'gone native' in their thinking and understanding about human beings at work. Such people, according to Kuhn, would have come to the point where they were 'thinking and working in, not simply translating out of, a language that was previously foreign'.[5]

Unfortunately, many of the Australian managers who were attracted to the progressive concepts of worker participation during the height of the movement in the 1970s and 1980s didn't make the 'going native' transition. Deep down they really believed that only a special class of employees—those destined to become managers—were actually capable of being motivated, responsible people. And so, after initial enthusiasm, they returned to more mechanistic and legalistic control systems of organisation that were consistent with their unchanged paradigms about human nature.

Why did this happen? After all, we are all rational beings who do that which we have good reason to do—aren't we?

By the mid-1980s it was becoming more and more obvious to me that the opposite is true. We are not essentially rational beings at all. Rather, we are *rationalising* beings—we are all 'spin-doctors' regarding our own behaviour. Although we may sometimes have difficulty doing the things we have good reason to do, or have difficulty living up to the ideals and values we espouse, we generally have very little difficulty providing rational reasons for what we end up doing.

It appears that we don't know the *real* reasons why we do things. This is because the causes of our actions lie not in the conscious mind, but at the *deeper, subconscious level* that acts as the storehouse of our more implicit beliefs, assumptions and theories about why things are the way they are. When we explain why we do things, we are not providing the real reasons. We are explaining our behaviour in terms of our 'personal theory' of behaviour.

We are, in a sense, all behavioural scientists who learned the essentials of our science in our earliest childhood. We think in terms of what our naïve mind perceived to be true, or in terms of the psychological myths or unquestioned beliefs handed down to us, from generation to generation, by others who also learned them in the same naïve fashion.

Around the same time, from experiences and lessons I learned in the clinical work setting, it became more obvious to me that, because these myths *mostly* work effectively enough to provide a modicum of social harmony, they are rarely questioned. It became apparent that it generally takes a catastrophic failure of the old paradigm before there is even a possibility of a new paradigm taking its place. And when the old paradigm catastrophically fails without a new paradigm being available to reinterpret and give new meaning to the important data of a person's life, it sometimes results in emotional or physical suicide.

I was coming to realise that what determines the effectiveness of our day-to-day interactions with others within organisations and other social systems is not our espoused values, or how we consciously think we *should* or *should not* behave, or even what we think would be best for us or for those around us. Rather, we relate to our world in terms of a highly interactive combination of the following:

**1** The *core motive* at the driving centre of our life. This acts as an interpretive filter that determines the meaning we give to every person or event that could impact upon our personal wellbeing.

*The mind cannot see what the heart cannot afford to accept.*[6]

**2** Our deeply held *implicit assumptions*, which we have been learning since early childhood and that provide the explanations as to *why* we act and feel the way we do.

*Only the theory decides what one can observe.*[7]

And this brings me back to the nature of human choice and free will.

Though strongly resisted by my ego and the 'sense' that I was my own personal creation, it became patently obvious to me that we have no individual free will regarding the creation of any specific cognitive content that we observe arising in our conscious minds. That all comes from the personally unchosen circumstances of our genetic, biological and social histories. For example, I challenge you to think of one single thought that is not in some way connected to your past! If you can do so at all, then there should be no limit to your capacity to create your own cognitive content, in which case you should be able to speak in any language and on any topic. And yet, we still feel *as if* we have a free and autonomous mind.

Neither do we have free will regarding the cognitive *decision-making* activity that evaluates that content according to criteria that we also obtained from our past. My students at the university where I was teaching at the time would often protest that they were not just products of their past; that they evaluated their experience and their past and gave more value to some aspects of that experience than others and replaced things that they did not like. Yes, I would reply, but what criterion did you use for this evaluation? Where did you get it from, other than from that same unchosen experience pool that you are attempting to evaluate? I was not being difficult or facetious, and I really did want them to investigate this question. It appeared to be getting near to the centre of the personal and interpersonal adjustment problems that all individuals, social groups, organisations and society in general had to face on a daily basis. And it was also becoming obvious that 'lack of intellectual ability' or 'genuine desire for a solution' were not the essential blockages that stood in the way to a solution to this fundamental problem.

So if there is no free will in these two areas (that is, either in the creation of conscious content or in the conscious evaluation of that content which does appear in the arena of your own mind), can it be found somewhere else? This is the question that had bothered me for over 30 years, because a satisfactory answer would help resolve the most pressing unresolved question in philosophy and psychology: 'Who am I and how do I rise above the unchosen circumstances of my unchosen life and do so in a fashion that does not prevent others from doing the same?'

### 'Maybe we need to take a closer look at what drives us'

In the late 1980s I took a closer look at Clark L Hull's simple but eloquent formula for human behaviour that had been presented in my Psychology 101 class all those years ago: Behaviour $=f$(drive × direction).[8] That is, *behaviour* is a function of the interaction between *drive* (core motive) and *direction* (the shaping potentials inherent in our present circumstances and past history).

At the same time I stumbled across an interesting quote from Albert Einstein:

> *Everyone has two choices. We're either full of love . . . or full of fear.*[9]

It seemed to me that when Einstein contrasted 'fear' and 'love', what he had in mind was that *fear* motivates the decision-making mind to view others as objects to be gained from or protected against; and *love* recognises the commonality of life and motivates the mind towards collective wellbeing.

The connection between Hull's formula and Einstein's 'choice' was suddenly apparent to me. Previously, I had always looked for human autonomy and responsibility on the 'direction' side of Clark's formula, based on the assumption that the 'drive' would *always* be self-preserving fear. It now occurred to me that the real choice that allows us to influence, even though indirectly, the ongoing process of decision making in our lives is a choice between two fundamentally opposed drives or core motives:

- *fear*—core motive oriented towards individualised self-preservation

- *love*—core motive oriented towards collective wellbeing and the transcendence of individualised self-preservation.

Nothing in our world comes with its meaning attached. We give everything its meaning, and the meaning we give depends upon which of the two core motives (love or fear) drives the machinery of our thinking and decision-making processes. This is the one area where we may truly have free will and choice in our lives—a choice that influences every significant decision we make as we respond to the unchosen circumstances of our world. And the dynamic struggle between the motive forces of 'fear' (individualised self-preservation) and 'love' (collective wellbeing) inherent in the collective process ultimately determines the success or failure of all our collective systems of human activity.

What became clear to me, however, was that the choice that determines the core motive or drive in the behaviour equation was not in any sense a *conscious* decision made at the cognitive level of our thinking. In other words, it was not one that an individual could make or refrain from making simply by deciding to do so or not do so at some particular point in time—no matter how good their conscious reasons for doing so, or how much they desired it from the motive of their existing paradigm! Rather, it is more akin to a shift at the very core of your being (similar to the paradigm shift described by Thomas Kuhn and which I will explain more fully).

Furthermore, it is this fundamental shift that *permits* the adoption of new beliefs and assumptions. The mind cannot understand what the existing paradigm does not permit. In other words, any conscious attempt to understand the assumptions inherent in some new paradigm *in terms of the assumptions of the old paradigm it is meant to replace* is going to be met with frustration and failure. The change process that allows a new paradigm to enter is very different and it is this difference that lifts education above mere training.

The whole structure of our thinking and learning is dependent upon the orientation of our core motive. What blocks a new paradigm from entering is the fear that arises when an old and cherished paradigm, one that has previously served to reduced the fear of a chaotic and unpredictable world, is being challenged.

All fear is essentially a fear of 'the unknown' (that is, fear of not knowing how to react in situations that may unsettle our predictable world).[10] Hence, fear is an almost impenetrable barrier to the adoption of new paradigms, especially if they threaten the implicit belief systems that currently protect us against the possibility of 'not knowing' how to relate to our world. For example, even though managers may sincerely agree to and espouse more effective ways of relating to workers, if fear is the underlying core motive of those managers, then they will not 'go native' in their thinking. Fear of the unknown will prevent them.

Incompatible core motives will result in inconsistency between the various levels of learning and will hinder the development of any long-term organisational cultural change.

The success of any leadership attempt at fostering a paradigm shift in employee core motive will be highly influenced by the motivational climate fostered by the leadership team (who set the tone for the organisation as a whole). For example, in an organisation promoting team-based, collective wellbeing, if the leaders are driven by fear (and therefore have not 'gone native' in their own thinking; in their implicit beliefs and assumptions), then it is highly unlikely that they will be able to set the tone necessary to encourage employees to move beyond individual self-preserving fear towards full involvement. Indeed, if employees *believe* (rightly or wrongly) that fear is the predominant management philosophy, then fear will become the controlling dynamic.

In addition, according to renowned organisational psychologist Edgar Schein, heightened learning anxiety (which is driven by fear—fear of failure, not knowing what to do, looking like a fool, losing the safety of old habits, and being seen as a deviant from established group norms) also inhibits learning. Although, paradoxically, Schein goes on to say that organisational learning rarely takes place where there is little or no survival anxiety—'the horrible realisation that, in order to make it, you're going to have to change'.[11]

It is certainly not hard to see why W Edwards Deming always felt that 'drive out fear' was the most important of his famous fourteen points for good leadership for Total Quality Management.[12]

## On influencing the paradigm shift from fear to love

Before attempting to describe more clearly the nature of this Kuhnian-type choice (that is, one that is more akin to a paradigm shift than a conscious decision) it is important to point out a very real limitation to such a process.

Given that a paradigm shift is a change in 'seeing' that results in a change in 'thinking'—rather than the other way around—any description of such a change in orientation that is offered in purely cognitive or language-based terms is in danger of leaving the impression that the choice is essentially cognitive and conscious rather than experiential and 'conversion-like'. Hence, it must be recognised that any description will be inadequate that describes the actual 'metaphysical choice' or 'paradigm shift' that confronts the individual. The term 'metaphysical' is used to describe the choice for the obvious reason that physical systems operate by physical laws and are not open to any notion of genuine freedom. Hence, any such choice—if one exists at all—must, of necessity, be described as metaphysical and therefore as 'mystical'.

When a paradigm shift occurs, the whole interpretive frame of reference encompassing that set of data changes. As Kuhn stated, such a change occurs 'all at once (though not necessarily in an instant) or not at all'.[13]

Paradigm shifts in the thinking of managers (or employees) regarding the nature of what it means to be human will produce a situation in organisations akin to that described by Kuhn when discussing the consequences of paradigm shifts in the thinking of scientists:

> *Practicing in different worlds, the two groups of scientists [read: 'managers' or 'employees'] see different things when they look from the same point in the same direction. Again, that is not to say they can see anything they please. Both are looking at the world, and what they look at has not changed. But in some areas they see different things, and they see them in different relations one to the other. This is why a law [read: a new 'way' of organisational management based on trust] that cannot even be demonstrated to one group . . . may occasionally seem intuitively obvious to another.*[14]

Kuhn also makes the point that members of a community who have not made the paradigm shift to the set of assumptions that underpin the 'new way' of doing things within the community may still make a valuable contribution to the operational use of the new paradigm so long as there are 'natives' already there. He suggests, however, that the effectiveness of such individuals will be dependent upon their opportunity to feed off the intrinsic understanding of the 'natives', because they themselves 'lack the constellation of mental sets which future members of the community will acquire through education'.[15]

## The role of the leader in influencing change

Organisational cultures are ultimately expressions of their embedded assumptions.[16] Or to put it another way: 'It is these unconscious, undebatable assumptions that (are) the culture of an organisation.'[17] So if a program of cultural change does not reach the *deeper levels* of employee cognitive structures, real long-term success will not eventuate. Sooner or later, values, attitudes and behaviour—the upper manifestations of culture—will revert to the old, more deeply held, unchanged assumptions.

Unfortunately, rational-economic notions regarding the freedom and intentionality of human motivation (that is, that employees will rationally choose the best path that brings them the greatest economic gain) towards behaviour change are still alive and well. They are strongly in evidence in the way many managers and leaders attempt to implement cultural change programs within their organisations.

Edgar Schein, the great 'assumption confronter' of organisational psychology, alluded to this in 2002, when he said:

> *I would like to emphasise that unless leaders become learners themselves—unless they can acknowledge their own vulnerabilities and uncertainties—then transformational learning will never take place. When leaders become genuine learners, they set a good example and help to create a psychologically safe environment for others.*[18]

Schein moves right away from the idea that organisational learning leading to long-term change is something that is done by one group of people to another group of people. Instead, the most effective way for leaders to influence others to learn to change is, to use Kuhn's terminology, to first 'go native' in their own thinking—that is, to *lead by example*.

Although it is true that no leader can influence others towards a deep-structure change in thinking *beyond* that which they themselves have personally experienced, it is also true that any leader who has personal experience of such a deep-structure paradigm shift in their own motivation—from individualistic self-preserving fear to collective wellbeing—will *inevitably* have a profound influence upon the lives of others they live and work with. Such a change, arising from both the conscious *and* subconscious levels of their thinking and decision making, will be naturally manifested in all their behaviours towards others within the sphere of their influence.

If a program of organisational learning and change is to be successful, leaders must ensure that their espoused values are fully consistent with their own more deeply held assumptions regarding human nature. The best way for leaders to do this is to become *deep-structure learners themselves*; that is, as unsettling as it may first appear to be, they need to investigate the deep-structure foundations of their own behaviour. Is their deep structure consistent to the core, or are there inconsistencies between espoused and manifest values? Any deep structure that is consistent to the core will be less likely to manifest defensive routines in the face of difficulty. In the words of the late Syd Durrington, it will be more likely 'to accept pressure without stress, frustration without defeat, failure without blame, people without condition, rejection without defeat, truth without fear'.[19]

By becoming deep-structure learners, leaders will have little need to force-feed employees by constantly preaching about the new values. They will demonstrate or model the values, both consciously and unconsciously, during the stresses and strains of day-to-day business operations and interpersonal relationships. In other words, effective leaders become living examples of the new culture and in so doing 'set the tone' for a more natural learning process.

By the way, despite my earlier comments that espoused values don't create their own behavioural reality, gaining agreement on values is a useful step in the learning path of any organisation seeking to foster a new working culture. If people at all levels agree on values, there is then a common framework for discussion about the ethical 'oughts' and 'ought nots', 'shoulds' and 'should nots' that operate at the conscious level. This will enable employees to identify more fully with the agreed behavioural norms. They can then jointly formulate self-imposed behavioural guides, checks and guards to help coordinate team action. In fact, if the behavioural norms are set by the team members themselves, they will replace the rules previously set and imposed top-down by management.

Explicit and espoused values and norms are held at the conscious level but, as previously discussed, most of our behaviour is governed and controlled by the more deeply held implicit beliefs and assumptions that reside at the subconscious level. It is for this reason that espoused values must be constantly revisited and reaffirmed at all levels of the organisation, to ensure that they are effectively aligned with employees' deeper core motives, implicit beliefs and assumptions.

## Conclusion

Central to this discussion has been the assertion that the choice between fear (core motive of self-preservation) and love (core motive of collective wellbeing) is not a conscious decision in relation to any externalised moral code, organisational rules or espoused group values. Rather, it involves a fundamental shift in the interpretive filter through which an individual views his or her relationship to others within their social world.

Organisational change programs put great pressure on employees to 'translate' new ideas into their daily routine. When individual employees espouse the new ideas, they gain approval and favourable attention from the leadership team. However, as many writers have pointed out, all too often there is no long-term change in the person's natural behaviour. Fervent espousal of the new way of working does not necessarily reflect any real change in attitude or perception by the employee.

For real long-term change to be consistent at all levels in the deep structure of our behaviour, a fundamental paradigm shift *may* need to occur at the 'metaphysical' core of our very humanity. We may need to experience a shift in the deepest driving motivation of our life—from fear-driven individualistic self-preservation to a deep sense of collective wellbeing, where the value of your life is not placed above that of others (or, as Einstein expressed it, from *fear* to *love*). And would it not be true, at least in theory, that this is what social and organisational life is really all about? When this happens, we may discover, as Kuhn says, 'the scales falling from the eyes'.[20] Though such a paradigm shift is most likely to occur as a response to catastrophic failure of your old paradigm, I believe it can also occur simply because you pursue it as the essential goal of your life.

One of my early teachers used to say: 'What gets your mind, gets you'. Although on the one hand we seem to be witnessing a rising tide of fear that captivates the minds of many people in the world, it is also the case that we are witnessing a growing discussion relating to the deep-structure questions of meaning and spirituality, and the importance of these questions as they impact on day-to-day life. It is perhaps not surprising, given that the greatest proportion of our waking lives is spent in workplace settings, that this discussion seems to be taking place in work-related conferences and seminars rather than in the more traditional religious and political settings.

Like the theme of the cult movie *The matrix*, we are faced with a stark choice between two pills—a blue pill and a red pill. We can take the blue pill and go back to sleep and wake up to remember none of this. Or we can take the red pill and make the difficult journey of discovery to find out just how deep the 'rabbit hole' of control goes and what we can do about it. Just as Morpheus told Neo—this may be our last chance to take the red pill!

## Challenges for leaders wishing to influence fundamental change

*In this chapter I have argued that any long-term culture shift and fundamental change is more likely to be effective if it is supported by leaders who have been willing to honestly explore the deep structure of their own thinking and motivation and thereby become exemplars of the change process they espouse.*

*The late Syd Durrington[21] proposed some simple challenges or 'tests' for leaders, based on situations they (and most other people) often face. They could be considered to be important tests of robust psychological maturity.*

*These challenges are roughly graded in difficulty. They are all difficult. At the emotional level they are truly challenging. None can be met without detachment—but with indifference, none of them is a test at all.*

1 *To accept pressure without distress*
   Pressure stimulates creative action only if it is not invalidated by stress.

2 *To accept frustration without defeat*
   Frustration is inevitable and should be accepted calmly and with humour, if possible. Do not get emotionally involved or stressed. On the contrary, choose and take effective action and accept the consequences.

3 *To accept failure without blame*
   Blame reinforces failure. There will always be some failures. Accept them and use them as learning points for future action. The attribution of blame and deliberate intent to others for their failures also leads to an inability to be of value to them. It reinforces their failure.

4 *To accept people without condition*
   Do not attempt to manipulate people to satisfy your own imagined emotional needs. This does not mean you must accept whatever people do. However, you should at all times evaluate ideas and contributions and not people.

5 *To accept rejection without resentment*
   Clearly, your ideas will be rejected sometimes. It is even tougher to accept rejection of yourself, but this too will be experienced as a reaction from 'fearful' people. In every situation there is an opportunity.

> 6 *To accept truth* without *fear*
> This is the toughest test of all. History has proved this beyond the slightest shadow of a doubt. It is very easy and noble to assert, but something else to actually do.

## For further exploration

- DL Coutu, 'The anxiety of learning', *Harvard Business Review*, vol. 80, March 2002, pp. 100–6.
  This article features an interview between Diane Coutu and the organisational psychologist Edgar Schein, in which Schein discusses how elevated learning anxiety, when associated with organisational learning, hinders the development of the learning process.
- TS Kuhn, *The structure of scientific revolutions*, 2nd edn, University of Chicago Press, Chicago, 1970.
  I highly recommend this classic. In just over two hundred pages it can change your whole thinking about education that goes beyond training. It did for me. You will also realise why 'arguments' between well meaning people are mostly just cross-paradigm discussions (each person correct within the limits of his or her own paradigm, but unable to see that another paradigm may exist). These arguments are impossible to resolve until a paradigm shift occurs—and it never occurs by force of logical argument or by the power of emotive pressure!
- T Scott & P Harker, *The myth of nine to five: work, workplaces and workplace relationships*, Universal, Sydney, 2002.
  Ted Scott, founding CEO of the multi-awarded Stanwell Corporation, and I wrote this book after many years of working together as organisational business leader and innovator and organisation consultant. It relates to our attempts to come to grips with what is really happening in the deep structure of any successful organisational change or development process and expands many of the central ideas expressed in this brief chapter. Described by *AFR Boss* magazine as 'for the thinking manager', but 'not for the psychology-phobic'!

## Acknowledgments

I wish to acknowledge the many years of dialogue with Ted Scott on the key topics covered in this chapter, as well as his role as an exemplar of 'deep-structure' transformation and organisational leadership. I also wish to acknowledge Professor Greg Hearn, my friend and graduate studies supervisor from QUT, for his help in the early formulation, refinement and expression of my thinking on these topics.

Earlier versions of some of the material in this chapter appeared in:

- T Scott & P Harker, *Humanity at work*, Phil Harker & Associates, Brisbane, 1997.
- T Scott & P Harker, *The myth of nine to five: work, workplaces and workplace relationships*, Universal, Sydney, 2002.
- P Harker, Managerial assumptions regarding human nature, and the success or failure of organisational culture change programs, PhD thesis, Queensland University of Technology, Brisbane, 1997.

## Notes

1. C Argyris & DA Schön, *Organizational learning II*, Addison-Wesley, Reading, MA, 1996.
2. © Phil Harker & Associates Pty Ltd.
3. TS Kuhn, *The structure of scientific revolutions*, 2nd edn, University of Chicago Press, Chicago, 1970.
4. P Davies, *About time*, Viking, London, 1995, p. 199.
5. TS Kuhn, 1970 (see note 3), p. 204.
6. Albert Einstein, quoted in G Holton, 'Werner Heisenberg and Albert Einstein', *Physics Today*, vol. 53, no. 7, July 2000, p. 40.
7. Albert Einstein, quoted in G Holton, 'Werner Heisenberg and Albert Einstein', *Physics Today*, vol. 53, no. 7, July 2000, p. 40.
8. CL Hull, *Principles of behaviour*, Appleton-Century-Crofts, New York, 1943.
9. Albert Einstein, quoted in J Canfield & MJ Hansen, *Dare to win*, Berkley Books, New York, 1994, p. 77.
10. JB Peterson, *Maps of meaning: the architecture of belief*, Routledge, New York, 1999.

**11** DL Coutu, 'The anxiety of learning', *Harvard Business Review*, vol. 80, no. 3, March 2002, p. 100.
**12** WE Deming, *Out of the crisis*, MIT Press, Cambridge, Mass., 1986.
**13** TS Kuhn, 1970 (see note 3), p. 150.
**14** TS Kuhn, 1970 (see note 3), p. 150.
**15** TS Kuhn, 1970 (see note 3), p. 204
**16** For more on this concept, see the work of Edgar Schein. A full listing of his publications can be found on his MIT website at <http://web.mit.edu/scheine/www/pubs.html>.
**17** D Lewis, 'Communicating organisational culture', *Australian Journal of Communication*, vol. 19, 1992, p. 49.
**18** DL Coutu, 2002 (see note 11), p. 100.
**19** Syd Durrington was a remarkable engineer and philosopher with whom I worked in the electricity generation industry in Queensland in the latter half of the twentieth century. These few words are a very brief summary of a seminar he delivered to a group of his colleagues on 'The Tests of Maturity and Professionalism'. Used with permission.
**20** TS Kuhn, 1970 (see note 3), p. 122.
**21** See note 19.

# Index

Page numbers in **bold** print refer to main entries.

3M innovation, 172

abundance, law of, 138
affective factors, *see* emotional factors
agreed values, 235–7, 247–8
Akwari, John, 213
alliances, *see* strategic alliances
anxiety, 244
appearance, physical, 83–4
appreciation, *see* recognition
Aristotle, 30–1, 48
*Art of war* (Sun Tsu), 205
assumptions, 177–8, 237–42, *see also* beliefs
 deep-structure learning and, 227, 246
 meaning and, 228
 mental models for sizing people up, 74–5
 paradigm shifts in, 243–4, 246
attention giving, 78, 80, 89–90
 in master networking, 144–5
attitudes, 234, *see also* persuasion
 instilling, 212–15
 positive and resourceful, 87–9
attractiveness, *see* charisma; physical appearance
audience, 50–6
 for media reports, 113–14, 121–2

behaviour
 appropriate, 231–2
 conscious control of, 231–2, 234, 240–3, 248
 deep structure of, 229–44, **230**
 rationalising, not rational, 239–40
behavioural change, *see also* change processes
 assumptions and, 237–42
 attitude change, 233–5
 influencing, 196–220, 227–51
 leading, 198–203
 messages influencing, 199–203, **199–200**
 rational-economic notions and, 246
 superficial, 231–3
 values and, 235–7

behaviourism, 233
beliefs, 228, 243–4, *see also* assumptions
body management, 83–4
Bohm, David, 238
brand integrity marketing, 105–6
brand trajectory model, 101, 109–12, **112**
brands, 111, 115
Branson, Richard, 43, 102, 105, 113
bullying, 23–5
business cards, 148
business coaches, *see* coaching
business 'etiquette', 90
business leaders, *see* leadership

calmness under pressure, 216
campfires, 183–4
caring, 54
case studies
 Bill Clinton, 116–19
 Carly Fiorina, 57–60
 hammer thrower's story, 107–9
 Jack Welch, 60–1
 radio station, 150
 values credibility gap, 236–7
 Wallabies, 202
 Western Power, 122–3
categorisation (sizing people up), 74–5
category bias (labelling), 83
centre of attention, 80
change processes, 203–17, **204**, *see also* behavioural change; influence; leadership
 developing, 209–15
 maintaining momentum, 215–17
 planning, 205–9
 resistance to, 196–7
charisma, 69–97
 increasing, 77–85, 96–7
 perceivers' standards, 73–7
'charismatic clicks', 71
charity sponsorship, 142
charm, 85–94
Churchill, Winston, 72
Clinton, Bill, 55, 78–80, 89, 116–19
clothes, 84–5
coaching, 185–6, 214–15

coercive power, 20–2
cognitive factors, 234, 241, 243, 245
collaboration, 184, *see also* strategic alliances
    learning, **171**, 173–4
    collective wellbeing (love), 242–3, 245–7, 249
    commitment in alliances, 153–4
    communication, 14–15, *see also* media communication; messages
        audience for, 50–4, **52**
        coaching, 185–6
        creating safe spaces, 178–80
        during change processes, 215
        expressing convictions, 82–3
        giving recognition, 146–8
        identification and, 48
        master networking, 144–6
        media release objectives, 113–14
        Myers-Briggs style and, 51–3, **52**
        non-verbal, 55–6, 85
        positive spin, 101–32
        profiles, 57–62, 116–19
Compaq merger with HP, 57–8
comparative socialising forces, 232
competence, 12
compliant learning, 170–2, **171**
compliments (praise), 91–3
composure, 216
confidence, 86–8
connections, *see* networking
conscious control, *see* behaviour, conscious control of
contextual level spin, 103
control, soft, 46–7
cooperation, *see* strategic alliances
core motives (drive), 240, 242–4, 248, *see also* motivation
correction (direction realignment), 217
cosmetics, 85
courage (valour), 88–9
courtesy, 90–1
'creative class' (Florida), 46, 53–4
credibility, 12, 54–5
    values credibility gap, 236–7
crisis management, 119–24
'crystal balls', 206–7
cultural change, *see* organisational learning
curiosity, 88

customer service case study, 150
cyanide spill, media reports of, 121

Darwin, Charles, 78
Davies, Paul, 238
debriefing, 156
decision making, 150, 214, 241–3
deep structure of behaviour, 229–44, **230**
deep learning, 227, 246–51
dependence, 27–8
determinism, 233
devious strategies, *see* Machiavellian power
direction (component of behaviour), 242
direction, sense of, 13–14
'disruptive brands', 105
dress, 84–5
drive, *see* core motives (drive)
Dumbledore, Albus, **10**
Durrington, Syd, 247, 250–1

Eales, John, 194
educational processes, *see* organisational learning
ego, 89–90, 174–6
Einstein, Albert, 242
electric shock studies, 18–19
electricity power crisis, 122–3
emotional factors, 182–3, 212, 234
    expressing sentiment, 82–3
    facial expressions, 78–9
emotional intelligence, 12, 88
employees, 25, 231–2
    change and, 209–12, 239, 245
    identification, 47–8, 49, 50, 84–5
    recognition of, 146–8
    relationships, 26–9, 168–9, 211–12
empowerment, 6–7, 16, 46–7, *see also* power
    intrinsic motivation from, 21
    networking and, 149–50
energy, charisma and, 79–81
environmental factors as stimulus for change, 198
equity, 15–16
espoused values, 235–7, 247–8
ethics (morality), 248, *see also* values
    networking alliances and, 141–3, 153
    spin and, 106–9
*ethos*, 30, 48, 54

exit clauses, 156
expectation, law of giving without, 138
*Das Experiment*, 18–20
expert power, 17–18, 22, 54, *see also* knowledge
extrinsic motivation, 21
eye contact, 55–6, 77–8, **79**

facial appearance, 78–9, 85
failure, 87–8
favouritism, 15
fear (individualised self-preservation), 242–7, 249
fictional characters, leadership qualities of, **10**
Fiorina, Carly, 42, 57–60
Florida, Richard, 46, 53–4
formal authority, *see* legitimate (positional) power
Forster, Nick, 2
frameworks for sizing people up, 74–5
friendship, 145
fundamental behavioural change, *see* behavioural change
future visions, 13–14, 206–8

Gates, Bill, 140
GE (General Electric), 60–1, 210
giving without expectation, law of, 138
goal setting, 61, 207–9
'ground truth', 176–8
group membership, 231–2, *see also* identification
Guilfoyle, Desmond, 68

hammer throwing, 107–11, **110**
Harry Potter stories, **10**, 23
Hatcher, Caroline, 40
Henderson, Robyn, 136
heuristic cues (decision rules), 44–5
Hewlett-Packard, *see* Fiorina, Carly
honesty, 10, 12
housing development vision, 207–8
Hull, Clark L, 242
human behaviour, *see* behaviour
humanism, rationalist, 233
humour, 16–17

identification, 47–8, **49**, 50, 84–5
imagination, 88
impression management, 75
influence, *see also* change processes; leadership; networking
  behaviour model, 230, **230**
  changing perceptions, 228–9
  charisma and, 69–97
  crisis management, 119–24
  defined, 4, 228
  good and bad of, 4–7, **5**
  integrity marketing, 124–30, **125–9**
  master networking, 143–59
  persuasion and, 41–63
  power and, 3–32
  sources of, 7–22
information gathering, 149, 176–8
inspiration, 12–13
integration (consistent persona), 89
integrity, 10, 12, 141–3
integrity marketing, 101, 105–6, 124–30, **125–9**
intentions, concealing, 29
interaction styles, 53–4
interpersonal exchanges, *see* social exchanges
interpretive filters, 228, 240
intrinsic motivation, 21, 47, 183

judgments, categorisation and, 74–5

knowledge, 165–88, *see also* organisational learning
  expert power, 17–18, 22, 54, 168–9
  sharing, 167, 182–3
knowledge agenda, 169–70, **171**
knowledge contribution styles, 169–74, **171**
knowledge flow, 170, **171**, 188
Kotler, Phillip, 124
Krispy Kreme, 115
Kuhn, Thomas, 237–9, 245–6

labelling (category bias), 83
language (rhetorical skill), 44, 59
law of abundance, 138
law of giving without expectation, 138
law of reciprocity, 138

leadership, 4–5, 8–17, **9–11**, 47–8, *see also* change processes; influence
change and, 196, 198–203, 209–15, 220, 244, 246–51
ethical, 107
fictional characters, **10**
misconceptions and truisms, 214
origin of words, 13
persuasion as, 42
praise and, 27
'learned self-helpfulness', 87
learning, *see* organisational learning
legitimate (positional) power, 18–21, 166
Lincoln, Abraham, 16
listening, 88–90, 144–5
logic and reason, 21, 239–40
*logos*, 30, 48, 59
love (collective wellbeing), 242–3, 245–7, 249

Machiavellian power, 22, 25–9
magnetism, *see* charisma
manifest values, *see* values-in-use
manipulative behaviour, 94
marketing, *see also* spin
'buying a network', 142–3
integrity marketing, 101, 105–6, 124–30, **125–9**
media releases, 113–14
master networkers, *see* networking
mastermind groups, 157–9
*Matrix, The*, 249
meaning, 228, 242–3, *see also* spin
media communication, 113–16
during crises, 119–24
membership, 231–2, *see also* identification
memories, *see* storytelling
mental models, *see* assumptions
mentoring/coaching, 185–6, 214–15
merit, 231
messages, *see also* communication
influencing behavioural change, 199–203, **199–200**
media crisis plans, 120
meta-messages, 45
spin, 103
metaphysical choices, 245, 249
Milgram studies, 18–19

mining company, media reports of cyanide spill, 121
mirroring in communication, 55–6
mirrors, *see* 'room of mirrors'
mistakes, learning from, 87–8
morality, *see* ethics
motivation, 12–13, 242–4, 246, *see also* core motives (drive)
goal setting and, 208
knowledge sharing, 182–3
personal level spin, 103–4
movement, 80–1, 84
Murrell, Thomas, 100
Myers-Briggs assessments, 51–3, **52**

'name calling', 144, 146
networking, 137–61, *see also* strategic alliances
connections, 144–6
integrity and, 141–3
master networkers, 139–41, 143–59
power of, 139–41
non-verbal communication, 55–6, 85
normative socialising forces, 232
Nudie (juice company), 104–5, **112**

obesity, 83
office politics, 168–9
organisational behaviour, 240–1
organisational identification, 47–8, **49**, 50, 84–5
organisational learning, 229, *see also* knowledge
core motives and, 243–4
deep-structure learning, 227, 246–51
knowledge contribution styles, **171**
values and, 235
organisational value alignment, 124–9, **125–9**

paradigm shifts, 238–40, 243–9
parity, 15–16
Parramatta City Council, MAD program, 183
passion, 46, 50, 88
as competitive advantage, 42
passionate collaborative learning, **171**, 173–4
pathfinders, leaders as, 13

*pathos*, 30, 48, 59
peers, *see* mastermind groups
Penglase, David, 124
perceptions, 73–7, 228–9
permission category model, 180–1
personal level spin, 103–4
personal power, 8–17, 22
personality, 89, *see also* charisma
    toxic, 23–5, 28
persuasion, 41–63, *see also* attitudes; charisma; influence; spin
physical appearance, 78–9, 83–4
Picard, Jean-Luc, **10**
playfulness, 93–4
politeness, 90–1
positional power, *see* legitimate (positional) power
positive spin, *see* spin
positive states of mind, 87–9
power, 3–32, *see also* empowerment
    Aristotle on, 30–1
    good and bad of, 4–7, **5**, 22–30
    knowledge as, 168–9
    Machiavellian, 22, 25–9
    sources of, 7–22
praise (compliments), 91–3
presentations, 82–3
pressure, composure and, 216
prison experiment, 19–20
profiles, *see* case studies
project learning, **171**, 172–3
psychology, 233–4
psychopaths, 23–4
punishment, *see* coercive power

'quality time', 149
quick wins, 178

radio station case study, 150
rational-economic notions of motivation, 246
rationalist humanism, 233
reason and logic, 21, 239–40
reciprocity, law of, 138
recognition, giving, 146–8, 155–6
referent power, 69–70, 94–7, *see also* charisma
    perceivers' standards, 75–7, 85
    power postures, 79

relationships, 26–9, 168–9, 211–12, *see also* social exchanges
reputations, 26–7, 53
    strategic alliances, 153
    *Sydney Morning Herald* test, 141
resourceful states of mind, 87–9
responsibility, personal, 213
return on investment (ROI)
    mastermind groups, 158–9
    strategic alliances, 153
reward power, 20
rewards, goal setting and, 209
rhetorical skill, 44, 59
risk management, *see* crisis management
role modelling, 150–2
role-play experiments, 18–20
'room of mirrors', 205–6, 216–17
Rylatt, Alastair, 164

safe spaces, creating, 178–80
Schein, Edgar, 244, 246
scientific progress, 238, 245
secretive learning, **171**, 172
self-concept, *see* ego
sense of caring, 54
sense of direction, 13–14
sense of humour, 16–17
shared views, 44
silence, 28–9
situation (message delivery), 51
Skinner, BF, 233
SMART checklist for goal setting, 209
smiling, 81–2
Smith, Dick, 115
social exchanges, 69, 93–4, *see also* referent power
social games, 26
social psychology, 234
socialising forces, 232
soft control, 46–7
sole focus, 149
speaking/speeches, 28–9, 55, 82–3
    Clinton case study, 116–19
Spence, Liza, 195
spheres of influence (master networkers), 139–41, 143–59
spin, 101–32, *see also* persuasion
    Clinton case study, 116–19
    ethics and, 106–9

power of, 102–5, 113–16, 131–2
rationalising behaviour, 239–40
sponsorship, 142–3
sport, 107–9, 213, 216
St James Ethics Centre, 107
staff, *see* employees
Stanford prison experiment, 19–20
states of mind, *see* attitudes
storytelling, 105–6, 177–8
strategic alliances, 152–7, *see also* networking
strategic level spin, 103
stretch targets, 61
structural power, *see* legitimate (positional) power
*Structure of scientific revolutions* (Kuhn), 237–8
'sufficiency' principle, 45
Sun Tsu (*The art of war*), 205
survival anxiety, 244

target audience, *see* audience
team environments, 203–17, **204**
project learning, 173
self-selection, 210
team building, 179
values case study, 236–7
technology, 59, 177
thought, *see* cognitive factors
threats, *see* coercive power
timeframes in alliances, 154
toxic personalities, 23–5, 28
transformational learning, 244
trust, 54, 176–7, 180–2
integrity marketing, 105–6
trilogy of trust, 140–1

truth, 176–8, 181–2

underhand strategies, *see* Machiavellian power
undiscussables, 181–2
uniforms, 84–5

valour, 88–9
values
behavioural change and, 235–7, 247–8
brands, 111
high performance individuals, 210–11, **211**
integrity marketing, 106, 124–9, **125–9**
values-in-use (manifest values), 235–7, 247
valuing people, *see* recognition, giving
victim mentality, 213
Vincent Fairfax Fellowship, 107
Virgin Blue, 102, 105
vision for the future, 13–14, 206–8
voice, *see* speaking/speeches

'walk your talk', 151
Walker, Lang, 207–8
Wallabies case study, 202
wardrobe, 84–5
website collaboration, 184
Welch, Jack, 43, 60–1, 210
Western Power case study, 122–3
wisdom, *see* knowledge
workplaces, *see* employees

X factor, *see* charisma

# MANAGEMENT TODAY

## WHAT'S HAPPENING IN MANAGEMENT TODAY?
## **SUBSCRIBE** AND FIND OUT.

*Management Today*, the Australian Institute of Management's national monthly magazine, keeps you in touch with all the issues that matter – leadership, globalisation, strategic thinking, governance, e-management and much more. It is Australia's only magazine focusing on the profession of management and is a 'must read' for managers at all levels.

A free subscription to *Management Today* is one of the many bonuses of AIM corporate and personal membership. However, additional or new subscriptions are available for $55.00 (GST included) per year (ten issues including postage and handling).

To subscribe
phone (07) 3227 4888 ...
or visit our website www.aim.com.au

# MANAGEMENT
### TODAY SERIES

*The Heart and Soul of Leadership*

A thought-provoking read for leaders and aspiring leaders. This multi-authored book draws together the themes that define the 'heart and soul' of Australian leadership. It pulls apart what it means to be a leader in an Australian organisation, with the emphasis on leadership as a personal journey.

*The Uncertain Art of Management*

Management author Harry Onsman provides a commonsense guide to management practice with this lively analysis of 32 issues that confuse, concern and exasperate managers at all levels. Management fads are debunked, gurus challenged, theories dissected and best practice explained.

*The 7 Heavenly Virtues of Leadership*

Eight accomplished management thinkers explore the quintessential Australian leadership virtues of humility, courage, integrity, compassion, humour, passion and wisdom. This book investigates how 'good character' translates into leadership behaviours that can ripple through the entire organisation and positively affect performance.

*The Power of Culture: Driving Today's Organisation*

This multi-authored book explores how to understand, assess, manage and lead organisational culture. It will provoke managers to rethink their approach to the human dynamic of the organisation, and shows how to turn the 'soft stuff' of the organisation into a competitive advantage.

*Innovation and Imagination at Work, 2nd edition*

Totally revised and expanded. Eight articles examine what Australian managers and leaders need to know to create innovative organisations. Includes 'future-thinking' and scenario planning; generating new ideas; encouraging staff creativity; strategic, operational and practical issues; and entrepreneurship for organisations.

All in paperback. RRP $32.95 each

**McGraw·Hill Australia**
*A Division of The **McGraw·Hill** Companies*